Chemistry
of New
Materials

DAVID E. NEWTON

Facts On File
An imprint of Infobase Publishing

Chemistry of New Materials

Copyright © 2007 by David E. Newton

Facts On File, Inc.
An imprint of Infobase Publishing
132 West 31st Street
New York NY 10001

ISBN-10: 0-8160-5278-6
ISBN-13: 978-0-8160-5278-3

Library of Congress Cataloging-in-Publication Data
Newton, David E.
    Chemistry of new materials / David E. Newton.
        p. cm.—(New chemistry)
    Includes bibliographical references and index.
    ISBN 0-8160-5278-6
    1. Materials—Popular works. 2. Chemistry, Technical—Popular works.
I. Title.
    TA403.2.N49 2007
    620.1'1—dc22   2006035943

Facts On File books are available at special discounts when purchased in bulk quantities for businesses, associations, institutions, or sales promotions. Please call our Special Sales Department in New York at (212) 967-8800 or (800) 322-8755.

You can find Facts On File on the World Wide Web at http://www.factsonfile.com

Text design by James Scotto-Lavino
Illustrations by Anja Tchepets
Project editing by Dorothy Cummings

Printed in the United States of America

MP CGI 10 9 8 7 6 5 4 3 2 1

This book is printed on acid-free paper.

One Last Time . . .
for

John McArdle, Lee Nolet, Richard Olson, David Parr,
David Rowand, Jeff Williams, and John D'Emilio

Thanks for the memories!

◆ CONTENTS

Preface   vii
Introduction   ix

1 THE EVOLUTION OF MATERIALS   **1**
    Early Materials   1
    The Birth of Modern Chemistry and the Discovery
        of New Materials   5
        John Wesley Hyatt (1837–1920)   *10*
    New Metals on Demand   12
        Sir Henry Bessemer (1813–1898)   *14*
    The Future of Materials Research   18

2 COMPOSITES   **20**
    The Nature of Composites   20
    Composites in Nature   22
    Composites in Human History   24
    Advanced Composites   25
        Stephanie Kwolek (1923–)   *26*
    Applications of Advanced Composites   32
        Owens-Corning Fiberglas®   *36*

3 BIOMATERIALS   **40**
    History of Biomaterials   41
    Tissue Engineering   45
        Ioannis V. Yannas (1935–)   *48*
    Replacement Parts   52
    Artificial Blood   62
        Thomas Chang (1933–)   *63*

4   NANOMATERIALS   **68**

   What Is Nanotechnology?   69

      Richard Feynman (1918–1988)   *70*

   Drexlerian Nanotechnology   73

   Reactions to Drexler Nanotechnology   76

      K. Eric Drexler (1955–   )   *78*

   Risks and Benefits of Nanotechnology   80

   Nanotechnology Research Tools   81

   Results of Nanoscale Research   93

5   SMART MATERIALS   **105**

   What Are Smart Materials?   106

   Types of Smart Materials   109

   Piezoelectric and Electrostrictive Materials   110

   Magnetostrictive Materials   120

   Electrorheological and Magnetorheological Effects   125

      Jacob Rabinow (1910–1999)   *126*

   Shape Memory Alloys   130

   Photochromism   136

   Intelligent Gels   141

      Toyoichi Tanaka (1946–2000)   *142*

6   NEW POLYMERS   **149**

   Polymers from Addition Reactions   151

   Polymers from Condensation Reactions   154

   Thermoplastic and Thermosetting Polymers   159

   Recent Developments in Polymer Science   162

   Conductive Polymers   162

      Hideki Shirakawa (1936–   )   *164*

   Dendrimers and Hyperbranched Polymers   170

   Synthetic Proteins   178

      David A. Baker (1962–   )   *186*

CONCLUSION   **190**

Glossary   193

Bibliography   201

Index   205

PREFACE

The subject matter covered in introductory chemistry classes at the middle and high school levels tends to be fairly traditional and relatively consistent from school to school. Topics that are typically covered in such classes include atomic theory, chemical periodicity, ionic and covalent compounds, equation writing, stoichiometry, and solutions. While these topics are essential for students planning to continue their studies in chemistry or the other sciences and teachers are correct in emphasizing their importance, they usually provide only a limited introduction to the rich and exciting character of research currently being conducted in the field of chemistry. Many students not planning to continue their studies in chemistry or the other sciences may benefit from information about areas of chemistry with immediate impact on their daily lives or of general intellectual interest. Indeed, science majors themselves may also benefit from the study of such subjects.

The New Chemistry is a set of six books intended to provide an overview of some areas of research not typically included in the beginning middle or high school curriculum in chemistry. The six books in the set—*Chemistry of Drugs, Chemistry of New Materials, Forensic Chemistry, Chemistry of the Environment, Food Chemistry,* and *Chemistry of Space*—are designed to provide a broad, general introduction to some fields of chemistry that are less commonly mentioned in standard introductory chemistry courses. They cover topics ranging from the most fundamental fields of chemistry, such as the origins of matter and of the universe, to those with important applications to everyday life, such as the composition of foods and drugs. The set title The New Chemistry has been selected to emphasize the extensive review of recent research and advances in each of the fields of chemistry covered in the set. The books in The New Chemistry set are written for middle school and high school readers. They assume some basic understanding of the principles of chemistry that are generally gained in an introductory middle or high school course in the subject. Every book contains a large amount of material that should be accessible to the interested reader with no more than an introductory understanding of chemistry and a smaller amount of material that may require a more advanced understanding of the subject.

The six books that make up the set are independent of each other. That is, readers may approach all of the books in any sequence whatsoever. To assist the reader in extending his or her understanding of each subject, each book in the set includes a glossary and a list of additional reading sources from both print and Internet sources. Short bibliographic sketches of important figures from each of the six fields are also included in the books.

INTRODUCTION

Nature has a remarkable variety of ways of assembling atoms and molecules to form natural products, and people still have a great deal to learn from these processes. But natural methods provide no more than a hint of the host of new products that can be made. These new products are changing—and will continue to change—the way in which scientists and engineers build the substances that make human civilization what it is today. *Chemistry of New Materials* reviews some of these exciting fields of materials research.

The level of a human civilization, it might be argued, is largely a function of the materials with which it has to work. Nature has provided a bountiful supply of materials, such as mud, stone, and wood. So humans have never suffered for lack of substances with which to build their homes, construct their boats, fashion their weapons, make their tools, design their kitchen implements, and produce the myriad other objects needed for everyday life.

Early on, people learned how to combine natural materials in a variety of ways to make them more useful. They found that the combination of mud and straw (bricks) was a stronger and more permanent building material than either material by itself. And, thus, one of the first *composite* materials was born. The importance of societies' ability to manipulate natural materials is evident in the fact that the earliest human civilizations have actually been named for the primary substances with which they worked: stone, iron, copper, and bronze.

Many of the new materials developed by early humans were modeled on substances found in nature. The first alloys, for example, were little more than artificial copies of substances produced when fire, lightning, or some other natural source of energy caused the fusion of naturally occurring materials on the Earth's surface. Over time, however, people learned how to modify these processes to produce new alloys and other materials that were superior to those found in nature. This pattern has dominated materials research since the dawn of time. Many of the best new materials available today were created when scientists discovered how nature makes its composites and found new and better ways to duplicate those processes. One of the most exciting fields of materials research today involves the development of new *biomaterials,* substances similar to naturally occurring products found in living organisms that can be used in a host of new ways by medical workers.

Perhaps the most promising field of materials research today aims to understand and imitate the way in which nature produces materials at its most fundamental level, that of atoms and molecules. The field of *nanotechnology* promises to revolutionize materials science in a way that has no precedent in human history. For the first time ever, scientists are learning how to construct new materials from the "bottom up," beginning with individual atoms and molecules, rather than from the "top down," as has always been the case in the past. This research promises not only to revolutionize existing fields of science and technology, such as computer science, but also to open up entirely new ways of thinking about, designing, and building synthetic materials.

Another field of materials science that has become identified with rapid and sometimes startling change is the development of so-called *smart materials*, materials that can sense changes in the surrounding environment and, in many cases, change their own character in response. Once no more than an optimistic dream of how materials *could* be used, smart materials have begun to appear in a virtually endless number of everyday applications, ranging from automotive airbags that protect riders with greater efficiency, to skis that "read" the snow and ice over which they travel and make appropriate adjustments in their shape, to concrete highways that measure the weight of trucks that pass over them.

Even in fields in which materials science had become somewhat routine and boring, such as the development of new *polymers,* unexpected and promising breakthroughs have occurred. The invention of polymers that conduct an electrical current—once considered a contradiction in terms—has made possible new substances with many of the advantages of traditional polymers and the added benefit of electrical conductivity. Like most other fields of materials research today, polymer research is turning out products with almost unheard of molecular structures, such as *dendrimers* and *hyperbranched polymers.* These products are so different from any natural or previously manufactured substance that researchers scarcely know the applications in which they may be employed.

1

THE EVOLUTION
OF MATERIALS

People have long defined civilizations in terms of the materials societies have used to build and make objects. Historians often divide human history into periods such as the Old, Middle, and New Stones Ages; the Bronze Age; the Iron Age; and, much later on in history, the Age of Plastics.

In the earliest stages of human history, people and their hominid ancestors relied on easily obtainable natural materials, such as wood, stone, and clay. They developed techniques for fashioning these materials into the weapons, tools, buildings, and household items needed in their everyday lives. The earliest recorded tools date to 3.1 to 2.5 million years ago from the Hadar region of Africa. These tools were made of volcanic rock and were probably used to shape household items, weapons, and other tools. If the earliest humans made and used tools of organic materials, such as skin or rope, they would all have decayed, and no record of them remains today.

Early Materials

It appears that clay may have been the first material to be treated and reworked by humans so as to produce new properties. This development was possible after the discovery of fire and the development of techniques for its control and use. Once natural clay was formed into some useful shape (such as a pot), it was heated. The new, hard product had applications not possible with the softer natural material. Archaeologists believe that the use of human-made clay products probably dates to the eighth millennium B.C.E.

The use of native metals, such as gold, silver, and copper, goes back even further than the first stone tools. Native metals are elements that occur in the Earth's surface in uncombined form. Examples of decorative objects made of silver, for example, date as early as the eighth millennium B.C.E. in Anatolia, the fifth millennium B.C.E. in parts of North America, and the second millennium B.C.E. in South America. Vedic scripture and other religious writings refer to the use of gold, silver, copper, tin, lead, and iron (although not necessarily in the forms known today) by humans at least three millennia ago.

The first artificial materials were almost certainly fashioned after similar materials found in nature. For example, natural glass is formed when sand is heated to high temperatures, as when it is struck by lightning. One can imagine that early humans witnessed this phenomenon and decided to replicate that process themselves. By the fourth millennium B.C.E., Egyptian artisans had learned how to make glass beads and other objects, although the manufacture of useful objects, such as vases, apparently did not occur until about 1500 B.C.E.

The first significant breakthrough in metallurgy occurred some time after the fourth millennium B.C.E. Metallurgy is the study of metals and the process by which they are extracted from the Earth and converted to useful objects, such as alloys. This event was the discovery of methods for the production of bronze, the first alloy. An alloy is a mixture of two or more elements (at least one of which is a metal) with properties different from those of the elements themselves. Bronze is made from copper and tin in a ratio of at least 9 parts copper to 1 part tin. The temperature required to convert the two elements into the alloy is relatively low (slightly more than the melting point of copper, 1,083°C) and could be attained in ovens available at the time.

Early artisans knew nothing, of course, about the chemical process by which bronze was formed. The first step in that process is usually the conversion of copper and tin oxides to the pure metals. Carbon present in a fire (in the form of charcoal) is the reducing agent in this process:

$$2CuO + C \rightarrow 2Cu + CO_2$$

and

$$2Cu_2O + C \rightarrow 2CO_2 + 4Cu$$

and

$$SnO_2 + C \rightarrow Sn + CO_2$$

The molten copper and tin that result from this process then form a liquid solution that solidifies to form an alloy (bronze) that is stronger and easier to mold than either copper or tin. The advantages of bronze over copper and all other naturally occurring metals soon became obvious, and artisans improved techniques for making the alloy artificially. As the technology for making bronze spread throughout the world, the alloy became the most popular metallic substance for the production of weapons, tools, kitchen implements, and other practical objects. The specific period during which bronze making proliferated differed in various parts of the world, but probably dates to about 3500 B.C.E. at the earliest in some parts of the Middle East. Such techniques did not reach parts of Europe until another 1,500 years later.

The Bronze Age lasted until about 1200 B.C.E., when iron became the new metal of choice for the manufacture of objects. As with bronze, iron was probably produced accidentally in campfires long before it became widely popular. Iron ores occur commonly in nature, and they are reduced at relatively modest temperatures in reactions similar to those for copper and tin. For example:

$$2Fe_2O_3 + 3C \rightarrow 4Fe + 3CO_2$$

and

$$2FeO + C \rightarrow 2Fe + CO_2$$

The iron thus produced does not *appear* to be a useful material, however, since it occurs as spongy material mixed with slag and ash. It is only after these impurities have been removed and the iron has been hammered into a solid mass that it becomes useful for the manufacture of weapons, tools, and other implements. This technology apparently first appeared among the Hittites in about 1500 B.C.E., after which it diffused throughout Anatolia and, eventually, other parts of the world.

Over the next millennium, iron gradually replaced bronze throughout most of the world. One of its great advantages was that iron ores are much more abundant than those of copper and tin, so the manufacture of iron was also much less expensive. Far more people could afford to make or buy tools made of iron than they could tools made of bronze. In addition, iron could be an even stronger, tougher material than bronze, depending on the method by which it was manufactured. Although unknown to people of the time, the form of iron produced by the smelting of iron ores varied greatly depending on the presence of impurities, primarily carbon (from charcoal). Indeed, many centuries later, it was the understanding of how such impurities affect the properties of iron (in forms that we now know of as *steel*) that iron truly became the king of metals during the Industrial Revolution.

By about 500 B.C.E., the discovery and invention of new materials had largely come to an end. The great Greek and Roman civilizations depended almost entirely on materials that had been known and developed in the millennia preceding their appearance, materials such as clay, stone, wood, copper, gold, bronze, and iron. Only one major new innovation occurred during this period, the discovery of hydraulic concrete. Hydraulic concrete was an improvement on a much older building material, lime mortar. Lime mortar is made when limestone (calcium carbonate) is heated to a high temperature, driving off carbon dioxide and leaving behind quicklime (calcium oxide).

$$CaCO_3 \text{ (heated to about 900°C)} \rightarrow CaO + CO_2$$

The quicklime is then mixed with water to form slaked lime (calcium hydroxide).

$$CaO + H_2O \rightarrow Ca(OH)_2$$

As the slaked lime dries, it reacts with carbon dioxide in the air to produce limestone, the raw material from which the final product was made.

$$Ca(OH)_2 + CO_2 \rightarrow CaCO_3 + H_2O$$

The final product, lime mortar, is an excellent building material and was probably one of the first artificial materials to have been manufactured and used by humans. The Romans, however, discovered a variation of this process that made the final product stronger and longer lasting. They found that the addition of other materials, especially the oxides of aluminum and silicon, greatly enhanced the building properties of the lime mortar. In this improved form, it became known as hydraulic concrete and was used by Roman engineers in many building projects throughout the empire. For example, the Colosseum, Pantheon, Baths of Caracalla, and at least one major aqueduct (the Pont du Gard) were all constructed with hydraulic concrete. The strength of the material is reflected in the fact that even today, 2,000 years after their construction, many of those buildings are still standing and, in some cases, in use.

The Birth of Modern Chemistry and the Discovery of New Materials

With the fall of the Roman Empire and the dawn of the Middle Ages, little or no progress was made in the development of new building materials. Indeed, some technologies were actually lost or virtually forgotten. The use of hydraulic concrete for construction, for example, was rarely used again until the late 18th century, when the technique for its manufacture and use was rediscovered by an English bricklayer named Joseph Aspdin (1788–1855). In 1824, Aspdin applied for a patent for his method for making hydraulic concrete, which later became known as Portland cement. There is little evidence that Aspdin understood the chemistry underlying his method of making cement, but his rediscovery of the product once more made it widely popular as a building material.

By the late 19th century, however, interest in a whole new range of synthetic materials had begun to grow. A strong impetus for this change was the development of a new field of chemistry, organic chemistry. At first, organic chemistry was a relatively limited and not particularly challenging field of chemistry. Organic chemists focused on a study of the chemical compounds contained in plants and animals, in contrast to those found in inorganic, or nonliving, materials. The challenges they assumed were to determine what chemicals were present in living organisms, how much of each was present, the chemical structure of such compounds, and so on. The major difference between organic and inorganic chemistry was that practitioners of the former science made no effort to synthesize the compounds they found in living organisms, only to analyze them.

The reason for this approach to organic chemistry was a dominant philosophy about the nature of organic and inorganic substances. At the time, philosophers and scientists believed that the substances that make up living organisms are, in a very important way, special and different from those that make up inorganic substances, such as rocks and metals. They assumed that organic chemicals contained some special quality, some "breath of life" imparted by a creator god. Given this theory of vitalism, it would have been absurd and even blasphemous for a human chemist to attempt to make organic compounds.

Then, in 1825, the German chemist Friedrich Wöhler (1800–82) made a quite astounding discovery. Upon heating a relatively common inorganic mineral, ammonium cyanate (NH_4CNO), Wöhler found that he was able to produce another compound known as urea [$(NH_2)_2CO$]. The remarkable point about this discovery is that urea is an organic compound, a common excretory product of many animals. As one can see from the formulas of the two compounds, heating of ammonium cyanate apparently causes a rearrangement of the atoms of which it is made, producing urea. Shortly after making his discovery, Wöhler wrote to one of the leading chemists of the day, Jöns Jakob Berzelius (1779–1848), "I must tell you that I can prepare urea without requiring kidneys or an animal, either man or dog." Berzelius wrote back, "It is quite an important and nice discovery which Herr Doktor effected and I was indescribably pleased to hear of it."

But how could such a result be achieved if organic compounds are produced only by the act of some supernatural being? There are only two answers to that question: Either Wöhler was, himself, a creator god (which most colleagues were eager to deny), or the traditional theory of vitalism was incorrect.

Of course, no single experiment is ever sufficient to demolish a long-held and popular scientific theory. Nonetheless, Wöhler's work led other chemists to think about synthesizing organic compounds, an act that would have seemed a waste of time before his discovery. Before long, these chemists began to obtain similar results. They began to synthesize in the laboratory chemical compounds that had only been found in living plants and animals or their products previously. It quickly became apparent that, from a chemical standpoint, there was really nothing "special" about organic compounds after all. They could be formed by reactions and processes well known to and widely practiced by chemists, and they were apparently subject to all the same laws and principles well know to chemists.

A floodgate was opened. Chemists suddenly found a whole new field of research available to them: the synthesis of organic compounds found in living organisms and, even more important, other compounds *similar* to those found in plants and animals but *not* actually found in the natural world.

Most of the early work in organic chemistry focused on questions with little or no practical application. Chemists were intrigued with the possibility of synthesizing a whole range of compounds that occurred naturally in living organisms, or that were similar to such compounds. It was not long, however, before organic chemists began to see the possibility of their work having some impact on industry and the everyday concerns of ordinary people.

A classic story of this line of research was the discovery of a method for the manufacture of the dye now known as mauve by the English chemist Sir William Henry Perkin (1838–1907). In 1856, Perkin was an 18-year-old student of the great German chemist August Wilhelm von Hoffmann (1818–92), superintendent of the Royal College of

Chemistry in London. For more than a decade, von Hoffman had been investigating the use of coal tar for the manufacture of new, commercially important chemicals. Coal tar had become a plentiful and inexpensive raw material after the development of the gas-lighting industry in the early 19th century, which generated vast amounts of coal tar as a by-product.

One of the research projects that von Hoffman suggested to his students was an investigation of the possibility of producing quinine from coal tar. Quinine is a valuable drug for the treatment of malaria. Perkin decided to take on this task and tried to convert both allyl toluidine and aniline (coal tar derivatives) into quinine. His experiments failed, but he noticed that an ugly black sludge was left behind on the bottom of the reaction flask in the aniline experiment. Curious about the residue, he added ethanol (ethyl alcohol) to the flask. A beautiful, deep purple solution formed when the sludge dissolved in the alcohol.

The color was so distinctive that Perkin wondered if the product could be used as a dye. In 1856, he sent samples of the chemical to a dyeing company, Pullars of Perth, who responded that the dye appeared to have commercial potential. Perkin immediately applied for a patent on the dye, which rapidly became very popular in Great Britain and especially in France. It was the French, in fact, who gave the dye the name by which it is now known, *mauve* (the French word for the plant from which the natural and similarly colored dye alizarin is produced). As a consequence of the dye's huge commercial success, the decade of the 1890s is now referred to as the Mauve Decade.

Perkin's discovery was important not simply because he found a new and very useful dye. In the first place, Perkin (in collaboration with his father) opened a chemical factory to manufacture mauve on a large scale. The business was so successful that the younger Perkin was able to retire from the business in 1874, at the age of 35, to devote himself full time to chemical research on topics of interest to him. Second, Perkin's success inspired many other chemists in Great Britain and on the Continent to look for other potentially lucrative synthetic dyes. Over the next decade, a host of such dyes were discovered, patented, and put into production. For example, in 1859, the French chemist Emanuel Verguin (1814–64) discovered a dye consisting of a mixture of triphenylmethane compounds that he named magenta (after a town in northern Italy where Napoleon III had recently won a great victory), which is known today as fuchsin. Within a decade, other synthetic dyes, such as aniline black, Bismarck brown, alizarin, indigo, methylene blue, methylene green, Congo red, and Primuline yellow, were also discovered and put into production in many cases within a matter of months.

These discoveries were important not only because of the individual new compounds, but also because they totally changed the nature of the dyestuff industry. Since the dawn of civilization, humans had relied on natural products (plants and animals) as dyes to color clothing and other fabrics. With the dawn of the Mauve Decade, such dyes very quickly became abundantly available at rather modest costs.

The Mauve Decade also saw the rise of another branch of organic chemistry that was to have enormous impact on the development of new materials: the field of polymer chemistry. Polymer chemistry is the science that deals with very large molecules consisting of hundreds or thousands of repeating units called *monomers*. Possibly the single most familiar class of polymer in use today is the group called plastics.

The first true synthetic polymer was probably a material produced in 1865 by the English inventor Alexander Parkes (1813–90). Parkes synthesized this material by reacting cellulose (a natural polymer) with nitric acid and dissolving the product (called pyroxylin) in a mixture of alcohol, camphor, and castor oil. Parkes called his product parkesine, or Xylonite. Although the material had many desirable qualities (for example, it could be shaped and molded easily while still warm), it was too expensive to be a commercial success, and, perhaps more important, no one quite knew how to use the product.

More than a decade later, Parkes's invention was rediscovered by the American inventor John Wesley Hyatt (1837–1920). Hyatt was attempting to win a $10,000-prize offered by the Phelan and Collender

◁ JOHN WESLEY HYATT (1837–1920) ▷

Mother Nature has provided humans with a mind-boggling array of natural products with nearly every conceivable set of physical properties and, therefore, an apparently endless variety of uses. And yet, human inventors have always tried to go Mom one better, producing synthetic products that are longer lasting, less expensive, more attractive, or preferable to "the real thing" in some other way. Such has been the case, for example, in the more than century-and-a-half development of plastics. One of the earliest pioneers in the evolution of the plastics industry was John Wesley Hyatt, an inventor who spent his whole life trying to devise new and better materials and improved methods for getting jobs done.

Hyatt was born in Starkey, New York, on November 28, 1837. He had only the most basic education, attending elementary schools in Yates County before moving to Illinois at the age of 16. He worked briefly in Illinois as a printer before becoming enchanted by the challenges of invention. Hyatt received his first patent at the age of 24 for a knife grinder and sharpener.

Before long, Hyatt returned to his native New York state, where he settled in the Albany region. There he founded a number of companies, including the Albany Dental Plate Company, the Celluloid Manufacturing Company, and the Albany Billiard Ball Company, all with his two brothers

Company, makers of billiard balls. Previously, billiard balls had been made of ivory obtained from elephant tusks. Because of the devastation of the elephant population in Africa, however, ivory was becoming more difficult to obtain, and Phelan and Collender were looking for an inexpensive substitute. Hyatt discovered that substitute when he found a way (nearly identical to that of Parkes's) to dissolve nitrated cellulose in a mixture of alcohol, ether, and camphor. Hyatt called his product celluloid. Although he was not awarded the $10,000-prize, he was honored later in life for this and other discoveries with the Perkin Medal of Honor from the Society of Chemical Industry.

Some historians argue, however, that credit for inventing the first truly synthetic polymer should go to the Belgian-American chemist Leo Hendrik Baekeland (1863–1944). They point out that the

Charles and Isaiah. All three companies grew out of his most famous invention, celluloid.

Hyatt was first drawn to the problem of finding a synthetic substitute for natural ivory by the $10,000 prize offered by the Phelan and Collender Company of New York City in the early 1860s. He knew about Alexander Parkes's earlier work, which had resulted in the invention of parkesine, a compound produced from a combination of cellulose, nitric acid, alcohol, ether, and camphor. He found a way to make parkesine more stable and less expensive to produce. This accomplishment failed to win him the Phelan and Collender prize, but it led to the creation of a healthy new industry, the production of celluloid, as he named his product. Celluloid soon became a popular material in the manufacture of a wide variety of consumer goods, including not only billiard balls, but also combs, shirt collars and cuffs, baby rattles, dominoes, and photographic film.

Hyatt was issued more than 200 patents during his lifetime, covering a wide array of materials and devices. In addition to celluloid, he also invented a material made of bone and silica that he name *bonsilate,* later used for billiard balls, buttons, knife handles, and other articles. In 1881, he invented a system for purifying running water that is still in use throughout the United States and Europe. Hyatt was still active late in life, receiving a patent at the age of 63 for a sewing machine that was able to produce 50 lockstitches simultaneously. Hyatt died in Short Hills, New Jersey, on May 10, 1920.

Parkes-Hyatt invention of parkesine/Xylonite/celluloid begins with a natural product, cellulose. The polymer formed, critics suggest, is not therefore completely synthetic. Baekeland's product, however, is made entirely of synthetic materials.

In 1900, Baekeland began research to find a substitute for shellac, a clear, thick liquid secreted by an insect and widely used as a transparent, tough coating. In one attempt, he reacted two organic compounds, phenol (C_6H_5OH) and formaldehyde (CH_2O). The product he obtained was a thick, gummy material for which he could find no solvent. The hard, tough, dense material obviously could not be used as a shellac substitute if no solvent could dissolve it, but the very fact that it was so insoluble suggested another possibility for the material, which he called Bakelite. Perhaps its resistance to solubility could be put to use in other applications. By 1909, Baekeland had found a way to produce the new phenol-formaldehyde product and then mold it or shape it into some desired form. When the product cooled and solidified, it held its form and proved to be resistant to water and most other chemicals. It was also an electrical insulator. The product turned out to be ideal for a great variety of products, from radio cabinets to insulator caps on high-tension wires. Baekeland opened his own company, the General Bakelite Company. With the military demands created by World War I, it quickly became a huge success.

In spite of Baekeland's success, it was another two decades before the Age of Polymers can really be said to have been born. The 1920s and 1930s saw the invention and/or commercialization of a number of new polymeric products ("plastics") that most consumers now consider to be essential chemicals in their lives. These products include the urea formaldehyde plastics (1923), polyvinyl chloride (PVC; 1926), polystyrene (1929), nylon (1930), polymethylmethacrylate (acrylics; 1931), polyethylene (1933), the melamine plastics (1933), polyvinylidene chloride (Saran™; 1933), polyvinyl acetate (PVA; 1937), and tetrafluoroethylene (Teflon; 1938).

Although many people may not think of the 21st century as the Age of Plastics, the invention and development of new types of commercially useful polymers continues, and at a significant pace. Each year, dozens of new polymer products, usually with very specific properties and applications, are patented in the United States and the rest of the world.

New Metals on Demand

Organic chemistry was not the only field of chemistry that experienced dramatic growth during the late 19th century. Scientists also began to take a new look at the production of metallic products especially designed to meet a variety of industrial needs. The Industrial Revolution, which began in the late 18th century, created a need for new materials for the mechanization of many processes that had once been carried out by direct human labor. Perhaps no field of metallurgy advanced more rapidly than the invention and design of new alloys.

An alloy is a material consisting of two elements, at least one of which is a metal, with properties different from any of its constituent parts. Most of the early alloys known to and used by humans, such as bronze, brass, and pewter, had been discovered accidentally. By the late 19th century, however, scientists had begun to realize that they were capable of designing a variety of alloys with special properties needed for the host of metallic products then being produced. At first, their attention focused on alloys of iron.

Iron had been known and used for the manufacture of products as early as about 1200 B.C.E. in some parts of the world. The iron used during this period usually occurred in a form known as *wrought iron*. Wrought iron is a relatively pure form of iron, containing no more than about 1 percent carbon, the most common impurity in iron. The carbon in wrought iron, along with other impurities, can be removed rather easily simply by hammering the metal while it is still soft. The product of this process has many desirable properties, but the method by which it is produced is very labor intensive and can be used for the production of only certain sizes and shapes of iron.

An alternative method for producing iron at high temperatures was known as early as the Middle Ages, but the technology for producing such temperatures was sufficiently lacking that the process was not widely used. The form of iron produced by this method is known as *cast iron*. Cast iron contains a much higher percentage of carbon (about 5 percent) and is much harder than wrought iron. Unfortunately, it is also much weaker and more brittle (easily broken when bent).

By the mid-19th century, scientists and industrialists had finally begun to understand the role of carbon and certain other impurities in determining the properties of iron made by various processes. They realized that the iron needed for construction projects needed to have enough carbon in it to make it strong and malleable, but not so much as to make it brittle. Such a product soon became known as

◁ SIR HENRY BESSEMER (1813–1898) ▷

Though it oversimplifies matters, one could say that the Industrial Revolution that began in Great Britain in the 18th century was dependent primarily on the development of two materials: coal, which powered the steam engines that drove all kinds of new machinery, and steel, from which those machines were built. The success in Henry Bessemer's discovery of an efficient, inexpensive way to make good steel in large quantities was, therefore, a major element in the growth of the new industrial way of life.

Bessemer was born in Charlton, Hertfordshire, England, on January 19, 1813. Bessemer's father was the son of an engineer, and Bessemer inherited his father's interests in making new kinds of devices. One of his first inventions was a device he made when he was 17 years old for stamping deeds that saved the British government more than £100,000 (about $450,000) a year. Much to Bessemer's disappointment, however, the government failed to compensate him for the invention.

In spite of this disappointment, Bessemer continued to develop new inventions, eventually receiving 110 patents for his ideas. Among these inventions were a way of compressing soft plumbago (lead) dust for use as the "lead" in "lead" pencils, a method for embossing velvet in order to produce a luxurious type of wallpaper, a machine that made artificial brass powder for use in embossing leather, a hydraulic device to extract juice from sugarcane, a steam-driven fan for ventilating mines, and a special furnace capable of making glass by the sheet.

Bessemer's method of producing steel was prompted by an earlier invention he had made in the 1850s, a new type of cannonball. The cannonball he made was designed to spin as it traveled through the air, giving it a longer and more accurate trajectory. The British government was not interested in the cannonball, but Bessemer was able to convince the French Army to try it out. The cannonball worked well, but the French reported that their cannon were not strong enough to fire the new type of missile. The fit between cannonball and cannon had to be so tight that the cannon often blew up when it fired the ball. Bessemer realized that he had to develop a new and stronger material from which to make cannon if his cannonball were ever to be used.

The problem was that cannon were then made with cast iron, a form of iron that contains relatively large amounts of carbon. Cast iron is very hard, but it breaks very easily. The only substitute available for cast iron at the time was wrought iron, which is nearly pure iron. Wrought iron, however, was not suitable for making cannon (or almost anything else) because it was too soft.

The ideal middle-ground material was steel, which has less carbon than cast iron but more carbon than wrought iron. It combines the hardness and strength of cast iron with the durability of wrought iron. The problem was that no one had found an inexpensive and effective way to make steel with just the right amount of carbon.

Bessemer's idea was to blow air through molten cast iron. He knew that oxygen in the air would react with carbon in the cast iron to form carbon monoxide and carbon dioxide. If the blast of air could be carefully controlled, he could burn off as much or as little carbon as he wanted. He could produce a type of steel that had the correct balance of carbon between cast iron and wrought iron.

Bessemer's colleagues had little faith in his idea. They warned him that blowing cold air through molten cast iron would cool the iron and make it solidify too soon. In that case, the whole process would come to an end with no result. When Bessemer actually tried the process, however, he made a fascinating discovery. Instead of cooling the molten cast iron, a blast of air increased the temperature of the mixture. His critics had overlooked the fact that heat would be released when oxygen combined with carbon, making it unnecessary to add heat from an outside source once the reaction had begun. Bessemer's blast furnace turned out to be a great success because it made possible the production of steel with a precise amount of carbon in it at a much lower cost than had been possible before. Bessemer received a patent for his invention in 1857 and founded Henry Bessemer & Company to market the new product. The company lost money in its first two years of operation, 1858 and 1859, but soon turned the corner and became a huge financial success.

In recognition of his many accomplishments, the Royal Society made Bessemer a Fellow in 1879, and Queen Victoria knighted him in the same year. He died in London on March 15, 1898.

steel. The correct amount of carbon needed in most types of steel then in use ranged from about 0.1 to 0.5 percent. Finding a method by which steel of the correct composition could be made became a critical challenge to inventors. The first person to make an important breakthrough in this research was the English metallurgist Sir Henry Bessemer (1813–98). In 1855, Bessemer discovered that steel of the proper composition could be made by blowing hot air through molten iron. Combustion of the carbon impurities in the iron provided sufficient heat to melt the iron for pouring and molding. This "air-boiling" process solved two problems at once: It removed just the right amount of carbon from the molten iron, and it converted the iron to a state in which it could be formed into almost any desired shape. The Bessemer process revolutionized the production of steel.

The Bessemer process, as important as it was, produced only one kind of steel, carbon steel. Carbon steel consists primarily of iron with varying amounts of carbon added to produce a variety of properties. Today, carbon steels come in various forms, known as high-carbon, medium-carbon, low-carbon, extra-low-carbon, and ultra-low-carbon steels, each with a characteristic amount of carbon, ranging from more than 0.5 percent carbon at the high end to less than 0.015 percent carbon at the low end.

It was not long, however, before metallurgists realized that iron could be alloyed with elements other than carbon and that those alloys often had very desirable properties for special uses. In 1868, for example, the Scottish metallurgist Robert Forester Mushet (1811–91) developed a method for adding a small amount of tungsten to iron being treated in the Bessemer process, producing an alloy that hardened in the open air, was harder and tougher than carbon steels, and had a lifetime five to six times that of steels produced by the usual Bessemer process. Mushet marketed his invention as Robert Mushet's Special Steel. It became the first steel especially designed for and used in tools, the forerunner of today's steels used in high-speed operations.

Chromium alloy steels had been formulated and produced in laboratory quantities as early as 1819 by the English chemist Michael

Faraday (1791–1867) and the London cutler John Stodart. Six decades later, chromium steel was being made commercially in France for use in armor plating. By far the most important chromium alloy steel, however, was *stainless steel,* discovered in 1912 by the English inventor Harry Brearley (1871–1948). While trying to find a way of eliminating rust from gun barrels, Brearley accidentally discovered that the addition of a small amount of chromium to steel vastly improved its ability to resist oxidation. He gave the name *rustless steel* to his invention, although the product later became known as stainless steel.

By 1900, a variety of steels were available commercially, alloys of iron with carbon, tungsten, chromium, silicon, manganese, cobalt, nickel, and other metals. So popular had steel become as a building material that its annual production increased from about 500,000 tons in 1870 to more than 28 million tons in 1899. The success of steel alloys, however, had a secondary effect of increasing inventors' interests in other types of nonferrous alloys—alloys that did *not* contain iron. One of the first of these alloys to be discovered was duralumin, patented in 1908 by the German engineer Alfred Wilm (1869–1937). Wilm found that a mixture of aluminum metal with 3.5 percent copper, 0.5 percent magnesium, and 0.5 percent manganese dramatically improved the hardness and tensile strength (the load a material will take without breaking) of aluminum while only slightly increasing its density. The alloy soon became popular in the construction of airplanes and lighter-than-air dirigibles, such as the Zeppelins.

Another alloy discovery that transformed an industry was that of nichrome, invented in 1905 by the young American engineer Albert Marsh (1877–1944). Nichrome is an alloy of nickel and chromium that is tough and ductile (capable of being drawn into wires), and very resistant to oxidation and melting with a very low electrical conductivity. These properties make the alloy ideal for a very special application: use as wires in a toaster.

Crude methods for making toast had been available for centuries, the simplest being to hold a piece of bread over a flame. By the early 1900s, inventors had envisioned the use of heat generated by an electric current to replace the flame in the toasting process, but no one had been able to find a metal from which to make the electricity-carrying wires in the new toaster design. Thomas Edison himself had spent a considerable amount of time testing a variety of wires for this purpose, but without success. Marsh's discovery solved this problem and made the electric toaster a reality and, today, a presence in nearly every kitchen in the United States.

The Future of Materials Research

Research in traditional fields of materials science, such as those described in this chapter, continues today and will undoubtedly go on in the future. Chemists are synthesizing thousands of new organic compounds and dozens of new alloys every year, many with promising new applications in everyday life. But research is also being directed at the synthesis of entirely new kinds of materials, some with analogues in the natural world (such as composites and biomaterials), and some with little or no connection to natural materials (such as smart materials and photonics). And, in what may be the most dramatic revolution of all, scientists have now begun to explore the use of an entirely new way of synthesizing materials, beginning with individual atoms and molecules, a process used extensively in nature but never achieved by humans until the last few decades. The advent of these new materials presages a striking new era for human civilization.

One of the most exciting fields of research involves the study of composites, materials with two or more components with properties different from those of the components. Composites have revolutionized fields as diverse as sports and recreation and air transportation and military equipment. Another active field of research focuses on biomaterials, synthetic or semisynthetic products that have applications in living systems. Today researchers are developing artificial skin, blood, nerves, and other body components that can be used for the repair of damaged tissues. Nanotechnology is perhaps the most revolutionary of all areas of materials research. The subject deals with components of very small dimensions, comparable to those of atoms and molecules. Smart materials are yet another topic of interest to materials scientists. Smart materials are substances that seem to have "a mind of their own" and that are able to provide "intelligent" responses to stimuli such as changes in temperature and pressure. Finally, polymer chemistry has once more become a field of active research in which strikingly new products with remarkable physical and chemical properties are being discovered.

2
COMPOSITES

What do bamboo stalks, mud bricks, steel-belted radial tires, fiberglass fishing rods, *reinforced concrete,* and the heat tiles on a space shuttle have in common? The answer is that these materials are all composites. A composite is a material consisting of two or more components with overall properties different from and superior to either or any one of the individual components. For example, many pleasure boats today have hulls made of a composite material called *reinforced plastic* that contains glass, plastic, carbon, or some other type of fiber embedded in plastic. The composite material is stronger, more durable, and less dense than the fibers or plastics of which it is made.

These qualities are highly desirable, and today about 3 billion pounds (1.4 billion kg) of synthetic composites are produced in the United States each year. These products are manufactured at about 2,000 plants that employ more than 150,000 people. About two-thirds of these composites are made from glass fiber embedded in polyester or vinyl ester plastics. The remaining third of composites include a large variety of mixtures.

The Nature of Composites

The two essential constituents of a composite are the *matrix* and the *filler.* The matrix of a composite is the material that gives it body, shape, and bulk and that holds the material together. The filler is the material embedded into the matrix. Fillers determine the internal structure and augment the physical properties of the matrix. In any composite material, the properties of the filler complement and augment those of the matrix, and vice versa. For example, in a reinforced plastic, the fiber fillers have very high tensile strength, but they tend to be brittle. By contrast, the plastic matrix in which the fibers are embedded has good resistance to bending but poor tensile strength. The composite made of fiber and plastic, then, combines the best qualities of both constituents, having both high tensile strength (due to the filler) and high bending strength (due to the matrix). In addition, this composite and most others have other desirable properties, such as low density and high resistance to wear and fatigue damage.

Fillers can take many forms, including particles, fibers, flakes, and whiskers. Whiskers are individual crystals that act like tiny fibers. In the pleasure boat example, the glass, plastic, carbon, or other fiber constitutes the filler of the composite, and the plastic makes up the matrix.

One characteristic feature of composites is that they have distinct boundaries between matrix and filler. That is, they are nonhomogeneous. In this regard, they differ from alloys, materials in which two or more metals are completely mixed with each other, forming a homogeneous combination. In brass, for example, one is unable to distinguish the copper and zinc that make up the alloy, while in a pleasure boat composite, the glass fibers or other fiber fillers can be clearly distinguished from the plastic matrix.

In some composites, filler and matrix are in direct contact with each other. An example from nature is a sedimentary rock, in which pebbles and small rocks (the filler) are embedded in a sandstone matrix. In many composites, however, there is an intermediary zone—an *interphase*—between filler and matrix. An example of an interphase is the adhesive that holds filler and matrix together in a laminated (layered) composite.

The properties contributed to a composite by the filler and matrix (and interphase) can often be augmented by introducing structural changes in the material. For example, the product or some part of it may be produced as a foam or generated in a honeycomb shape to add strength to the final product while reducing its density.

Researchers who design composites tend to focus on a variety of physical properties of the materials with which they work. Some of these properties include strength, *toughness,* resistance to wear, and thermal and electrical properties. In many cases, the most important of these properties is density. Other factors being equal, it is usually preferable to have a high strength-to-density, toughness-to-density, or similar ratio. In this context, the term *toughness* refers to the ability of a material to absorb energy by bending or otherwise changing its shape property without breaking. In airplane and automobile design, for example, an important goal is to obtain the strongest, toughest airframe or body per kilogram of material. In this respect, many modern composites are far superior to metals and alloys traditionally used for airframes, wings, engines, auto bodies, and other structural parts of the vehicle.

Composites in Nature

Composites occur abundantly in nature, two of the most common being bone and wood. Bone is a very complex but well-ordered material with at least two levels of composite structure. The more fundamental of these two levels consists of an inorganic filler embedded

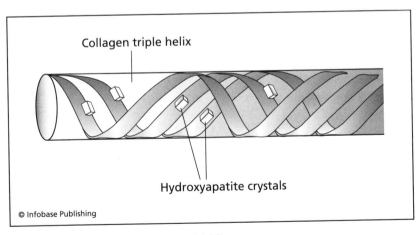

Collagen triple helix

Hydroxyapatite crystals

© Infobase Publishing

Collagen interspersed with precipitated dahlite

in a matrix of protein molecules. The inorganic filler is a form of the mineral apatite $[Ca_5(PO_4)_3(OH,F,Cl)]$ in the shape of flat crystals. The crystals are similar to the hydroxyapatite $[Ca_{10}(PO_4)_6(OH)_2]$ found in teeth and largely responsible for their toughness and strength. But the bone form of the mineral is carbonated and contains impurities, such as ions of sodium, magnesium, and potassium, as well as the biphosphate ion (HPO_2^{2-}). Its formula has been determined to be similar to that of the mineral dahlite $[Ca_5(PO_4,CO_3)_3F]$. The mineral is very strong, with an estimated value of 110 GPa (gigapascals) for its Young's modulus. Young's modulus is a measure of the amount of deformation a material will undergo, under some given force, before it breaks. For comparison, the Young's modulus of aluminum metal is about 70 GPa, that of brass is about 110 GPa, and that of stainless steel about 200 GPa.

The matrix at this lower level of organization in bone is the protein collagen. Collagen is the most abundant protein found in animals. It consists of a triple helix, with three long ropelike *polypeptide* molecules wrapped around each other, as shown in the diagram on page 22. Each polypeptide chain contains about 1,000 amino acids and has a molecular weight of about 100,000. Collagen is a soft, pliable, but not very strong material, with a Young's modulus of about 1.2 Gpa. Composite bone material develops over time as dahlite crystals are precipitated in spaces between bundles of collage molecules. These crystals gradually grow outward, replacing water molecules originally interspersed among the collage molecules, until they form continuous sheets. These sheets act as the filler for the collagen material, giving it strength and toughness.

This model of bone as a composite material, while correct as far as it goes, is insufficient. Measurements of actual bone strength do not conform to those predicted by the dahlite-collagen model. Researchers now believe that a higher level of organization must be considered to explain the effectiveness of bone as a composite. At this higher level, the fillers in bone are thought to be hollow structures known as *osteons* (also known as *Haversian systems*) embedded in a matrix consisting of mucopolysaccharides. Mucopolysaccharides are polysaccharides the monomers of which are sugar molecules, amino sugars, and uronic acid (altered forms of simple sugars).

The structure of this material is generally similar to that of reinforced concrete, which contains steel rods embedded in concrete. Researchers are currently attempting to calculate the predicted strength of the osteon-mucopolysaccharide composite and to compare it with observed values.

Like bone, wood is a complex composite consisting of a small number of basic materials, primarily cellulose, lignin, and hemicellulose. Cellulose is a long-chain polymer of glucose. As a plant grows, cellulose molecules arrange themselves in highly ordered crystal-like arrays known as *microfibrils,* which collect themselves into even larger structures, *fibrils.* Cellulose accounts for about half the mass of wood. As with glass fibers in reinforced plastics, cellulose fibrils are flexible with high tensile strength.

Lignin is a three-dimensional polymer of phenylpropane, in which a variety of groups can be substituted on any one of the three carbon atoms (the α, β, and γ carbons) in the propane chain. Hemicellulose is a less polymerized form of cellulose. These two materials, lignin and hemicellulose, constitute the matrix in which cellulose fibers are embedded. As a plant grows, chains of lignin and hemicellulose develop and link together bundles of cellulose microfibrils. Like the plastic in a reinforced plastic, these chains hold the fibrils together, providing stiffness to the final product.

Bone and wood are only two examples of the many composites found in nature. Others are teeth, shells of sea and land animals, plant structures, and exoskeletons of insects. In every instance, natural processes have evolved that combine the qualities of matrices and fillers to form strong, durable, flexible materials used for a variety of purposes by living organisms.

Composites in Human History

Possibly the first synthetic composite to be used by humans was brick. Brick is a mixture of straw and clay that has been heated and dried. In their original form, bricks were made of clay only. Such bricks, properly called mud or clay bricks, were among the first building materials to be used by humans. The raw material, clay, was readily available in most parts of the world, easily shaped when wet, and strong for most purposes. For example, in the walls of a house, the dominant force is downward (compressive), a force that dried clay resists quite well, but dried clay by itself does not withstand twisting or bending forces very well. Strike a mud brick sharply on one end, for example, and it is likely to shatter quite easily.

By trial and error, people found that they could augment the properties of a mud brick by adding straw. A piece of straw is flexible, and it has great tensile strength. It can bend or be pulled on opposite ends without breaking or tearing apart very easily. By embedding straw in wet clay and allowing the mixture to dry, one adds straw's tensile and bending strength (also known as its *modulus of rupture*) to clay's compressional strength. The resulting composite is superior to simple mud bricks for most building purposes.

Advanced Composites

Researchers developed relatively few synthetic composites throughout history. One exception was the discovery by French inventor Joseph Monier (1823–1906) that implanting steel rods in concrete after it had been laid greatly increases the strength of the final product. That discovery introduced the age of *reinforced concrete,* making available a product that is still used extensively throughout the world.

The modern age of composites can be dated to the 1940s, however, when a confluence of factors led to the rapid development of a number of new materials. Perhaps the most important of these factors was the demand for a variety of new materials created by World War II. The construction of aircraft and projectiles, in particular, required better strong, light-weight materials than were currently available. The growth of the polymer industry, which occurred simultaneously, provided some of the materials needed to effect this changeover from traditional materials to new composites. Finally, the chemical industry itself experienced an enormous growth spurt during and just after the war, providing an even wider array of materials for use in the manufacture of new composites.

◄ STEPHANIE KWOLEK (1923–   ) ►

The 1940s marked the beginning of the age of polymer chemistry. During preceding decades, the discovery of new products such as Bakelite, nylon, rayon, celluloid, polyvinyl chloride, polyethylene, Saran™, and Teflon convinced chemical corporations that such products held the key to an exciting and profitable future based on a host of amazing new "miracle" materials. Research departments around the world began the search for new materials with properties designed to meet a variety of special needs. One chemist who succeeded in this kind of project was Stephanie Kwolek.

Stephanie Kwolek was born in New Kensington, Pennsylvania, on July 31, 1923. Her father died when she was 10, and her mother took a job at the Aluminum Company of America (Alcoa) to support the family. After graduating from high school, Kwolek entered the Women's College of Carnegie-Mellon University, planning for a career in medicine. She graduated in 1946 with a B.S. degree in chemistry but was unable to continue her medical studies because of a lack of money. Instead, she accepted a job at DuPont, one of the world's largest and most prestigious chemical companies, where she was first assigned to the Rayon Department at the company's plant in Buffalo.

Kwolek's task at DuPont was to find a new kind of fiber that was resistant to acids and bases and that would remain stable at high temperatures. In 1964, she discovered such a product, an aromatic polyamide that was five times as strong as steel with half the density of fiberglass. The material was given the name aramid. Aramid was later marketed under the trade names of Kevlar® and Nomex®. Today, aramid is one of the most widely used substances in polymer matrix composites.

Kwolek remained with DuPont for the rest of her working life, retiring in 1986. She has remained active in the field of chemistry since her retirement. She serves as a consultant to DuPont and to the National Research Council of the National Academy of Sciences. Kwolek was inducted into the National Inventors Hall of Fame in 1995, only the fourth woman to be so honored, and received the National Medal of Technology in 1996. She was also awarded the Perkin Medal in 1997, only the second woman to receive that award.

As a result of this impetus, interest in composite design has shifted to a new class of materials known as *advanced,* or *high-performance,* composites. Advanced composites are structural materials designed for applications for which more traditional materials, such as aluminum alloys and steels, are not strong enough, able to withstand heat, sufficiently durable, or unsatisfactory in other ways. Such applications include automobile, airplane, and spacecraft frames and components. Advanced composites typically offer greater stiffness, strength, and durability, along with lower density, than their metallic counterparts.

Like other composites, advanced composites can be organized according to the types of fillers (also called *reinforcements*) and matrices that make them up. The properties of an advanced composite depend primarily on the type, length, shape, and orientation of the reinforcing (filler) material. By far the most common type of reinforcement is glass, largely because it is the least expensive filler commonly available. Glass fibers are also, however, the least rigid and the most dense of such materials. Their use is therefore limited to nonstructural, low-performance applications, as in the panels that make up the body of a pleasure boat.

Carbon fibers are the most rigid and strongest of commonly used reinforcements. They are produced by the pyrolysis (high-temperature decomposition) of natural and synthetic materials, such as rayon, polyacrylonitrile (PAN), and pitch (the tacky residue left from the distillation of petroleum or coal tar). Carbon fibers are commercially available in a variety of formats, including single strands and bundles (known as *tows*). They are midway in density between glass and polymer fibers and are the most expensive of commonly used reinforcements.

In theory, almost any polymer can be used as a reinforcement in an advanced composite. By far the most common polymer fiber, however, is aramid, better known by its trade name, Kevlar. Developed originally for use in belted radial tires, aramid is an aromatic polyamide in which benzene fragments (C_6H_4) alternate with peptide groups ($NHC = O$) in forming a polymeric structure:

$$-[-NH-C_6H_4-NH-\ CO-C_6H_4-CO-]-$$

It is produced from a liquid solution in a process similar to that by which viscose rayon is made. The final product consists of long fibers with the lowest density of all commonly used reinforcements. Aramid's rigidity and strength are intermediate between those of glass and carbon.

A variety of inorganic materials are also used as reinforcers. These include boron, silicon carbide (SiC), silicon nitride (Si_3N_4), titanium carbide (TiC), and aluminum oxide (Al_2O_3). These materials are usually made by the vapor deposition of raw materials. For example, when a halide of boron (such as boron trichloride, BCl_3) is heated on a hot tungsten wire, it decomposes to form elemental boron and the corresponding halogen. The boron then condenses as a thin wire, which can be used as a filler. Boron fibers were one of the first fillers to be used in advanced composites, but they are more expensive, less rigid, and weaker than carbon fibers.

Aluminum oxide fibers have use in specialized advanced composites because of their high strength and rigidity, high melting point, and exceptional resistance to corrosion. They are usually produced by the extraction of aluminum oxide from a liquid solution, followed by drying and spinning into rodlike fibers.

Researchers are constantly searching for new materials that can be used as fillers in advanced composites. For example, the U.S. Department of Agriculture (USDA) is currently sponsoring research on the use of wood fibers embedded in a polymer matrix. The problem is that relatively little is currently known about such systems, and products that have been developed are not competitive with existing composites. One of the most promising approaches developed at the USDA so far begins by treating wood fibers with styrene-maleic anhydride (SMA). A matrix is then prepared by reacting polypropylene with maleic anhydride to form a *copolymer* with a variety of similar chemical structures, all of which involve various combinations of styrene ($C_6H_5CH=CH_2$) fragments interspersed with fragments of maleic anhydride ($C_4H_2O_3$). The wood-SMA fibers bond strongly with the polypropylene-maleic anhydride matrix to form a strong, durable product.

At Imperial College, London, researchers are studying the properties of composites made of a natural or modified flax fiber embedded in a variety of matrices, such as polyester and high- and low-density polyethylene. A major challenge at this point is to improve the adhesive qualities between flax fibers and polymer matrices in such materials. If the fibers do not bond strongly to the matrix, the material breaks apart easily and has no practical applications.

Fibers of almost any kind can come in a variety of lengths, from a few microns to a few centimeters. They can be classified as particulate, discontinuous (short), or continuous. Particulate fibers are small and of roughly the same dimension in all directions. Embedding tiny grains of sand in a plastic matrix would produce a composite of this type. In general, short fibers provide greater strength to a composite than do long fibers. To attain such strength, however, the fibers should all be aligned in the same direction, a difficult fabrication challenge.

Reinforcements can be made with one-, two-, or three-dimensional shapes. A threadlike glass or carbon fiber, for example, has only one dimension: length. But reinforcements can also be made with two dimensions (length and width), as in thin, crystalline plates, or even three dimensions, as in a mineral crystal. The mechanical properties of such materials typically vary—often dramatically—in different directions. For example, some types of silica fibers may have a tensile strength of 110,000 psi (pounds per square inch) in a direction parallel to that of the fiber length to only 14,000 psi in a direction perpendicular to that of the length. In this case, a hammer blow to the side of the material would be about eight times as likely to break it as would a "head on" blow of the same force. In the design of a composite material, therefore, the direction in which the fibers in the matrix lie must correspond to the direction of loading forces that will act on the material.

The most common materials used for making matrices today are polymers, long-chain organic molecules consisting of many (usually thousands of) or repeating units, the monomer(s). For example, polyethylene is made in a series of reactions in which individual ethene (ethylene; $CH_2 = CH_2$) molecules are added to a growing chain, one unit at a time:

$$CH_2=CH_2 + CH_2=CH_2 \rightarrow CH_3CH_2CH=CH_2$$

$$CH_2=CH_2 + CH_3CH_2CH=CH_2 \rightarrow CH_3CH_2CH_2CH_2CH=CH_2$$

$$CH_2=CH_2 + CH_3CH_2CH_2CH_2CH=CH_2 \rightarrow CH_3CH_2CH_2CH_2CH_2CH_2CH=CH_2, \text{etc.}$$

In some cases, the polymer may be formed by the reaction of two different monomers, as in the case of the reaction between phenol (C_6H_5OH) formaldehyde (HCHO):

$$C_6H_5OH + HCHO \rightarrow C_6H_4(OH)CH_2OH$$

$$C_6H_4(OH)CH_2OH + C_6H_4(OH)CH_2OH \rightarrow C_6H_4(OH)CH_2C_6H_3(OH)CH_2OH + H_2O, \text{etc.}$$

Polymers that consist of only a single polymer are called *homopolymers,* while those that contain two different monomers are known as *copolymers.*

Polymers can be classified into one of two general categories: *thermoplastic* and *thermosetting.* Thermoplastic plastics are formed from liquid solutions that eventually become solid. When heated, these solid polymers soften and can be reshaped. By contrast, thermosetting polymers, once they become solid, cannot be resoftened or reshaped. If they are reheated, they crack, break, or otherwise deform. For most applications, thermosetting *resins* are preferred because they are very durable and resist wear and attack by chemicals. On the other hand, thermoplastic polymers have the advantage of being more resistant to fracture than thermosetting resins. They can also be recycled and produce fewer environmental pollutants during manufacture.

The most common advanced composites are made of thermosetting resins, such as epoxy polymers (the most popular single-matrix material), polyesters, vinyl esters, polyurethanes, polyimids, cianamids, bismaleimides, silicones, and melamine. Some of the most widely used thermoplastic polymers are polyvinyl chloride (PVC), PPE (poly[phenylene ether]), polypropylene, PEEK (poly [etheretherketone]), and ABS (acrylonitrile-butadiene-styrene). The precise matrix selected for any given product depends primarily on the physical properties desired for that product. Each type of resin has its own characteristic thermal properties (such as melting point and thermal conductivity), chemical resistance, electrical properties, resistance to combustion, adhesive characteristics, durability, and density.

Metals and *ceramics* (claylike materials) are also used as matrices in advanced composites. In most cases, metal matrix composites consist of aluminum, magnesium, copper, or titanium; alloys of these metals; or intermetallic compounds, such as TiAl and NiAl. The reinforcement is usually a ceramic material such as boron carbide (B_4C), silicon carbide (SiC), aluminum oxide (Al_2O_3), aluminum nitride (AlN), or boron nitride (BN). Metals have also been used as reinforcements in metal matrices. For example, the physical characteristics of some types of steel have been improved by the addition of aluminum fibers. The reinforcement is usually added in the form of particles, whiskers, plates, or fibers.

Metal-matrix composites may have a number of desirable properties, including high strength at relatively low weight; high compression strength; excellent performance at high temperature; and resistance to fatigue, creep (weakness that develops in a metal over time), abrasion, and other forms of wear. An important advantage of metal-matrix composites is their electrical conductivity, a property often not found in traditional polymer-matrix composites. It is not unusual for some metal-matrix composites to demonstrate electrical conductivity much greater than that of most steel alloys and up to half that of pure aluminum metal.

So far, relatively few applications have been found for ceramic-matrix composites. The major problem is that such products tend to be very brittle. However, the search for improved materials is an active field of research, and a number of interesting and promising new materials have been developed. For example, particles, whiskers, plates, or fibers of silicon carbide (SiC) can be embedded in a matrix of silicon nitride (Si_3N_4) to produce a composite that tends to be very rigid and tough even at very high temperatures. One form of the product retains these properties at temperatures in excess of $1,400\,°C$. The high-temperature attributes of ceramic-matrix composites makes them useful in automotive and aircraft engines and in energy generation facilities.

Some of the most common combinations used in the development of new ceramic composites involve the use of silicon carbide, silicon nitride, aluminum oxide, silicon dioxide, and mullite (a form of aluminum sulfate $(Al_2[SO_4]_3)$. Each of these compounds can be used either as the reinforcement or as the matrix in a composite.

Recent research has explored a wide variety of filler-matrix combinations for ceramic composites. For example, scientists at the Japan Atomic Energy Research Institute have been studying a composite made of silicon carbide fibers embedded in a silicon carbide matrix for use in high-temperature applications, such as spacecraft components and nuclear fusion facilities. Other composites that have been tested include silicon nitride reinforcements embedded in silicon carbide matrix, carbon fibers in boron nitride matrix, silicon nitride in boron nitride, and silicon nitride in titanium nitride. Researchers are also testing other, less common filler and matrix materials in the development of new composites. These include titanium carbide (TiC), titanium boride (TiB_2), chromium boride (CrB), zirconium oxide (ZrO_2), and lanthanum phosphate $(LaPO_4)$.

One of the most promising forms of advanced composites is the carbon-carbon composite, which consists of continuous carbon fibers embedded in a carbon matrix. The product has excellent strength and toughness up to temperatures of 2,000°C. These properties make it useful in applications such as motor parts and exhaust cones on rockets and space vehicles. As researchers begin to solve the many technical problems associated with the design of new composites, those products will begin to see a number of new applications in a wide range of commercial fields, including the space program, military applications, air transportation, sports and recreation, and construction.

Applications of Advanced Composites

Some basic principles involved in the production of composites have been known since ancient times. The ancient Egyptians developed methods for incorporating glass fibers in vases and other types of containers. Such applications were largely decorative, however, providing little if any structural support to the objects. The birth of modern composite technology dates only to the 1940s, when a Russian father-and-son team, K. L. and D. L. Biryukovich, began experimenting with glass fiber–reinforced concrete. Their initial results were promising but ultimately led nowhere: It turned out that their product degraded rapidly over time. At about the same time, the first fiber-reinforced composites were being developed, although World War II prevented the immediate application of this technology to actual structures.

It was only with the end of the war that progress in the development and use of advanced composites began to take place. One of the most powerful forces bringing about this development was the U.S. government, which demanded new and improved materials for use in aircraft and the nation's young space program. Supporters of the burgeoning aircraft industry realized that the cost of air travel could be reduced only if new materials could reduce the weight of airplanes and, hence, the cost of operating them. And administrators of the space program recognized that a very substantial portion of the cost of placing objects into orbit around the Earth was related to the energy needed to lift heavy masses through Earth's atmosphere.

The special needs of the space program motivated the search for composite materials for other reasons also. For example, during tests of the first Atlas ICBM (intercontinental ballistic missile), engineers were concerned that the rocket's metallic components would not survive the missile's reentry into the atmosphere; they feared it would melt down because of the intense heat to which it was exposed. By the late 1950s, therefore, aerospace researchers had begun to look for satisfactory substitutes for metal alloys for such applications. With that research, the modern field of composite design was born. One of the first composites tested consisted of pieces of glass embedded in melamine, purported to be the first composite material developed for aerospace applications.

An important breakthrough in the development of advanced composites came in the late 1960s: the invention of boron and carbon filaments in the United States, the United Kingdom, and Japan. These fibers were soon incorporated into some of the earliest fiber-reinforced polymers (FRPs) for use in aerospace vehicles. The first application of such composites was the horizontal stabilizer in the U.S. Navy's F-14 fighter in 1970. Shortly thereafter, FRPs were used in the construction of the U.S. Air Force's F-15 and F-16 fighters.

Even today, air, space, and related military applications continue to account for the largest single use of advanced composites. Such materials have dozens of applications in airplanes and space vehicles. On some aircraft, for example, they are used for the radar dome that covers the nose of the aircraft, for cabin floor panels, on access doors and handles, for horizontal and vertical stabilizers, and on fairings throughout the aircraft. Fairings are structures whose primary function is to produce a smooth contour, reducing drag. Composite fairings can be found on aircraft doors, air brakes, fins, wings, and other parts of an airplane.

The reason military aircraft account for the largest single use of metal matrix composites is that these materials are considerably more expensive than traditional alloys. Such composites are currently used in jet engines because of their superior strength and stiffness over a large range of temperatures. Some automakers have attempted to adapt this technology for use in diesel engines, but costs are still too high to allow their widespread use in most commercial automobiles. It is possible, however, that metal matrix composite technology can be improved for future use in specific applications, such as the "skin" and engines of high-speed aircraft and for propeller shafts, bearings, pumps, transmission housings, gears, springs, suspension systems, and other mechanical components of aircraft, space vehicles, commercial automobiles, and high-speed machinery.

Other military applications continue to account for a large fraction of all types of advanced composites produced today. Such materials are used, for example, in the construction of missile systems, their ammunition components, and their launch systems. Missile-related components that use composites include launcher tubes, armor-piercing penetrators, and stanchion and torpedo tubes used in submarines.

Although few applications have so far been found for ceramic matrix composites, they have shown considerable promise for certain military applications, especially in the manufacture of armor for personnel protection and military vehicles. Historically, monolithic ("pure") ceramics such as aluminum oxide (Al_2O_3), boron carbide (B_4C), silicon carbide (SiC), tungsten carbide (WC), and titanium diboride (TiB_2) have been used as basic components of armor systems. Research has now shown that embedding some type of reinforcement, such as silicon boride (SiB_6) or silicon carbide (SiC), can improve the mechanical properties of any of these ceramics.

Military and aerospace applications have often been the first uses of advanced composites. But soon after these military, air, and space composite technologies were developed, they began to appear in civilian products. For example, the National Aeronautics and Space Administration (NASA) created the Aircraft Energy Efficiency (ACEE) program in 1975 to improve airplanes' efficiency. By 1982, composite technology developed for military aircraft had been incorporated into the stabilizers of a commercial aircraft, the Boeing 737. As the decade progressed, other composite technologies were used in the design of many other commercial aircraft, including the Boeing 757 and 767; the McDonnell-Douglas MD-82, -83, and -87; and the Airbus 300 and 310. As they replaced traditional alloys, these composites reduced the weight of such aircraft by up to 30 percent.

For many Americans, composites' contribution to new product design is most prominent in the field of sports and recreation. Credit for the construction of the first boat made of composite material is sometimes given to Ray Greene, an inventor from Toledo, Ohio, who built a fiberglass dinghy in 1942. By the early 1950s, composite technology for boats was well developed and widely discussed. Nonspecialists could read about such boats in general circulation magazines such as *Popular Mechanics.* Within two decades, fiberglass and other composite watercraft (boats, yachts, kayaks, canoes, and others) had become far more popular than their wooden counterparts.

◄ OWENS-CORNING FIBERGLAS® ▷

Throughout the history of science, one can point to a single individual who deserves credit for making an important breakthrough discovery or invention. As scientific research has become more complex and more expensive, however, scientists are less likely to work independently and to make discoveries that they can claim for their very own. Instead, important inventions and discoveries are often credited to teams of researchers, in some cases large teams of scientists. And in many cases, those teams work under the auspices of some major industrial research laboratory. Such is the case with the development of the product now known as fiberglass.

Techniques for spinning thin wires of glass have been known for centuries, but little progress was made toward the development of a commercial product, or even toward the recognition of the commercial applications of such a product. In the early 1930s, however, one of the world's major glass manufacturing companies, Corning Glass of Corning, New York, began to explore the possibilities of turning spun glass into a major commercial product. Their earlier research throughout the 1920s had convinced company officials that the product could be made economically and that it held the potential for a number of practical uses.

In 1935, officials of Corning approached a smaller glass-making company in Illinois, known as Owens-Illinois, about the possibility of joining forces in the development of fiberglass and fiberglass products. Owens-Illinois had been formed only six years earlier through the merger of the Owens Bottle Company, founded in 1903, and the Illinois Glass Company, established in 1873. Agreement was reached, and a new corporate entity, Owens-Corning Fiberglas®, was created on November 1, 1938. By the end of the first year, the company was employing 632 men and women and reported sales of $2,555,000.

The combination of strength, durability, and light weight have also made composites popular for many other types of sporting equipment, including bicycle frames; snowboards; golf clubs; tennis, badminton, and squash rackets; surfboards; archery bows and arrows; fishing poles; hockey sticks; in-line and ice skates; hang gliders; skis and ski poles; racing cars; and athletic footwear.

World War II provided a host of new opportunities for the young company. In 1939, the U.S. Navy Bureau of Ships chose Owens-Corning fiberglass as the standard insulating material for all new ships being constructed under its direction. By the end of 1942, the company had produced more than 22 million square feet (2.04 million m²) of the product for navy use. Other products developed by the company for wartime use included sewn blankets, electrical wire insulation, metal mesh blankets, battery separators, and wool insulation. It also invented new materials for use in airplanes, including laminates made from fiberglass cloth impregnated with resin for use in structural aircraft parts.

As the war drew to a close, Owens-Corning began to plan for peacetime uses of its fiberglass products. In 1946, it introduced fiberglass-reinforced fishing rods, serving trays, acoustical tiles, and pleasure boats. And in 1953, it announced production of the first commercial automobile, the Chevrolet Corvette, with a body made entirely of polymer matrix composite, a fiberglass reinforced plastic.

On January 2, 1996, Owens-Corning Fiberglas® Corporation changed its name to simply Owens Corning, a change reflecting the growth in the range of technology developed and used by the company over its 30-year history. By 1999, corporate sales had reached more than $5 billion. By that time, however, the company was suffering severe financial reversals as the result of a very large number of asbestos lawsuits filed against it. The company filed for bankruptcy in 2000 but has since begun to recover from this difficult period in its history. Whatever its future, Owens Corning has already secured its place in the history of chemical technology with the development of one of the commercially most important and successful composites ever made, fiberglass.

One of the most interesting applications of composites has been in the area of infrastructure, the system of public works in a city, county, state, or nation. One of the serious problems facing many government bodies, for example, is the deterioration of bridges. Yet the cost of repairing and/or replacing bridges can be more than the governments can easily afford. One approach to solving this problem has been to make use of strong, durable, high-density composites in place of steel, concrete, and other traditional bridge-building materials. Today, there are literally hundreds of bridges around the world that have been built or repaired using composites rather than traditional materials. Some examples include a light-weight vehicular bridge built in the Philadelphia zoo; a pedestrian bridge at the Antioch Golf Club in Antioch, Illinois; a pedestrian walkway over the Chicago River in Chicago; a highway bridge near Edmonton, Alberta; a retrofitted Foulk Road Bridge in Wilmington, Delaware; and the new Tech 21 bridge in Butler County, Ohio.

Composite materials have also been used to add seismic protection against earthquakes to existing bridges. The first such project involved the use of a glass-aramid composite to wrap 34 support columns in the parking garage of the Nikko Hotel in Beverly Hills, California, in 1993. When an earthquake struck the area two years later, a number of the unprotected columns in the garage were damaged, but those that had been wrapped with the composite survived without damage.

Composites are also being used in a number of other construction programs. In 1995, for example, a large order of polymer matrix composite was used in the construction of a new offshore oil drilling platform off the coast of Louisiana. The material was used because it has a high resistance to flame and high temperatures with low thermal conductivity, making it possible to withstand exposure to a fire without serious long-term damage.

Although relatively unimportant in terms of the total mass used, composites now appear in a very large variety of industrial, mechanical, tool, and other applications. Some examples include antennas; drive shafts; light poles; oil field tubing; tool handles; beams, shafts, and columns; modular toilet units; doors and window frames; containers for chemical storage; radar domes; pressure vessels; a variety of electrical and electronic equipment, such as motors, generators, and printed circuit boards; drive shafts; cutting tools; signs and display boards; *sensor* devices; movie camera bodies; ceiling panels; decking; lightweight boxes and storage containers; robotics; undersea vehicles; and furniture. The list goes on and on.

The development of new composites over the past half century has dramatically enhanced the variety of materials available for construction, manufacturing, and other purposes. These materials are generally lighter, stronger, and more durable than traditional composites or pure materials, such as steel, cement, and plastics. They can also be engineered for use in products that were once available only at high cost, or not available at all. Future research on composites will almost certainly further expand the range of materials available for use in roads and bridges, homes and office buildings, factories, airplanes and space vehicles, sports equipment, and countless other applications.

3

BIOMATERIALS

The 1970s saw the introduction of a very popular series of three television motion pictures, followed by a television series on the same theme: *The Six Million Dollar Man*. The motion pictures and series starred Lee Majors as a test pilot whose airplane crashed, resulting in the loss of both legs, an arm, and an eye. Majors's character, Steve Austin, was rebuilt by a skilled physician named Dr. Rudy Wells using advanced biomedical body parts at a cost of $6 million (hence the name). In a follow-up series, Lindsay Wagner played Austin's counterpart, Jaime Sommers, in *The Bionic Woman*. Sommers was seriously injured in a parachute jump and, like Austin, is provided with a number of engineered body parts that give her extraordinary physical powers.

In the 1970s, these stories were generally viewed as "far-out" science fiction, a view of what medical science *might* be able to accomplish some day, probably far into the future. Only three decades later, however, many of the most unlikely forms of biological engineering imagined by author Martin Caidin, creator of the bionic man concept, have come to pass. Indeed, modern research in biomaterials has begun to surpass many of the wildest dreams of chemists, physicians, surgeons, biologists, and others interested in the design of synthetic biological materials and body parts. While that research has not yet found the range of applications that scientists expect, it has shown the possibilities for future progress in replacing body parts with synthetic substitutes.

A number of definitions have been offered for the term *bioma-terials*. One of the most common is the following: Biomaterials are nonviable (nonliving) materials used in a medical device, intended to interact with a biological system. Other authorities prefer a broader definition that includes the use of synthetic, semisynthetic (or hybrid), and/or living (rather than strictly nonviable) materials designed to serve some function in a biological system.

In general, biomaterials can be subdivided into three major categories:

1. Those that are essentially inert chemically and biologically, that is, that produce no response (or virtually no response) from tissues and other biological substances with which they come into contact;

2. those that play some active role in the body by bonding to or reacting with surrounding tissue or other biological material; and

3. those that are degradable (that is, that essentially dissolve) or that are absorbed (that is, that are incorporated into the body) over a period of time.

Some of the biomaterials that fall into one of these categories are synthetic skin, blood, nerves, tissues, and organs.

History of Biomaterials

Humans have been using crude forms of biomaterials for a very long time. One of the most common uses of biomaterials has been the replacement of broken or diseased teeth with implants made of various types of material. For example, archaeologists have found Egyptian skulls dating to 2000 B.C.E. containing gold implants for lost teeth. Early Egyptian dentists also appear to have used sea shells hammered into the jaw to replace lost teeth.

The use of wood or metal for the manufacture of simple prosthetic devices also has a very long history. The technology needed to replace an amputated leg, for example, is not very difficult since the prosthetic simply has to support the weight of its wearer. Wooden legs and hooks or claws for arms are familiar to readers of both fiction and nonfiction. As early as the fifth century B.C.E., the Greek playwright Aristophanes included a part in his play *The Birds* for an actor wearing a leg prosthesis.

In 2000, archaeologists at the Ludwig Maximilian University in Munich reported finding the mummified remains of a 50- to 60-year-old Egyptian woman with a prosthetic big toe on her right foot. The woman's death was dated at between 1550 and 700 B.C.E. The researchers concluded that the woman had had her toe amputated and the prosthetic toe installed during her lifetime. The prosthesis was made of three separate components, was functional, and had even been painted brown to match the color of her other toes.

For nearly four centuries, one of the most active fields of research on biomaterials has been the search for blood substitutes. Not long after the English physician William Harvey (1578–1657) discovered the process by which blood circulates in the body, people began searching for substitutes for natural blood for treatment of those who had been wounded or had lost blood in some other way. At first, those efforts had little scientific basis and centered on certain apparently logical connections. For example, wine was sometimes used to replace human blood because blood and wine have a similar color. Milk was also used as a blood substitute because both milk and blood are naturally occurring bodily fluids.

In 1868, two German biologists known today only by their last names of Ludwig and Schmidt developed a technique for using gum acacia as a blood substitute in certain of their experiments. That product continued in use for certain types of emergency circumstances for more than four decades. During World War I, for example, medical researchers working for the U.S. Army explored the possibility of using an acacia solution as a blood substitute in battlefield emergencies. They found that a 6–7 percent solution mixed with a 0.9 percent solution of sodium chloride had the same viscosity and osmotic pressure as normal blood. It also did not seem to induce immune responses in the person who was infused with the solution, nor did it causes the formation of blood clots. It could also be easily sterilized without destroying the solutes. Gum acacia was unable to take over the oxygen-transporting properties of normal blood, but it was able to maintain other vital blood functions. In spite of this research, the product was never used in actual practice by the military.

In spite of the long history of dental implantation, blood substitutes, and prosthetics, the history of modern biomaterials dates only to the beginning of the 20th century. One of the earliest researchers to attempt the replacement of interior tissues and organs with synthetic materials was the French physician Alexis Carrel (1873–1944). In the early 1900s, Carrel attempted an amazing array of experiments on the transplantation of blood vessels and organs and on vascular suturing (the stitching of blood vessels), research for which he was awarded the 1912 Nobel Prize in medicine or physiology. Among his many experiments, Carrel designed and tested the use of tubes made of rubber, glass, metal, and a specially made absorbable form of magnesium as substitutes for damaged blood vessels. In one experiment, he replaced a portion of the thoracic aorta in a dog with glass and metal tubes covered with paraffin. The dog survived for 90 days in "perfect health," as Carrel reported in his Nobel lecture.

Probably the first successful and widespread clinical use of biomaterials occurred in the early 1900s, when a number of metals and alloys were developed to stabilize bones that had been fractured. These materials were used to form bone plates that held the broken ends of bones in place until they grew back together. After healing, the plates were removed, if possible, or, if not, left in the patient's body.

The first metal alloy developed specifically for use in bone plates was vanadium steel, invented in about 1905. Over the next two decades, a number of other alloys and metals were tried as bone plate materials. In 1926, another alloy designed especially for bone plates was invented. It was a type of stainless steel consisting of 18 percent chromium and 8 percent nickel. Later the same year, a slightly modified form of the alloy was introduced, called 18-8SMo, containing a small amount of molybdenum.

The problems experienced with these early types of bone plates foreshadowed the types of problems medical researchers could expect to encounter as they pursued their research on new biomaterials. Metals and alloys were often difficult to fit precisely with the living material (bone and tissue) they were designed to support. Also, the human body's immune system frequently reacted to these implants, resulting in infections and rejections of the metal or alloy. Finally, some materials designed for use as bone plates were attacked and dissolved by bodily fluids, resulting in their failure. These three problems—choice of material to be used, design of the device, and biocompatability—remain the three major issues with which biomaterials researchers have to deal.

One of the turning points in the history of biomaterials occurred during World War II, with the development of a range of new polymeric substances. The connection between the use of polymers and biological implants was illustrated in a somewhat peculiar way during the war. The English ophthalmologist Sir Harold Ridley (1906–2001) noticed that British Royal Air Force pilots who had survived plane crashes sometimes had shards of plastic from broken windshields embedded in their eyes. Surprisingly, these plastic shards remained in the eye for long periods of time without causing any apparent harm or discomfort to the men. Ridley got the notion of using this plastic, a substance called polymethylmethacrylate (PMMA), to form lenses that could be embedded into a person's eyes to improve vision. Although most of Ridley's professional colleagues in Europe and the United States spurned his idea, the implantation of intraocular lenses made of PMMA has now become standard procedure, and more than 5 million people worldwide have received this technology.

At the dawn of the 21st century, the invention, development, and use of biomaterials has become big business in the United States and around the world. According to a 2001 report in *Chemical and Engineering News,* more than 10 million Americans now have at least one kind of implanted medical device, and national sales generated by the biomaterials industry exceeds $50 billion per year. Industry analysts see an even larger future for the industry. For example, every year about 30,000 people die from liver failure while waiting for liver transplants, of which fewer than 3,000 become available every year. Modifications that would lead to acceptable liver substitutes would save the lives of many of these individuals.

One of the most important themes in modern biomaterials research is a shift from emphasizing human-made materials that take over normal bodily functions (such as replacing blood with some kind of blood substitute) to finding ways of encouraging the body to make its own repairs. A primary reason for this change in emphasis is the tendency of the body to reject, to at least some extent, almost any biomaterial that is embedded into it.

The presence of an implant almost always energizes the body's immune system, which sends out white blood cells to destroy the "foreign invader" (the implant). Even if a biocompatible material is used for the implant, inflammation caused by the surgical procedure used in its insertion may also cause an immune response. Although the immune system's macrophages are generally unable to eliminate the implant itself, they may cause scar tissue to form around the implant. The scar tissue often prevents the restoration of normal tissue at the site of the implant, which can prompt an early failure of the implant itself.

Today, much of the research on biomaterials can be classified into three major fields: *tissue engineering*, development of replacement parts, and creation of blood substitutes. Although there is some overlap among these fields, they serve well as organizing themes for recent developments in the science of biomaterials development.

Tissue Engineering

One of the youngest fields in the area of biomaterials is tissue engineering. Although some research in this field was taking place before the mid-1980s, the term *tissue engineering* itself was coined only in 1987, when it was proposed and defined at a series of meetings sponsored by the National Science Foundation as the following: "Tissue engineering is the application of principles and methods of engineering and life sciences toward fundamental understanding of structure-function relationships in normal and pathological mammalian tissues and the development of biological substitutes to restore, maintain, or improve tissue functions."

Two other definitions provided in a 2002 report by the International Technology Research Institute are:

"Tissue engineering is an interdisciplinary field that applies the principles of engineering and the life sciences toward the development of biological substitutes that restore, maintain, or improve tissue function,"

and

"Tissue engineering is the basic science and development of biological substitutes for implantation into the body or the fostering of tissue remodeling for the purpose of replacing, repairing, regenerating, reconstruction, or enhancing function."

The important theme in all of these definitions is the desire of the drafters to move away from the use of donor or artificial organs or tissues as replacement for damaged body parts and explore mechanisms by which the body can be encouraged to heal itself. This theme is reflected in two terms sometimes used as synonyms for tissue engineering: *regenerative medicine* and *reparative biology.*

The treatment of damaged skin has been a problem for medical workers for centuries. In some cases, skin damage results from a surgical procedure, such as during the amputation of some body part. Far more often, however, skin damage occurs as the result of a burn.

Burns are classified into one of three categories, depending on the severity and symptoms presented. The most serious type of burn, a third-degree burn, may actually be the least painful because nerves in the skin are destroyed, and the burn victim loses all sense of feeling in the affected area. But third-degree burns are also the most serious, since all three layers of skin, epidermis, dermis, and subcutis, are destroyed. Historically, third-degree burns over a large part of a person's body led almost inevitably to death.

Recorded efforts to deal with damage to skin tissue date to the second century B.C.E., when an Indian surgeon by the name of Sushruta (fl. sixth century B.C.E.) developed a method of grafting skin taken from one part of a patient's body to replace a lost nose. Amputation of noses was a common procedure at the time, partly because of injuries from knives and swords, and also because nose amputation was a common legal punishment.

Probably the most famous practitioner of grafting prior to the modern age was the Italian physician Gaspare Tagliacozzi (1545–99). Tagliacozzi developed a method for grafting skin from a person's arm to his or her nose by physically attaching the arm to the damaged nose until new skin began to grow back. He described his procedures in a now-famous text called *De Curtorum Chirugia per insitionem.* One reason the success of Tagliacozzi's work was important (although it was condemned by the church) was the spread of syphilis among the general population; a long-term consequence of untreated syphilis is deterioration and loss of the nose.

Grafts like those developed by Sushruta and Tagliacozzi are called *autografts.* Autografts are the most desirable form of grafting. Because it does not involve the introduction of tissue from a different person or a different species, the likelihood that a patient's body will reject an autograft is nearly zero.

Autografting is not always possible, however. For example, a person who has third-degree burns over more than half of his or her body does not have enough healthy skin to use for autografting. In such cases, replacement skin must be found from some other source. If the other source is human, the graft is called an *allograft* or *homograft.* The most common form of grafting makes use of skin taken from cadavers. Skin from animals other than humans has also been used to treat patients with damaged skin. Such grafts are called *xenografts* or *heterografts.* Traditionally, the most common animal used as a donor in xenografting treatment has been the pig.

Of all forms of skin grafting, autografting is by far the most likely to be successful. In other forms of grafting, a patient is likely to suffer not only from infections developing from the loss of skin, but also from immune responses as his or her body begins to reject the "foreign" implant, the skin from some nonself source.

The modern era of skin grafting using synthetic materials began in the late 1970s, when Dr. John F. Burke, then director of the Burn Center at Massachusetts General Hospital and Shriners Burns Institute, became frustrated at the inadequacies of existing

◄ IOANNIS V. YANNAS (1935–   ) ►

Scientific research today sometimes produces strange bedfellows, teams of scholars from fields that might seem very far apart and distinct from each other. Research on biomaterials is one area with many such examples. Someone interested in developing an artificial heart, a blood substitute, or a new material that can be used for bone must know a little something about many topics from biology, chemistry, and physics. Even better, such research can be carried out most efficiently when scholars from each of these fields is involved in a research program. One of the best examples of that point is found in the history of research on artificial skin, in which Ioannis V. Yannas made an important breakthrough.

Ioannis V. Yannas was born in Athens, Greece, on April 14, 1935. He attended Harvard College, from which he received his A.B. degree in 1957; MIT, where he earned an S.M. degree in 1959; and Princeton University, which awarded his M.A. and Ph.D. degrees in 1965 and 1966, respectively. Between 1959 and 1963, Yannas worked as a physical chemist at the chemical firm of Grace Company in Cambridge, Massachusetts. In 1966, Yannas was appointed to his position in the Department of Mechanical Engineering at MIT, a post he held until 1968. He was then promoted to associate professor and then full professor in 1978.

In the early 1970s, John F. Burke, then director of the Burn Center at the Massachusetts General Hospital (MGH) and the Shriners Burns Institute decided that traditional methods of treating serious burns were inadequate. Those methods were based on the philosophy that healers should wait until the patient's skin sloughed off on its own before healing could begin. Burke

grafting techniques in the treatment of seriously burned patients. He contacted Dr. Ioannis V. Yannas, professor of both polymer science and engineering and of biological engineering at the nearby Massachusetts Institute of Technology. Burke and Yannas discussed the development of new materials that could be used in place of human or other animal skin for the treatment of serious burns. By 1981, Yannas had devised such a material, and in that year it was first transplanted on a burn patient at Massachusetts General Hospital in Boston.

thought that a better approach might be to actually remove the patient's damaged skin. In order to adopt this procedure, however, Burke realized the necessity of having a skin substitute available that could be used to replace the lost skin.

As a physician, Burke knew a great deal about the biology of skin function, but not as much about the structural characteristics of a possible skin substitute. To help him with this part of his research, Burke turned to Ioannis V. Yannas, then assistant professor of fibers and polymers in the Department of Mechanical Engineering at the Massachusetts Institute of Technology (MIT), just across the Charles River from MGH. Working together Burke and Yannas developed the first successful skin substitute by 1977. In November of that year, they were awarded a patent for a "Multilayer Membrane Useful as Synthetic Skin."

Yannas has also held appointments as professor of materials science and engineering at MIT (1983–2000), professor in the Harvard-MIT Program in Health Sciences and Technology (1978–present), and professor of bioengineering and environmental health at MIT (1998–present). Yannas has also served as visiting professor at the Royal Institute of Technology in Stockholm (1974), at MGH (1980–81), and at Shriners Burn Institute (1980–81). He has published more than 200 research papers and a book, *Tissue and Organ Regeneration in Adults,* published in 2001. He has been awarded, on his own or with collaborators, 14 patents in the field of organ regeneration. Yannas is an active teacher and researcher with interests in a variety of fields, including biomaterials, tissue engineering, polymer science and engineering, design of medical devices and implants, cell-matrix mechanics, and deformation and fracture of polymers.

Yannas's invention mimics the structure and function of the upper two layers of natural skin. It consists of an upper layer about 0.023 mm thick made of an elastic silicone material that, like the human epidermis, acts as a barrier to the loss of moisture from the body. Silicones are siloxane polymers to which are bonded various organic radicals (groups of atoms that contain carbon). The chemical structures of siloxane and a typical silicone polymer are shown on page 50.

The lower layer of Yannas's artificial skin consists of a 2-mm thick matrix of collagen fibers, obtained from bovine tendons, and

Structures of siloxane and silicone

chondroitin sulfate, obtained from shark cartilage. Collagen is the most common protein in the human body. As explained in chapter 2, it is found in skin, muscles, and tendons and has a triple-helical molecular structure, similar to the appearance of a three-stranded rope. Each of the strands that make up this "rope," in turn, is a long polypeptide chain (a chain made of many amino acid residues) especially rich in the amino acids glycine, alanine, proline, and hydroxyproline. Chondroitin sulfate belongs to a family of hetero-polysaccharides (polysaccharides consisting of two or more differ-ent monosaccharides) called the glycosaminoglycans, or GAGs. The glycosaminoglycans are also sometimes known as mucopolysaccha-rides. The two monomers that make up the chondroitin polymer are D-galactosamine and D-gluconic acid.

When the collagen–chondroitin sulfate matrix is laid down over an area where skin has been lost, it begins to act like the *extracel-lular matrix* normally found there. Extracellular matrix is a complex mixture of molecules (the most common of which in humans is collagen) that are secreted by cells and that surround the cells that produce them. It has three major functions in the body: (1) providing structural support for cells, (2) providing substances needed by cells to migrate and attach themselves to other cells, and (3) regulating the development of cells and cell metabolism.

Yannas and his colleagues discovered that once the collagen-chondroitin sulfate matrix was in place, the recipient's dermal cells began to migrate into the matrix and attach themselves to collagen molecules, replicating the process by which natural skin is formed. Over time, the bovine collagen degraded and was replaced by human collagen identical to that found in natural skin. At the same time, blood vessels began to grow into the matrix, producing a tissue with essentially the same characteristics as the patient's original skin. Once the dermal layer had regenerated itself, the protective outer coating of silicone could be removed and replaced by a very thin transplant of epidermal tissue from elsewhere on the patient's body. Burke and Yannas patented their new product under the name of Integra® in 1980.

As promising as Yannas's original formulation was, it suffered from one major problem. In a patient who is severely burned, there may not be enough healthy skin tissue available to harvest the epidermis needed to replace the silicone coating on the artificial graft. Yannas's solution to this problem was to develop an artificial epidermis that could be implanted at the same time as the artificial dermis.

Yannas's procedure produces the artificial epidermis by taking basal cells from the patient's healthy skin. Since only the basal cells are needed in this procedure, only very small amounts of healthy skin are needed. The basal cells are seeded into a collagen matrix, which is laid onto the dermal layer (the collagen–chondroitin sulfate matrix); it replaces the upper layer of silicone used in the original formulation. Over time, the implanted basal cells multiply within the matrix, generating new epidermal tissue that incorporates blood vessels and nerves. The new skin, consisting of regenerated dermal and epidermal layers, is functionally identical to skin originally lost by the patient.

This explanation emphasizes the success of the Yannas procedure, but actually a number of technical problems had to be solved before Yannas's artificial skin functioned properly. For example, he discovered that the matrix had to be designed so as to degrade at precisely the correct rate. If it degraded too rapidly, the burn wound was exposed before new skin tissue had been formed. If it degraded too slowly, the new tissue intermixed with the engineered material in the matrix. Also, the molecular structure of the collagen proved to be a crucial factor in the effectiveness of the skin replacement process. The collagen molecule had to provide just the correct number of sites at which dermal cells could attach themselves before beginning to proliferate. While it is not clear why this relationship is true, experimentation demonstrated that it was.

Another form of tissue engineering begins with human skin cells harvested from infant foreskins. These cells grow and develop very rapidly and can be embedded into a matrix that can be overlaid on tissues exposed by burns, trauma, or other kinds of damage. In 1997, a company formed to develop and market synthetic tissue, Advanced Tissue Sciences, for marketing of its artificial skin product, Dermagraft-TC®, produced by this technology, and a second company, Organogenesis, received FDA approval in 1998 for a similar product, Apligraf®. Advanced Tissue Sciences has since discontinued operations, although Organogenesis remains in business.

Although progress in tissue engineering has been slow, many experts expect more rapid growth in the near future. This optimism is based on a number of factors, including the success achieved so far by Organogenesis's Apligraf®, growing interest in regenerative research and applications in many universities, the creation of a number of start-up companies working in the field, and growing interest in stem cell research, which has applications to research in tissue engineering.

Replacement Parts

Successes achieved in the young science of tissue engineering have encouraged researchers to consider the possibility of wholesale replacement of a number of body parts. For example, Ioannis Yannas's success with artificial skin has been one factor in his latest area of research, replacement of nerves.

One of the areas of greatest interest is the development of synthetic blood vessels. Heart disease is currently the number one cause of death among both men and women in the United States. The most common cause of heart disease, in turn, is atherosclerosis, a condition in which fatty deposits form on the inner walls of blood vessels, constricting the flow of blood. If it were possible to develop an artificial substitute for blood vessels damaged by atherosclerosis or other diseases, it would save the lives of millions of Americans each year.

Little progress was made in solving this problem in the four decades following Alexis Carrel's research during World War I. Then, in the mid-1950s, researchers began exploring a variety of techniques for producing synthetic blood vessels. One line of research relied on biological materials as the basis for the engineered vessels. For example, some researchers tried transplanting blood vessels taken from cows into human patients, but these transplants usually degraded too rapidly to make them useful on a long-term basis.

In another line of research, scientists began to look for synthetic materials from which artificial blood vessels could be manufactured. Some of the earliest materials to be tried were synthetic fibers, such as nylon, vinyon (a polymer consisting primarily of vinyl chloride), and ivalon (a polymer of vinyl alcohol). These materials were largely unsuccessful because they tended to lose their strength too quickly after implantation.

The first really successful artificial material used in the manufacture of synthetic blood vessels was Dacron®, a polyester fiber made from polyethylene terephthalate (PET). The material is woven or knitted into thin tubes with dimensions similar to those of a natural blood vessel. The tubes are then treated with coagulated blood or with albumin, an important blood protein, to block the tiny holes in the fabric of which they are made. Over time, cells migrate into the blood or albumin trapped within the Dacron matrix and deposit collagen. As the blood or albumin degrades, it is replaced by the collagen, producing a vessel with some properties similar to those of natural blood vessels.

Another synthetic material used for the manufacture of artificial blood vessels is polytetrafluoroethylene (PTFE), a polymeric material widely known by its trade name, Teflon®. Teflon is produced in the form of an impermeable sheet that can be formed into small cylinders. Since it lacks holes like those found in Dacron, artificial blood vessels made from Teflon need no additional treatment to prevent the seepage of blood. In addition, the strongly electronegative charge on the surface of Teflon (which also accounts for its nonstick properties in a number of commercial applications) was thought to offer protection against the formation of blood clots in the artificial vessels. Initial hopes for Teflon vessels were disappointed in early trials, however, when it was found that the material had a tendency to "balloon out," producing aneurisms. In modified forms, where thicker walls are used or additives strengthen the walls, the material has gained wider use in the manufacture of artificial blood vessels today. The structural formula for Teflon is as follows:

$$-[-CF_2-CF_2-CF_2-CF_2-]-$$

Dacron, however, continues to be the most popular material used in the production of artificial blood vessels. When first used with experimental animals, treated Dacron appeared to induce the regeneration of interior walls of blood vessels (called *neointima*) in essentially the same way as the natural process. When implanted into humans, however, the same treated Dacron has a somewhat different effect, resulting instead in the formation of a thin (about 1 mm thick) layer of fibrin (or a pseudointima) on the inner lining of the blood vessel. While this thin layer of fibrin is of relatively modest concern in larger blood vessels, it can be a serious problem in vessels less than 5 mm in diameter. In such cases, fibroblasts from the blood stream attach themselves to the fibrin, and the blood vessel gradually becomes blocked.

Scientists continue to look for new and better materials out of which to form artificial blood vessels. In 1990, for example, the biomedical company Organogenesis began testing a material they called *living blood vessel equivalent* (LBVE), whose structure mimics the three-layer structure of natural blood vessels. The three layers, consisting of en-

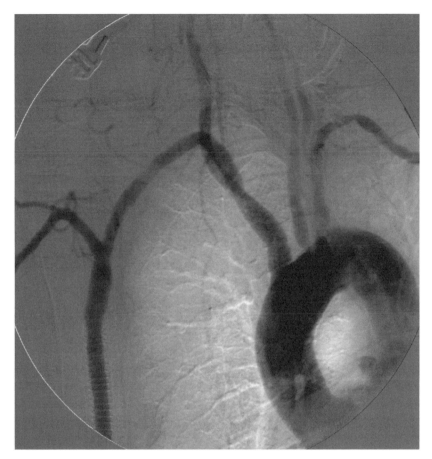

The blood vessel in the lower left hand portion of this angiogram is made of synthetic material. (Simon Fraser/ Freeman Hospital/Photo Researchers, Inc.)

dothelium, smooth muscle, and connective tissue cells, are held together and strengthened by a Dacron mesh woven through the three.

Also, in late 2002, scientists from Stanford University announced progress in the development of artificial blood vessels using only natural body cells. They made a two-layer sheet of material, one layer consisting of human fibroblast cells, which form the outer wall of blood vessels, and the other made of endothelial cells, cells that form the inner lining of blood vessels, taken from experimental animals. Researchers wrapped the two-layer sheet around a tiny cylinder to form the blood vessels, which were then implanted in rats and dogs.

Except in two cases, in which the two-layer sheet was found to be defective, no harmful effects were observed over a two-week period in the animals who received the implants. Thus far, experiments on human subjects have not been completed.

Another active field of research includes experiments designed to develop biomaterials that can be used to substitute for natural bone. In spite of its lifeless appearance, bone is a living material that consists of nerves, blood vessels, collagen, and three important kinds of cells: osteoblasts, cells that are responsible for synthesizing new bone; osteoclasts, cells that catalyze the degradation of old bone; and osteocytes, mature forms of osteoblasts that are no longer capable of producing new bone. This complex combination of living structures is embedded in a matrix of inorganic material that gives bone its strength and firmness. The primary component of this nonliving matrix is hydroxyapatite, $Ca_{10}(PO_4)_6(OH)_2$.

Artificial bone implants are used to deal with two distinct problems: fractures and bone loss. When a bone breaks, it immediately begins to heal itself by generating new bone material that will ultimately join the broken parts to each other. In simple fractures, a caregiver can assist this process by encasing the fractured area in a cast, which holds the bone parts in place until they heal naturally. But in some cases, a fracture is so serious that the broken segments may need to be held in place by some strong, stiff material until they have had an opportunity to grow back together. After that process is completed, the support may be removed, or, in some cases, it may be left in place for many years or for the life of the patient.

Bone replacement may also be necessary in older people because the natural process by which bone is replenished begins to fail. That is, osteoclasts continue to perform their function at a normal rate, breaking down old bone so that it can be replaced by new bone. But osteoblasts no longer operate as efficiently as they once did, and an inadequate amount of new bone is produced to replace that lost to the work of osteoclasts. In such cases, a person's bones may become thin and brittle, often resulting in the kind of deterioration and breakdown that cannot be solved by a metal pin, bar, or sheet, as would be used in the case of fractures. In such cases, surgeons may

This bioceramic material is made of hydroxyapatite that has been inoculated with bone marrow stromal cells. (Mauro Fermariello/Photo Researchers, Inc.)

suggest an entirely synthetic replacement for a knee, a hip, or some other joint that has been damaged beyond repair.

Probably the earliest example of bone replacement dates to 1668, when the Dutch physician Job van Meekeren (1611–66) transplanted a section of a dog's cranium into the skull of a soldier who had been wounded in battle. The implantation was apparently successful, but the solider later asked to have it removed. He had been told by the Catholic Church that the surgery was an affront to God because animal tissue had been inserted into the human body.

Joint replacement, caused by the ravages of arthritis and other bone diseases, has long fascinated medical inventors. Although surgical efforts to replace joints date as far back as the 19th century, virtually no progress was made in this field until at least the middle of the 20th century. In 1925, for example, Dr. Marius Smith-Peterson

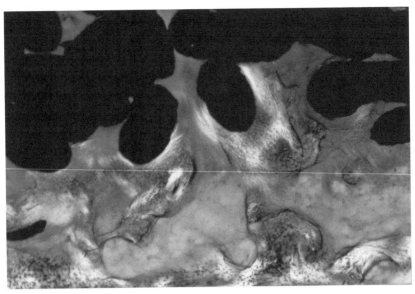

This material, made of titanium metal joined to a biocompatible substance, is used for hip and knee replacements. (Daculsi-CNRS/Photo Researchers, Inc.)

of the Massachusetts General Hospital designed a glass cup to fit on top of a femoral head damaged by arthritis in a patient's knee. The experiment was, however, a failure because the device failed.

A decade later, a group of new metals and metal alloys became available for the construction of artificial knees, hips, and other joints. These included stainless steel, cobalt, and titanium products. Since that time, these materials have been the most popular materials from which joint replacements, as well as supporting structures for the immobilization of fractures, have been made.

One of the most important discoveries leading to the adoption of these metals for bone replacements was made in 1952 by the Swedish orthopedic surgeon Per Ingvar Branemark. While working on an unrelated project, Branemark observed that a metal cylinder made of titanium metal inserted into a rabbit's thighbone was fully integrated into the bone, a process that later became known as *osseointegration*.

Currently, the materials of choice for most bone implantations are metals and metal alloys. These materials have the advantage of providing strength and support for a joint or fractured bone, while reacting to a surprisingly small degree with the biological tissue into which they are embedded. The most popular of these products are titanium and titanium alloys, although stainless steel 316L, alloys of chromium and cobalt, and nitinol (an alloy of nickel and titanium) are also widely used. The specific metal or alloy used in any particular implantation is determined by the function the material has to play in the body. For example, a major concern for a load-bearing structure will be strength, so a strong metal or alloy is chosen for the implant.

Metals and metal alloys are not without their disadvantages as biomaterials, however. Although they tend to be quite stable in a biological system, they are not completely inert. They do react to some extent, meaning the metal implant can deteriorate over time. A number of methods have been devised to reduce this problem. For example, metal implants are sometimes attached to existing bone with a ceramic material, which acts as a buffer between the metal and the living material in bone.

In recent years, however, there has been growing interest in trying to develop nonmetallic biomaterials that embody both the advantages of metals (strength and rigidity) while avoiding their disadvantages (reactivity with body tissues). One group of compounds that has been studied in some detail includes the polyglycolides (PGAs) and polylactides (PLAs), polymers of glycolic and lactic acids, respectively. The chemical formulas for these two compounds are shown below. Copolymers of the two substances (PGLA) have also been developed and tested.

Glycolic acid: $CH_2OHCOOH$
Lactic acid: $CH_3CHOHCOOH$

One advantage of these polymers is that they degrade slowly over time, producing only water and carbon dioxide as waste products. Also, while they are in place, they produce little or no antibody reaction from the host body's immune system, and new bone material grows in as the polymer degrades away. The major disadvantage of such materials is that they are not as strong as metals and alloys and cannot be used as replacement for bones that must bear significant body weight.

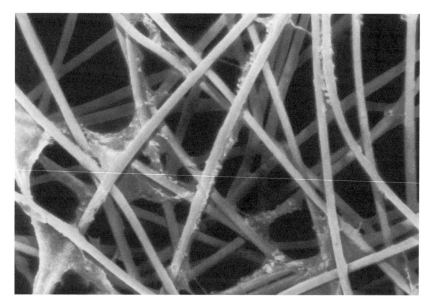

An electron micrograph showing the structure of artificial cartilage made with a matrix of polyglyolid fibers that hold embedded cartilage cells (David Mooney/ Photo Researchers, Inc.)

These polymeric materials are fabricated to mimic the shape of natural bone, in a form referred to as a scaffolding. The scaffolding provides open spaces in which the body's osteoblasts can begin the regeneration of new bone. When regeneration is complete, the new bone can take over the structural chores temporarily performed by the bone implant.

Researchers are also exploring ways of using inorganic materials, especially those closely related to natural bone material, for artificial bone filling. Interpore International of Irvine, California, for example, received approval in 1992 for its hydroxyapatite-based bone substitute called Pro Osteon. The material is made from coral that has been heated to temperatures of about 2000°C to obtain hydroxyapatite (a primary component of coral) of 95 percent purity. The material is then formed into a scaffolding resembling natural bone, and this final product is irradiated with gamma rays to sterilize it.

Another approach involves the synthesis of some bonelike material from simpler compounds. For example, in a process developed by the Osteo Medica company in the 1990s, calcium metal, calcium hydroxide, and phosphoric acid are heated together at temperatures of 700 to 8,500°C. The product of the reaction is a hydroxyapatite with pores whose size can be controlled by adjusting reaction conditions. The company plans to market the product under the name Megagraft 1000.

Other researchers are considering the possibility of using inorganic compounds similar (but not identical) to the natural hydroxyapatite found in bones. Thus far, more than two dozen compounds of calcium sulfate and calcium phosphate have been tested for use as possible bone substitutes. The sulfates have been found to be largely unsuccessful, while the phosphates appear to hold more promise. Their advantage is that they can be formed into scaffolding that will promote the growth of new bone cells, but they are not very strong and are currently quite expensive to make.

One approach developed by Isis Innovation Limited (a wholly-owned subsidiary of the University of Oxford) involves the precipitation of calcium phosphate onto collagen at room temperature. When o-phosphoserine is added to the reaction, the calcium phosphate precipitates onto the collagen in the form of small "needles." These structures provide abundant surface area on which osteoblasts and other bone cells can become established.

Finally, in 2002 the Japanese firm Olympus Optical announced that it had begun testing its OSferion artificial bone replacement material. The material consists of a highly porous β-tricalcium phosphate (β-TCP) scaffolding into which differentiated bone cells have been inserted. The presence of the bone cells is designed to initiate and promote growth of new bone material to replace the β-TCP scaffolding as it degrades.

Researchers have made amazing progress in the development of materials and structures for the replacement of nearly every possible body part. In most cases, however, those developments have been limited thus far to experimental use in a relatively small number of cases. A number of technical problems remain to be solved before engineered materials become reliable and inexpensive enough to be used commonly for the repair and replacement of structures damaged by injury and disease.

Artificial Blood

The synthetic biomaterial for which demand is greatest is artificial blood. Each year more than 12 million blood transfusions are performed in the United States. Many times that number are carried out in other countries around the world. The ideal substance to use in a blood transfusion, of course, is usually properly matched human blood, but, for a number of reasons, it has never been possible to rely entirely on human blood for transfusions.

In the first place, adequate supplies of blood may not be available when and where they are needed. For example, medical workers may not have enough human blood on hand to treat the victims of an accident or a terrorist attack, on a battlefield during wartime, or during some other major emergency. In addition, members of some religious groups are not permitted by their faith to accept blood transfusions from another person. Also, transfusions carried out with human blood may actually present health risks of their own, such as, for example, when blood contains viruses or other disease-causing organisms. Finally, supplies of blood from human donors are routinely inadequate in poor countries, where well-developed blood bank programs do not exist.

Human blood is a complex mixture with a variety of functions provided by four major components: red and white blood cells, platelets, and plasma. When a person begins to lose blood rapidly, the body can survive for at least a short time without the white blood cells (which are needed only to stave off infection), the platelets (of which there are large excesses in the body), and plasma (which can be replaced by an isotonic fluid, such as saline or Ringer's solution). But life cannot continue long with a replacement for the red blood cells. These are the cells that carry oxygen from the lungs to other cells, where it is used to carry out the metabolic processes that keep the body alive.

Actually, it is not the red blood cells themselves that are crucial to survival, but the hemoglobin molecules within them. Hemoglobin molecules are made up of two pairs of identical polypeptide chains, named the alpha 1 and 2 (α1 and α2) and the beta 1 and 2 (β1 and β2) chains. These four chains are bonded weakly to one another in an arrangement known as a *tetramer* ("four parts").

◁ THOMAS CHANG (1933–) ▷

Scientific research is not a pursuit for anyone who is interested in immediate returns on their work. Sometimes researchers spend a dozen years or more—and sometimes their whole lifetimes—before realizing a goal. This is often the case in biomedical research, where a discovery or invention alone is not the end of a research project. That discovery or invention then must typically go through a long and complex testing phase that may last 10 years or more. Such has been the story of the father of artificial blood cells, Thomas Ming Swi Chang.

Thomas Chang was born on April 8, 1933, in Swatow, a coastal town in southern China. His grandfather was a very successful industrialist, but Chang's family left Swatow for Hong Kong as refugees in 1950. Chang's decision to become a physician was a disappointment to his family, so he promised them that he would go to the best university in the world and "do something to make the family proud." He received his bachelor of science degree in physiology in 1957 and his M.D. in 1961 from McGill. More than 30 years later, in 1995, he was awarded his Ph.D. in physiology from McGill.

Chang first became interested in the possibility of building an artificial red blood cell in 1956, while still an undergraduate at McGill University in Montreal. "I thought, if artificial organs could be built—why not the basic unit, the cells?" he told a staff writer for the university's newsletter, *McGill News,* in 1996. And, in fact, he was successful in putting together an artificial cell 1 mm in diameter, with a membrane made of collodion that enclosed a molecule of hemoglobin. The cell did not function in an organism, however, the way natural red blood cells do.

Almost a half century later, Chang has not given up on his pursuit of a functional artificial red blood cell that can be used in blood substitutes. Although he has made a number of important breakthroughs in his research, he has not yet devised a product that functions properly in the body. He has not set his goals aside, however. "I'm a stubborn person," he told the newsletter reporter. "I don't give up too easily."

Chang has spent his entire academic career at McGill, serving as assistant professor (1966–69), associate professor (1969–72), and full professor (1972–present). He has written more than 400 scientific papers and 21 books and is currently editor in chief of the international journal *Artificial Cells, Blood Substitutes & Biotechnology.* In 1991, Chang was made an Officer of the Order of Canada, an award recognizing important contributions to the nation and the world.

Within each of the four chains is a *heme* group that contains a single atom of ferrous iron (iron(II), Fe^{2+}). In the presence of molecular oxygen, each atom of iron(II) can bond to a single oxygen molecule, forming a complex known as oxyhemoglobin. The bloodstream carries oxyhemoglobin to individual cells, where, in oxygen-poor environments, it breaks down to form the original hemoglobin molecule, releasing oxygen to cells.

One possible approach to the manufacture of synthetic blood might be simply to remove the hemoglobin from red blood cells and introduce it directly into the bloodstream of a patient who has lost blood. When these experiments were actually carried out, however, the results were disastrous. Free hemoglobin *outside* the protective coating of a red blood cell quickly breaks down into two parts; that is, the tetramers degrade into dimers ("two parts"), and the type of dimer that is formed is toxic to the kidneys! One of the body's most important life-giving and life-saving molecules, hemoglobin becomes a killer once removed from its "home" inside a red blood cell.

Since the discovery of this effect, researchers have attempted another line of invention, one in which pure hemoglobin is "bundled" in some way or another so as to prevent its toxic effects. These modified forms of hemoglobin are called *hemoglobin analogs.* They fall into two general categories: encapsulated hemoglobin and cross-linked hemoglobin.

The first encapsulated hemoglobin was invented in the mid-1950s by Thomas Chang (1933–), then an undergraduate student in physiology at McGill University in Montreal. Chang extracted hemoglobin from red blood cells and embedded it in an artificial cell whose membrane was made of the synthetic polymer pyroxylin. The first problems this product presented were related to its short half-life in the blood, generally only a few hours. In attempting to solve that problem, Chang and other researchers have used a variety of materials for the membranes of their artificial red blood cells, including cellulose nitrate, polystyrene, nylon, silicone rubber, polyamides, lipids alone, and various combinations of lipids with proteins, cholesterol, and polymers. Today, the most popular material used for the membrane is a liposome. A liposome is a microscopic pouch consisting of two layers of lipid (fatty) material that has both hydrophilic and hydrophobic properties. (Hydrophilic chemicals mix readily with water; hydrophobic ones do not.) The inside of the pouch contains an aqueous solution in which the hemoglobin is suspended.

Encapsulated hemoglobin has been studied for more than 50 years without progressing to advanced trials in humans. Its immediate outlook is not, therefore, very promising. Nonetheless, because the encapsulated hemoglobin is potentially so similar to a natural red blood cell, some specialists believe it holds the best long-term hope for the production of artificial blood.

A second, apparently more promising, approach to the development of artificial blood in the short term is a type of blood analog that introduces new chemical bonds *within* a single hemoglobin molecule or *among* two or more hemoglobin molecules. This cross-linking is intended to stabilize the hemoglobin molecule and prevent it from degrading into the dimeric, toxic form when introduced into the bloodstream.

The simplest cross-linking approach is to add bonds between the alpha chains and beta chains within the hemoglobin molecule to provide the needed stability. More commonly, researchers have bonded two or more hemoglobin molecules together to form a complex known in general as *polyhemoglobin*. Polyhemoglobin may consist of anywhere from a handful to a few thousand hemoglobin molecules bonded to each other. *Intra*molecular bonding may also be combined with the *inter*molecular bonding used to produce these larger arrays.

Research on polyhemoglobins has been going on since the 1960s, and a group of "first-generation" products is now available either for testing or, in some cases, for limited human use. The general problem with all such first-generation polyhemoglobins remains their brief residence time in the body. Researchers are now working on second-generation products that have an important property not available in first-generation polyhemoglobins: the inclusion of certain enzymes that protect against oxidants, such as free oxygen radicals. Oxidants tend to attack hemoglobin and convert it to a modified form known as methemoglobin, which is unable to bond to and transport oxygen.

Work has also begun on a third generation of polyhemoglobins in which a membranelike envelope will be developed to encase the polyhemoglobin-plus-enzyme system from second-generation research. The most optimistic observers predict that such products will be available at least for testing, and perhaps for actual human use, in the next decade or so.

As of late 2006, no hemoglobin analog had yet been approved for use in humans in the United States. A veterinary product, Oxyglobin®, produced by the pharmaceutical firm Biopure, has been approved in the United States and Europe. Its human counterpart, HemoPure®, was approved for human use in South Africa in 2001, making it the first hemoglobin analog to receive approval for human use anywhere in the world. South Africa granted its approval of the product for transfusions because the country's supply of human blood is at high risk of being tainted with the HIV or hepatitis C viruses.

HemoPure has also been used in the United States in about 40 compassionate-use cases. Compassionate-use is a special situation in which a patient's medical condition is so serious that the FDA may grant special, one-time permission to use a drug that has not yet otherwise been approved for human use.

Another artificial blood product named PolyHeme® was submitted for FDA approval by its manufacturer, Northfield Labs, in August 2001. PolyHeme is produced by extracting hemoglobin from red blood cells, filtering them to remove impurities, and then modifying them chemically to produce the polymerized hemoglobin analog.

Some researchers are exploring a totally different approach to the production of artificial blood that focuses on the synthesis of non-natural substances with bloodlike properties. This approach has the advantage of avoiding the use of human or animal blood or any of its components. One line of research makes use of a class of chemicals known as the *perfluorocarbons* (PFCs), hydrocarbons in which all hydrogens have been replaced by fluorine atoms. The first PFC to be marketed commercially was called Fluosol-DA, manufactured by the Green Cross Corporation of Japan. Fluosol-DA was a mixture of perfluorodecalin ($C_{10}F_{18}$) and perfluorotripropylamine ($C_9F_{21}N$) emulsified with Pluronic F-68, a copolymer of oxyethylene and oxypropylene.

In 1983 the FDA approved Fluosol-DA for limited use as a blood substitute in coronary angioplasty surgery. However, a number of problems were associated with its use. For instance, patients had to breathe nearly pure oxygen in order to obtain a satisfactory concentration of oxygen in the blood. Also, the product was found to accumulate in the body's reticuloendothelial system (RES), whose function it is to protect the body against infection. As a result of these and other problems, Green Cross ceased production of Fluosol-DA in 1994.

Research on PFCs has not ceased, however. Indeed, it has achieved some success in preventing the retention of these compounds in the RES, although the problem of the high oxygen concentrations needed for breathing has not yet been resolved. One of the most promising products appears to be a substance called Oxygent™, developed by Alliance Pharmaceutical Corporation. Oxygent is based on a slightly modified form of perfluorocarbons called perflubron, the brand name of perfluorooctyl bromide ($C_8H_{17}Br$) mixed with a small amount of perfluorodecyl bromide ($C_{10}F_{21}Br$). Both of these products are forms of perfluorocarbons in which a single terminal fluorine atom is replaced by a bromine atom. Oxygent is more stable than Fluosol-DA (stored at just above freezing, its shelf life is about two years), and it has a higher oxygen-carrying capacity (about five times that of Fluosol-DA). As of late 2006, Oxygent was in phase 3 clinical trials in the process of obtaining FDA approval for human use.

The day when a truly bionic man or woman can be produced by biomaterials engineers has still not been reached. If researchers have discovered anything at all in their work on artificial skin, blood vessels, bone, and blood, it is that living systems are far more complex and delicate than many scientists had believed, and efforts to replicate them with the best-known biological, chemical, and physical techniques still fall far short of the perfection obtained by nature itself. Still, impressive strides have been made in only a few decades, and one can be optimistic that another few decades from now will see the ready availability of synthetic skin, blood, and bone, along with many other synthetic body parts and materials.

4
NANOMATERIALS

In December 1959, the Nobel laureate Richard Feynman (1918–88) gave an address at the annual meeting of the American Physical Society (APS) he called "There's Plenty of Room at the Bottom." This speech remarked on the great revolutions in materials science. Rather than starting with large chunks of matter and manipulating them to get the shapes and properties desired, Feynman posed the possibility of manipulating individual atoms and molecules to achieve the precise structures people want. He concluded his speech with two challenges to the physics community: first, the construction of an operating electrical motor in the shape of a cube no larger than 1/64 inch per side; and second, a method for reducing a page of printed material to 1/25,000 standard size so that it could be read with an electron microscope.

Feynman was already known for his sly and sophisticated sense of humor. The fact that he offered a $1,000 prize for each challenge—then a small fortune for a college professor, even one of Feynman's stature—only confirmed the belief that he regarded them as insurmountable. To his surprise, Feynman did have to pay one $1,000 prize less than a year later, when an inventor presented him with the miniature motor described in his speech. Despite this accomplishment, his vision of a revolutionary new approach to materials science did not materialize in his lifetime. The reason for this neglect is clear: No one had the foggiest notion of how to pick up and move an atom.

Nearly two decades later, however, an undergraduate at the Massachusetts Institute of Technology (MIT) began thinking along similar lines. K. Eric Drexler (1955–) was not familiar with Feynman's famous speech at first, but he attended MIT at a time when the marvelous workings of DNA and RNA in the manufacture of proteins were first being studied. Drexler began to ask himself whether other kinds of molecules could gain the wonderful abilities of nucleic acid molecules to make exact copies of themselves and to produce new molecules. Suppose scientists could build both very small molecules with the ability to duplicate themselves (which Drexler called *replicators*) and other molecules that could manufacture specific molecular products (Drexler called these molecules *assemblers*). If they could, a whole new approach to materials science might be possible. This approach is now a reality known as *molecular manufacturing,* or *nanotechnology.*

What Is Nanotechnology?

The prefix *nano-* comes from the Greek word for "dwarf." A *nanometer* (nm) is 1 billionth of a meter (10^{-9} m), about 1 ten thousandth (10^{-4}) the diameter of a human hair. The term *nanotechnology* usually refers to the manipulation of materials in the low nanometer range, generally from about 1 to 100 nm. Many atoms and molecules have dimensions of a few nanometers or less. The diameter of a hydrogen atom, the smallest of all atoms, for example, is 0.078 nm. Most common biological molecules consist of thousands of atoms and have dimensions of a few 10s of nanometers or more.

The term *nanotechnology* is sometimes used ambiguously, however. In some cases, it is used simply to describe objects and events with "very small" dimensions, such as a few microns in size. A micron (μm) is a micrometer, or 1 millionth (10^{-6}) of a meter. Unarguably, a micron is a very small dimension; a human hair, for example, is about 10 μm in diameter. Still, a micron is 1,000 times as large as a nanometer, and research conducted at the micron level is more accurately known as *microtechnology.* Studies that involve objects

◁ RICHARD FEYNMAN (1918–1988) ▷

The world's literature is filled with science fiction stories attempting to forecast the future of human civilizations. Scientists and novelists alike have described such apparently fantastic concepts as flights to the Moon (such as Johannes Kepler's *Somnium* of about 1591), aircraft that could hover motionless in the air (Leonardo da Vinci's helicopter, late 16th century), and interplanetary battles between humans and invaders from other planets (H. G. Wells's *The War of the Worlds*, 1898). These stories may or may not be based on scientific information available to the author. But they almost always include a very large amount of creativity on the writer's part, and they may turn out to be very accurate predictors of scientific inventions that arise years, decades, or centuries later. Or they may prove to be nothing other than wild flights of imagination that never become realities. One of the great names that was added to this list of prognosticators in the 20th century was that of Richard Feynman, who predicted the field of nanotechnology.

Feynman was born in New York City on May 11, 1918. He attended the Massachusetts Institute of Technology (MIT), from which he received his bachelor's degree in 1939. He went on to earn a doctorate in physics at Princeton University in 1942. During World War II, Feynman worked on the Manhattan Project in Los Alamos, where he was in charge of a group working on problems of separating uranium isotopes by means of diffusion. After the war, Feynman accepted an appointment in the Department of Physics at Cornell University. In 1950, he took a similar position at the California Institute of Technology. Feynman's special area of expertise was the study of quantum electrodynamics. He was awarded a share of the 1965 Nobel Prize in physics for his work in this area.

and events in the submicron range (10–1,000 nm), however, may legitimately be thought of as either microtechnology or nanotechnology.

So what's in a name? Does it make any difference whether a researcher calls her work "microtechnology" or "nanotechnology"? In some cases, the answer is yes, and often for completely nonscientific reasons. Since the 1990s, nanotechnology has become a hot topic. In

In December 1959, Feynman gave a now-famous speech to the American Physical Society (APS). In it, he described a new way of making materials that was dramatically different from any approach ever attempted by humans. His audience listened to his address with uncertainty. Feynman was widely known for his impish sense of humor, and APS attendees could not decide whether their collective legs were being pulled when Feynman suggested that they start thinking about the possibility of making materials one atom or molecule at a time. He pointed out that throughout history, scientists had taken a brute force approach to materials science, beginning with large chunks of matter and then cutting, bending, twisting, and shaping them to achieve certain desired properties, but, Feynman observed, there was nothing in the laws of physics that prevented scientists from starting at the bottom, picking up and moving around individual atoms and molecules to produce the shapes and properties they wanted. Even a half century later, it is not completely clear to what extent Feynman was fantasizing and to what extent he was predicting the future of materials science.

Feynman was widely known as an outstanding teacher and interpreter of science and technology for the general public. His *Feynman Lectures on Physics* (in three volumes, with R. Leighton and R. Sands, 1963) is still one of the finest general introductions to the subject available. Feynman also wrote two enormously successful popular books about physics, *Surely You're Joking, Mr. Feynman* (W. W. Norton, 1985) and *What Do You Care What Other People Think?* (W. W. Norton, 1988). He is probably best remembered by many people for his work on the commission appointed to study the cause of the *Challenger* space disaster in 1986. He was the commission member selected to appear before television cameras to explain the O-ring failure that caused that disaster. Feyman remained at the California Institute of Technology from 1950 until his death in Los Angeles on February 15, 1988, after an eight-year battle with abdominal cancer.

the scientific community, in government and politics, and among the general public, nanotechnology is being viewed as the possible source of a number of important breakthroughs that may dramatically change human life and the environment in which we live. New research that can be labeled "nanotechnology" may have a better chance of funding than more traditional, less "revolutionary" projects.

Perhaps the most significant distinction in the way people think about microtechnology and nanotechnology, however, is not a matter of scale, but a philosophy of materials science. For almost all of human history, people have made new products by starting out with a hunk of material and hacking it down to just the right size and shape. Early humans used hard rock to chip bone, wood, and other materials into arrows and spearheads. Today, complex machinery is used to bend, twist, cut, meld, and otherwise shape aluminum, steel, and other materials into automobile bodies, skyscraper skeletons, refrigerators, and other objects.

As different as primitive and modern technologies may seem, they both depend on a "top-down" approach to the manufacture of objects. It begins with a mass of trillions upon trillions of atoms and molecules and uses brute force to arrange those atoms and molecules into some desirable form.

Richard Feynman seems to have imagined that the traditional top-down approach to materials science could be developed in such a way as to allow the manipulation of individual atoms and molecules. He envisioned *macroscale* devices (those the size of everyday objects) that could make smaller devices that could then make smaller devices . . . and so on until those devices were small enough to permit the manipulation of individual atoms and molecules, and the first electric motor invented to meet Feynman's first challenge was made in just that way. The problem is that without exception, this approach produces imperfect products, with cracks, holes, and other defects that eventually result in the failure of the product.

Eric Drexler had a very different view as to how atoms and molecules could be manipulated to produce new materials. He suggested starting at the bottom, with atoms and molecules, and constructing larger objects the way one builds with Tinkertoys or LEGO blocks. This approach can be described as the "bottom-up" method of manufacturing new materials. In this approach, atoms and molecules are assembled one at a time in some predetermined manner. Every particle goes into exactly the right position such that the final product will be an automobile frame, an I-beam, or a toaster with a perfect molecular composition. The product will have no flaws and will last many times longer than any product currently available. Research at the nanoscale that operates on a bottom-up philosophy is sometimes referred to as *molecular nanotechnology* in an effort to differentiate that approach from top-down nanoscale research.

Drexler was probably the first person to provide a comprehensive, cohesive description of a bottom-up approach to nanotechnology and materials science. He was certainly *not* the first person, however, to carry out this kind of research. Indeed, in the 1980s, a number of new technologies allowed scientists to begin carrying out the kinds of research that Drexler had described. Just a decade earlier, this work could only have been thought of as science fiction.

For example, in 1989, two researchers at the IBM Almaden Research Center, Donald M. Eigler and Erhard K. Schweizer, used a *scanning tunneling microscope* (STM; invented in 1981) to arrange 35 xenon atoms on a nickel crystal to spell out the company's logo, IBM. The "I" in the logo was made of nine xenon atoms and the "B" and "M," of 13 atoms each. If it accomplished nothing else, Eigler and Schweizer's research demonstrated that the manipulation of individual atoms was not purely science fiction.

Today scientists often distinguish between two types of nanotechnology. To most researchers, the term refers broadly to any type of research that involves objects and events at the nanometer level. That research may be done by any number of methods, some top-down and some bottom-up. Another type of nanotechnology, sometimes called Drexlerian nanotechnology, is more specific. It refers to a collection of specific nanoscale objects—including replicators and assemblers—manufactured by the manipulation of individual atoms and molecules. No materials scientist today doubts that nanotechnology in its broadest sense is a realistic possibility and that it is likely to be one of the most exciting fields of research in the next few decades. Many people question Drexlerian nanotechnology and suggest that, while it may be theoretically appealing, it will never provide the basis for any significant productive research in the real world.

Drexlerian Nanotechnology

Eric Drexler is widely regarded as the founder of bottom-up nanotechnology. That recognition is based largely on a book he wrote in 1986,

Engines of Creation: The Coming Era of Nanotechnology, which outlines the general principles involved in molecular manufacturing in terms laypeople can easily understand. Six years later, Drexler wrote a second book on molecular manufacturing, this one intended for the scientific community. In *Nanosystems: Molecular Machinery, Manufacturing, and Computation,* Drexler discussed the fundamental physical and chemical issues involved in the development of nanoscale devices.

Many (perhaps most) scientists would have little quarrel with the basic technical discussions Drexler presented in these two books. His extrapolation of these scientific principles to the direction of future research, however, has become the subject of vigorous and sometimes acrimonious debate. That debate centers on Drexler's belief that bottom-up technology can eventually result in the development of three new and powerful nanoscale devices: assemblers, replicators, and nanocomputers.

An assembler is a nanoscale device for carrying out some mechanical action, such as picking up an atom and moving it to another position. A comparable device, the disassembler, has essentially the same function as an assembler, except that it takes things apart rather than putting them together. Assemblers can take on many different shapes, depending on the function they are expected to perform. Most engineers would recognize the various types and components of assemblers from their macroscale counterparts. Some examples of assemblers and the parts of which they are made are pumps, bearings, cables, struts and beams, fasteners, drive shafts, gears, clamps, conveyor belts, motors, and containers. All of these devices are used in the everyday world to make, hold, and maneuver objects and materials. The only difference in such devices designed for the nano-level is size. They will consist of a few thousand or a few million atoms or molecules rather than the trillions and trillions of particles contained in everyday objects of the same kind. An example of a nanoscale machine is shown in the photograph on page 75. Each sphere in this computer model represents an individual atom in a molecular bearing that, in theory, operates in exactly the same way as a macroscopic bearing, except on a far smaller scale.

The availability of a wide variety of different kinds of assemblers will make possible the construction of any material by moving individual atoms and molecules according to any predetermined plan. Objects constructed by this method will have perfect structures in the sense that every atom or molecule is in exactly the correct place. No flaws will exist, and the object will, therefore, be much stronger and longer lasting than objects built by traditional top-down methods.

Replicators are a specialized type of assembler capable of making copies of themselves. They are similar in concept to one of the best-known of all biochemical molecules, deoxyribonucleic acid (DNA).

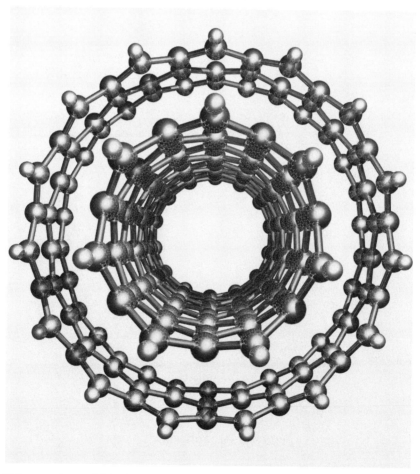

This computer model depicts a molecular bearing that performs the same functions as a macroscopic scale bearing, the only difference being the number of atoms contained within the device. (Alfred Pasieka/Photo Researchers, Inc.)

DNA molecules are capable of making precise copies of themselves; if errors are made during replication, they can even correct those errors to ensure an exact copy of the original molecule. But DNA molecules can be thought of as assemblers as well as replicators. They are capable of collecting raw materials in a cell and arranging them into some predetermined pattern required for the production of ribonucleic acid (RNA) molecules.

Nanocomputers are nanoscale devices that carry the instructions for the operation of assemblers, disassemblers, and replicators. Historically, there have been two types of computers: those that operate mechanically and those that operate electrically (electronically). The first computers to be built were mechanical, carrying out operations by means of moving rods, wheels, disks, and other devices that could represent numerical values. The first computer ever invented, Charles Babbage's difference engine (conceived by Babbage in 1821), operated on mechanical principles. Modern computers, by contrast, operate on electrical and magnetic principles. A pulse of electrical current causes a magnetic material to take one of two positions: magnetized or nonmagnetized; "on" or "off"; or "1" or "0." Electronic computers have the advantage of operating much more rapidly than mechanical computers, but they generate far more heat. At this point in time, it is still not clear whether nanoscale computers will operate more efficiently using mechanical or electronic principles.

To the nonscientist, Drexler's vision of replicators, assemblers, and nanocomputers has considerable appeal. It has inspired, for example, a number of science fiction books based on the premise that nanodevices will eventually be constructed and will have a significant impact on the world of tomorrow. Many scientists reject this vision, however, arguing that technical constraints make the construction of Drexlerian devices highly improbable, if not impossible.

Reactions to Drexler Nanotechnology

The possibility of a bottom-up approach to nanotechnology is no longer in question. Each month, many new advances in the development of nanoscale devices and phenomena constructed from fundamental particles are being reported. An active debate continues among scientists, however, over whether Drexlerian nanodevices such as assemblers and replicators can ever be produced. That debate has a long history dating to the publication of *Engines of Creation* in the late 1980s. In 1990, for example, journalist Simon Garfinkel wrote about what he called the "cult of nanotechnology" in an article in the summer issue of *Whole Earth Review*. Molecular nanotechnology, Garfinkel wrote, envisions "working with atoms the same way a model-maker might work with wooden sticks and Styrofoam balls." The problem, said Garfinkel, is that "atoms don't work that way."

Not himself a scientist, Garfinkel based his conclusion about molecular nanotechnology on interviews with a number of professionals in chemistry, primarily from the Massachusetts Institute of Technology (MIT). One criticism he heard came from Robert J. Silby, professor of chemistry at MIT, who pointed out that "molecules are not rigid, they vibrate, they have bending motions." This could lead one to conclude that physical devices like assemblers and replicators are not technically feasible.

The Garfinkel article was only the opening salvo in a long-running battle over the possibilities of Drexlerian nanodevices that has continued for two decades. The high point of that debate occurred in 2001, when Nobel Prize winner Richard Smalley wrote an article for *Scientific American* on Drexlerian nanotechnology. "Self-replicating, mechanical nanorobots," he said, "are simply not possible in our world." In a publication for the National Science Foundation (NSF) written in the same year, Smalley announced that "For fundamental reasons I am convinced that these *nanobots* are an impossible, childish fantasy. . . . We should not let this fuzzy-minded nightmare dream scare us away from nanotechnology. Nanobots are not real."

Drexler finally answered Smalley's arguments two years later in an exchange with the Nobel laureate in the "Point-Counterpoint" column of *Chemical and Engineering News*. The four letters that made up that column, two by Drexler to Smalley and two by Smalley to Drexler, provide a succinct, if highly technical, summary of the arguments as to why Drexlerian nanodevices are or

◄ K. ERIC DREXLER (1955–) ►

Those who attempt to predict the future of scientific progress run an enormous risk of being called a fool or a charlatan. Such individuals *sometimes* turn out to be correct, but they almost always encounter severe criticism from their colleagues and the general public early on in their careers. Name a field of enormous impact on our modern lives, and one can easily find naysayers who said "it can never be done." So is Eric Drexler a wild dreamer whose prognostications are likely to disrupt the progress of scientific research (as some of his critics complain), or is his vision one that will transform the nature of human society a century from now? No one can begin to answer that question today, but there is little doubt that his ideas about developments in nanotechnology have influenced a great many researchers and intrigued a number of laypersons.

Drexler was born in Oakland, California, on April 25, 1955. He grew up in Lafayette, Indiana; New Haven, Connecticut; Cincinnati, Ohio; Denver, Colorado; and Monmouth, Oregon. In 1973, he began studies at the Massachusetts Institute of Technology (MIT), from which he eventually earned his bachelor of science degree in interdisciplinary science in 1977.

When he entered MIT, Drexler was interested primarily in the subject of space travel and the possibility of establishing human civilizations in space. He eventually became a part of an informal group of students, faculty, and other enthusiasts from a variety of academic institutions. While still a freshman at MIT, he gave a presentation at the First Princeton Conference on Space Colonization, sponsored by Dr. Gerard K. O'Neil, one of the world's foremost authorities on the subject.

Drexler was (and is) not the kind of person, however, to limit his interests to a single topic. As he thought about the possibilities and potentials for space research, he began to see ways in which microfabrication of materials could be useful in the development and production of essential materials and structures. Before long, this line of thought led him to the idea that an entirely new method for producing materials might be possible, a method that involved constructing objects beginning with individual atoms and molecules placed carefully in exactly the correct places.

During his days at MIT, Drexler continued to develop his ideas about nanotechnology and to discuss and debate these ideas with other students and faculty. He was largely unaware of previous discussions of the subject, however, until 1979. In that year, he first found out about Richard Feynman's speech "There's Plenty of Room at the Bottom" given 20 years earlier. In it, Feynman had outlined many of the essential ideas about which Drexler had been thinking and talking over the previous six years. He knew it was time for him to write a paper in which he laid out his thoughts about an entirely new field of technology, nanotechnology.

Drexler's paper, "Molecular Engineering: An Approach to the Development of General Capabilities for Molecular Manipulation," was published in the *Proceedings of the National Academy of Sciences* in September 1981. The paper drew virtually no attention and apparently was not even cited until two years later. Nonetheless, it had laid down the general principles of a new approach to technology and a new field of research that had the potential to revolutionize life on Earth.

In September 1979, Drexler received a master's of science degree in engineering from MIT. He then worked as a research affiliate, first at the Space Systems Laboratory and later at the Artificial Intelligence Laboratory. In May 1985, he and his wife, Christine Peterson, left for California. The group with which he had been working on nanotechnology felt that California would be the most congenial place for them to continue meeting and working on their ideas for this new form of technology. After arriving in California, Drexler and his then-wife established the Foresight Institute with the purpose of ensuring the beneficial implementation of nanotechnology.

Drexler worked as a visiting scholar in the Stanford University Department of Computer Science from 1985 until 1991, when he and his colleagues established the Institute for Molecular Manufacturing (IMM) in Palo Alto. Since 1991, Drexler has carried out research on nanotechnology at IMM and has written three major books, many articles, and many technical papers on the subject for both technical and general publications. In 1991, he was granted his Ph.D. degree from MIT in the field of molecular nanotechnology, the first degree of its kind to be awarded anywhere. Drexler served as chairman of the Foresight Institute until 2003, when he resigned to become chief technical adviser of Nanorex, a company based in Bloomfield Hills, Michigan, that develops software for the design and simulation of molecular machine systems.

are not technically possible. The exchange is important not only because of the technical issues raised by the two men, but also because the thinly veiled personal attacks they include provide a glimpse of the passionate nature of the debate over Drexlerian nanotechnology.

Risks and Benefits of Nanotechnology

An underlying theme in much of the criticism of Drexler's writings has been the potential risks posed by nanotechnology. What are those risks? If assemblers and replicators can exist, those devices pose a number of dangers to the world. Replicators are designed to make copies of themselves using the simple building blocks supplied to them, such as atoms of hydrogen, oxygen, and carbon; assemblers are designed to use the same raw materials to construct new materials. Ideally, people would make available to replicators and assemblers just the atoms and molecules they need to carry out the functions for which they are designed.

But supposing that a replicator or assembler (again, *if* it could exist) were free to roam in the natural environment, it is easy to imagine that it could find these same building blocks everywhere around it. It could easily find the atoms of hydrogen, oxygen, and carbon (and anything else it might need) to carry out the functions for which it was designed. In theory, a "free-range" replicator or assembler could make an unlimited number of copies of itself or unlimited amounts of new materials. One might compare the process to what would happen if a single bacterium were placed in an environment where it had continuous access to an endless supply of food: It would reproduce exponentially, essentially forever.

The worst-case scenario in Drexlerian molecular nanotechnology, then, envisions free-range nanodevices (usually called nanorobots or *nanobots*) that gobble up endless quantities of the natural environment, producing a massive cloud of such devices. This hypothetical cloud has sometimes been referred to as *gray goo*. Gray goo, like a rain cloud, consists of individual particles each of which is itself invisible but which collectively, because of their vast numbers, is able to diffract light producing a visible cloud. Some researchers have attempted to develop models of the properties that gray goo would have and the impact it might have on humans and the natural environment.

As sometimes happens, those most interested in this question have been science fiction writers. In 1995, for example, Neil Stephenson wrote a novel called *The Diamond Age* describing a world in which Drexlerian nanodevices were part of one's daily existence. One function for which they were used by the government was as invisible spies that followed citizens wherever they went, going so far in some cases as to enter their bodies to conduct their spying functions.

Stephenson's book is still about as "far out" as one can imagine in writing about a future permeated by the products of molecular nanotechnology. Yet the political atmosphere in which such devices could be considered an asset had, by the early 21st century, already arrived. Terrorist threats and attacks have shown governments how vulnerable they are, and after the terrorist attacks of September 11, 2001, the desirability of a government-controlled gray goo, technically feasible or not, was widely recognized.

Probably the most famous fictional account of the gray goo problem has been Michael Crichton's 2002 novel *Prey*. In his book, Crichton tells of the escape of nanobots (replicators) into the surrounding environment from a research facility in the desert of Nevada. The nanobots then begin to replicate by attacking humans and other animals to extract the raw materials they need for their own reproduction. Crichton's book was on the *New York Times* bestseller list for months, and in 2002 Twentieth-Century Fox purchased film rights to the story.

While some scientists continue to debate how realistic Drexlerian nanotechnology is, a far greater number are moving ahead with research on techniques and devices at the nanometer level. Over the past two decades, it has become abundantly clear that whether or not the world ever sees an assembler or a replicator, it will certainly see a host of machines the size of atomic and molecular clusters.

Nanotechnology Research Tools

The greatest challenge to bottom-up research in nanotechnology has long been the availability of tools with which to manipulate individual or small groups of atoms and molecules. The first two such tools to have been developed for this purpose are DNA molecules and the scanning tunneling microscope (STM) and its various modifications.

DNA has long been a vital argument for proponents of a Drexlerian nanotechnology and for other researchers in the field. It is a naturally occurring molecule that has all the properties of an assembler and/or a replicator, with the ability to select specific building blocks (nucleotides) from its environment and use them to construct precise structures (RNA molecules and proteins) needed for the survival of living organisms. It also has the ability to make exact copies of itself with high reliability. Proponents of Drexlerian nanotechnology point out that DNA can, therefore, serve as a model on which synthetic nanodevices such as assemblers and replicators can be constructed. Critics counterargue that the way DNA functions in cells is so complex that its operations can never be reproduced by mechanical means.

In any case, some researchers have used and are now using DNA as a tool in the synthesis of functioning nanoscale devices. One of

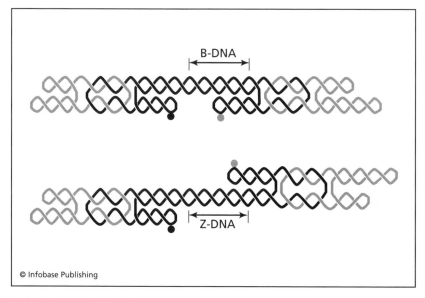

© Infobase Publishing

Nadrian Seeman's DNA robotic arm

the leaders in this field of research has been Nadrian Seeman at New York University. In some of his earliest work, Seeman explored the possibility of building rigid three-dimensional objects from strands of DNA. The diagram on page 82 shows one of these devices, a robotic arm consisting of synthetic DNA molecules specially designed for the device.

Seeman's device makes use of the fact that DNA can exist in a variety of geometric conformations. Two of these are known as the "B" and "Z" conformations. The B conformation is the one discovered by Francis Crick and James Watson in 1953, with a characteristic right-handed twist to its double helix. In Z-DNA, by contrast, the double helix has a left-handed twist.

Seeman's robotic arm consists of two rigid strands of double-crossover (DX) DNA in which the bonds between strands are very strong. The two rigid strands are connected by a short bridge of natural DNA in its B conformation. When the bridge DNA is changed from its B to its Z conformation, the molecule unwinds by 3.5 turns, producing the change shown in the diagram. To detect this change visually, Seeman attached two fluorescent dye molecules to inner ends of the rigid arms. Movement of the fluorescent molecules confirmed changes in the conformation of the DNA and, hence, the movement of the nanorobotic arm. Seeman points out that atoms and molecules other than those of fluorescent dye—metallic ions or proteins, for example, could also be attached at these locations, providing a method by which those particles can be moved from one position to another.

Two additional methods that use DNA to construct nanodevices were reported in late 2003. The first experiment was carried out at the Technion-Israel Institute of Technology under the direction of Erez Braun, professor of physics. The second was reported by a group of Duke University researchers.

The Technion experiment used DNA and protein molecules attached to *carbon nanotubes* to construct a simple nanotransistor. (A *transistor* is a device that controls the flow of electricity.) The first step in the process was to combine single-stranded DNA, double-stranded DNA, and the protein known as RecA in an aqueous solution, as shown in the first step of the diagram on page 84. The three molecules

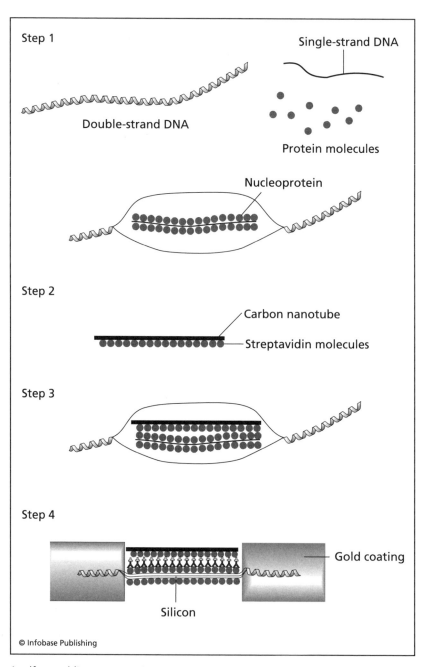

A self-assembling nanotransistor

are selected to be complementary, permitting binding between certain pairs. That is, the single-stranded DNA is synthesized so as to attract and bind to the RecA protein, forming a product known as a nucleoprotein. The single-stranded DNA is also designed to be complementary to a section of the double-stranded DNA; these strands bind together forming a three-stranded unit consisting of the double-stranded DNA bonded to the single-stranded DNA bonded to the RecA protein.

Next, the Technion team synthesized a compound molecule consisting of a carbon nanotube about 1 nm in diameter bonded to a molecule of the protein streptavidin, as shown in the second step of the diagram. (Carbon nanotubes are very small strawlike devices discussed in greater detail later in this section.) Streptavidin has a strong affinity for the RecA protein and binds readily with it. When the streptavidin-nanotube combination is mixed with the three-stranded nucleoprotein, the two molecules bind together tightly, forming a long filament, as shown in the third step of the diagram. Finally, the filament is laid on the surface of an oxidized silicon wafer and coated with gold. The gold coating makes the DNA and protein portions of the filament electrically conductive, which they would otherwise not be. Since the carbon nanotube portion of the filament acts as a semiconductor, the final product behaves as a transistor.

In the second line of experimentation using DNA-based nanodevices, a group of Duke University researchers prepared a number of single-stranded molecules of DNA, then mixed them with each other. The DNA strands were designed to be complementary, and when they were mixed, they self-assembled into a tile-like structure similar to that shown in the diagram on page 87. The "tiles" then assembled themselves into a variety of shapes, depending on the types of base pairs present at each end of the tile. In some cases, the tiles formed a wafflelike grid, and in other cases they formed a long ribbon. When the ribbon was coated with silver, it was able to carry an electrical current. When biotin molecules were added at certain points in the DNA grid, the grid became a detector for streptavidin molecules, to which biotin is strongly attracted. Researchers suggest that their DNA grids may eventually find a host of applications in nanoscale devices, sensors and even assemblerlike "factories" for the manufacture of nanoscale objects.

This nanotransistor is made of two tiny electrodes joined by a carbon nanotube that controls the flow of electric current through the system. (Digital Instruments/Veeco/ Photo Researchers, Inc.)

Despite these accomplishments in nanoscale technology using DNA, probably the single most powerful tool currently available to nanoscale researchers is the scanning tunneling microscope (STM) and its variants. The STM was invented in 1981 by Heinrich Rohrer (1933–   ) and Gerd Binnig (1947–   ), then researchers at the IBM Zurich Research Laboratory (IBM-ZRL). Rohrer and Binnig were awarded the 1986 Nobel Prize in physics for their invention.

The scanning tunneling microscope was invented as an observational tool, a device for examining the structure of materials at magnifications higher than those possible with an optical (light) microscope. The design of an STM is, in principle, relatively simple. The working part of the microscope consists of a very small tip, only a few atoms or molecules in diameter, attached to a piezoelectric shaft. A piezoelectric material is one whose dimensions change when an electric current flows through it. (For more on piezoelectric materials, see chapter 5.)

To use the STM, an operator brings the tip of the instrument very close to the surface of the material being examined. "Very close" in this case means a distance of about a nanometer or less. The tip normally does not actually come into contact with the surface because the force of separation between electrons in the tip and in the surface at this range is quite large.

At the tip's closest approach to the surface, electrons may flow from the instrument to the surface, or vice versa. According to the laws of classical physics, this flow of electrons is not possible because of the repulsion of like charges (in electron clouds) on the two materials. The laws of quantum mechanics, however, do allow some

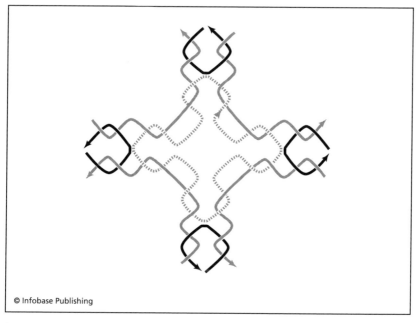

DNA nanotiles

electrons to "sneak through" or "tunnel under" that energy barrier, and an electrical current can actually be observed between surface and tip. This current is what gives the STM its name.

As the tunneling current flows between the microscope tip and the surface at a specific location, the microscope operator can detect and measure its change. The operator moves ("scans") the microscope across the surface of the material being studied by applying a voltage to the piezoelectric shaft, which changes its length. The STM records the topography of the surface by plotting the location and current that flows at that point.

Since 1981, researchers have developed a number of modifications of the STM for uses in which the original instrument is not suitable. For example, the atomic force microscope (AFM) was invented in 1986 by Binnig and Christoph Gerber at IBM-ZRL and Calvin Quate at Stanford University. The AFM can be used on nonconductive surfaces, such as organic materials, on which the STM cannot be used. Today the STM, AFM, and related devices are collectively known as *scanning probe microscopes* (SPMs).

Shortly after the invention of the STM and AFM, some researchers saw a different application for these instruments. They realized that SPMs can be used actively to move atoms and molecules around on a surface rather than passively to simply look at a surface. One of the earliest and most impressive breakthroughs in this line of research came in 1989 when Eigler and Schweizer constructed their IBM nanologo with 35 xenon atoms (as described earlier in this chapter).

These researchers cooled their apparatus to a temperature of about 3 K ($-270\,^\circ$C) to reduce thermal vibration of the atoms and make them stable enough to manipulate. They then used an STM in its imaging mode to search for xenon atoms on the nickel surface. When an atom was located, they lowered the STM until the tunneling current reached a maximum, making the xenon atom more strongly attracted to the tip than to the nickel surface. They then moved the tip across the nickel surface, dragging the xenon atom into its desired position. Finally, they switched the STM back to its imaging mode, reducing the force between the xenon atom and the STM tip, and the xenon atom was fixed to its new position. As simple as the process may sound in this description, the actual manipulation of xenon atoms was very time consuming, requiring a total of about 22 hours of work. At the time, it seemed difficult to imagine how the process could be adapted to the manufacture of any kind of useful device.

Since the discovery of this use of STMs, nanoresearchers have routinely used the devices to manipulate atoms, molecules, ions, and other particles. Today, however, such experiments are often completed in a matter of minutes rather than hours. And researchers are finding seemingly endless ways of using SPMs as "nanocranes" that shuffle particles back and forth across a surface, placing them in precisely determined positions.

For example, Wilson Ho and Hyojune Lee at Cornell University reported in 1999 on a method for making molecules of iron dicarbonyl $[Fe(CO)_2]$ from iron atoms and carbon monoxide (CO) molecules. They first deposited atoms of iron and molecules of carbon monoxide on a silver surface in a vacuum at a temperature of 13 K ($-260°C$). They then used an STM to scan the surface and locate both iron atoms and carbon monoxide molecules. When they encountered a carbon monoxide molecule, they lowered the tip of the STM and increased the voltage, attracting the molecule to the tip. At this point, Ho and Lee were able to pluck the carbon monoxide molecule from the silver surface and position it above an iron atom. They then reduced the voltage in the STM tip, and the attractive forces between the iron atom and carbon monoxide molecule were strong enough to bond the two, which formed a new molecule of iron carbonyl $[Fe(CO)]$. In a second stage of the research, Ho and Lee were able to repeat this process, adding a second molecule of carbon monoxide to an iron carbonyl molecule to form iron dicarbonyl $[Fe(CO)_2]$.

Another type of device used in nanoscale research, the carbon nanotube, is not so much a tool as an invaluable raw material from which to make nanoscale objects. Carbon nanotubes were discovered in 1991 by the Japanese electron microscopist Sumio Iijima (1939–). In his research, Iijima vaporized a sample of carbon between two electric arcs and then used an STM to analyze the soot formed. He found that the soot consisted of very large numbers of long cylinders only a few nanometers in diameter, but hundreds or thousands of nanometers in length. Iijima called these structures carbon nanotubes.

Carbon nanotubes can be thought of as sheets of graphene rolled up into cylinders. Graphene is a naturally occurring form of carbon consisting of flat sheets of carbon atoms bonded to each other. Since all carbon electrons are used in the formation of these bonds, none are available to bond to adjacent materials. Two graphene sheets placed on top of each other slide smoothly over each other with very little friction. (This property is put to use in the "lead" in pencils, which is really graphite. When the pencil point—the graphite—is rubbed against a piece of paper, some carbon easily rubs off the point and is deposited on the paper.)

Graphene sheets have two significant physical properties. First, they have the highest tensile strength of any material known. If a rope could be made out of carbon nanotubes, it would be the strongest material ever produced, 50 to 100 times stronger than steel. Second, the density of carbon atoms in a graphene sheet is greater than the density of any other two-dimensional material made of an element. Thus, under normal circumstances, a nanotube or nanorope would be essentially impermeable.

The first carbon nanotubes discovered in nature, such as those produced in Iijima's experiments, were multiwalled nanotubes (MWNT). Multiwalled nanotubes consist of a number of concentric carbon cylinders, a set of tubes nested inside each other. They are somewhat complex systems that are relatively difficult to study. An important step forward in research on carbon nanotubes occurred in 1993, when scientists learned how to make single-walled nanotubes (SWNT). Using the simpler SWNTs, scientists have learned quite rapidly a great deal about the electrical conductivity, tensile strength, flexibility, toughness, and other physical properties of carbon nanotubes.

Much research has now been done on the properties and possible uses of carbon nanotubes. An important center for this research has been the laboratory of Cees Dekker and his colleagues at Delft University in the Netherlands. In 1997, for example, one of Dekker's teams found that bent carbon nanotubes can function as electric wires. Their electric behavior is very different from that of ordinary macroscopic wires, however. In these familiar-sized wires, each small increase in voltage produces a correspondingly small increase in current. In other words, the relationship between voltage and current is linear. In carbon nanotubes, however, current increases as a stepwise function of voltage. That is, increasing the voltage may or may not cause a current to flow. Increasing the voltage in the

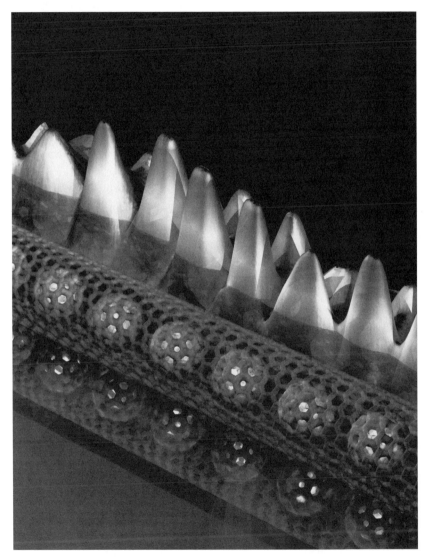

A computer model shows a row of buckyballs inside a carbon nanotube. (David Luzzi, University of Pennsylvania/Photo Researchers, Inc.)

nanowire for a short period of time produces no increase in current (the flat part of the stepwise curve), but another increase in the voltage then produces a significant increase in current (the vertical part of the stepwise curve).

Another major center of research on carbon nanotubes has been the Center for Nanoscale Science and Technology at Rice University. The center's director from 1997 to his death in 2005 was Richard Smalley, who was awarded a share of the 1997 Nobel Prize in chemistry for his part in the discovery of a new allotrope of carbon. The discovery, a 60-atom soccer ball–shaped particle originally named *buckminsterfullerene,* is more commonly known as a *buckyball.* The structure of a buckyball is shown in the photograph on page 91.

In a 1996 project, Smalley and his colleagues found that they could produce very long carbon nanotube "ropes" consisting of bundles of SWNTs that self-assembled into larger groupings. The ropes were produced when Smalley's team used a laser beam to vaporize a mixture of graphite and a nickel-cobalt catalyst. Microscopic examination of these ropes showed that they consisted of long chains of 100 to 500 SWNTs, 10 to 20 nm in diameter. One observer mused that it might one day be possible to produce continuous lengths of the nanorope that can be wound in a spool and used in the construction and operation of nanoscale devices.

Many researchers now believe that carbon nanotubes may provide an alternative to the use of semiconducting materials that now form the basis of electronic devices used in computing machines. An example of this line of research is a study conducted in 1999 by researchers at the University of Pennsylvania led by Alan Johnson. Johnson's team learned how to use an AFM like a pair of tweezers to manipulate SWNTs: moving them around on a surface, cutting them apart, and laying them on top of each other. One discovery of their research came when they laid one SWNT on top of a second SWNT at right angles: The electrical conductivity of the upper tube changed where it was in contact with the lower nanotube. This arrangement appeared to inhibit the flow of electrons, changing the tube from a conductor to a semiconductor.

These results suggest that it may be possible to arrange carbon nanotubes such that they can perform the same functions as those currently found on a silicon chip. Only a decade after their discovery, carbon nanotubes have become the focus of one of the most intense research efforts in the history of materials science, with new properties and applications of these objects being reported monthly.

The promise of bottom-up nanotechnology has always depended on solving the problem of having a way to move individual atoms and molecules into desired positions. The best method yet developed to solve this problem is the family of scanning probe microscopes, which are now being used to produce a host of nanosize devices, some of which are discussed in the next section. DNA molecules may also become a powerful tool in the manipulation of atoms and molecules, although their potential has yet to be fully developed.

Results of Nanoscale Research

Given its short history, the field of nanoscale research has already produced an impressive volume of results. Research goals have ranged from the solution of immediate problems in materials science, such as the manufacture of computing devices, to the pursuit of more remote goals, such as the design of nanoscale machines.

Arguably the single most powerful force driving nanoscale research today is the need for smaller, faster, and more powerful computing devices. For more than 30 years, scientists have been finding ways to cram more and more transistors, the basic units of a computing device, on a single chip. The simplest processors in the early 1970s, the 4004 and 8080 processors, contained fewer than 10 transistors per chip. By 2000, that number had risen to nearly 10,000 transistors per chip in the Pentium II and III processors and to 100,000 transistors per chip in the Pentium III Xenon processor.

This trend conforms to a pattern foreseen in 1965 by Gordon Moore (1929–   ), cofounder of the Intel Corporation. Moore predicted that the number of circuits on a silicon chip would double every year, a projection he later changed to a doubling every 18 to 24 months. Progress in chip design has followed Moore's Law with remarkable accuracy ever since. If that law continues to hold true, one can expect processors with a billion transistors per chip sometime before the year 2015.

The nanowires shown in this photograph are only about 10 atoms wide. (Hewlett-Packard Laboratories/Photo Researchers, Inc.)

To meet this demand, engineers will have to find ways of reducing electronic components, such as wires and logic gates, to dimensions even smaller than those used in current devices, dimensions of about 100 nm. Present-day technology is based on the use of intense laser beams for the construction of lithographic circuitry by etching lines into a *substrate.* That technology is probably capable of achieving these goals. The problem is the potential costs involved. By some estimates, a chip fabrication facility needed to make these improved processors could cost upward of $200 billion in 2015. Leaders of the computer industry have questioned investments of that magnitude and, as a consequence, have already begun to explore alternatives to traditional solid-state computing devices. One of the most powerful of those alternatives is molecular electronics.

The term *molecular electronics* refers to the design and construction of electronic devices consisting of a single molecule or small groups of molecules. These devices include such familiar components as wires, rectifiers, switches, and memory devices.

As least two major approaches to the manufacture of molecular wires have been suggested: the use of carbon nanotubes and the use of of polyphenylene chains. To make carbon nanotube molecular wire one need only find a way of creating a carbon nanotube of some desired length capable of conducting an electric current. An example of this approach is the work of Hongie Dai and his colleagues at Stanford University in 2000. Dai's team first etched the surface of a silicon dioxide plate with a laser beam and then passed heated methane (CH_4) over the material in the presence of a metal catalyst, such as cobalt and/or nickel. Under these conditions, the methane decomposed, forming hydrogen and carbon, and the carbon condensed on the lines etched on the silicon dioxide surface, forming long carbon nanotube wires. Dai's team then measured the conductivity of these carbon nanotube molecular wires.

The second method of making molecular wires starts with phenylene groups, benzene molecules in which two hydrogen atoms have been removed. The loss of these two hydrogens leaves a molecule with two free (unbonded) electrons, represented by the formula $*C_6H_4*$, where the asterisks represent the unbonded electrons. The free electrons allow the bonding of the molecule at these two positions. When two or more phenylene groups bond with each other, they form a long chain of many such groups known as polyphenylene, with the structure

$$*C_6H_4\text{-}C_6H_4\text{-}C_6H_4\text{-}C_6H_4\text{-}\ldots\text{-}C_6H_4\text{-}C_6H_4\text{-}C_6H_4\text{-}C_6H_4*$$

The value of polyphenylene as a molecular wire stems from the relative mobility of some of the electrons in each benzene ring. If an electrical *potential* is applied at one end of the chain, it initiates the dislocation of those electrons throughout the chain, resulting in the flow of an electrical current. The first functioning molecular wire of this design was made in 1996 by a group of researchers headed by James Tour, then at the University of South Carolina, and David Allard and Paul Weiss, at Pennsylvania State University.

The polyphenylene wire has some potentially attractive characteristics. A variety of chemical groups can be inserted at various positions in the chain to increase or decrease the wire's conductivity. Insertion of an electron-rich molecule, such as acetylene (HC≡CH), for example, increases the number of electrons available in the chain and, hence, the wire's conductivity. Insertion of a molecule with tightly bound electrons, such as a saturated hydrocarbon like methane (CH_4), by contrast, reduces the number of electrons available in one segment, producing an insulating effect in that segment.

A second essential part of any electrical circuit is a switch, a device that can be turned ON to allow the flow of current or OFF to stop that flow. The simplest imaginable switch would consist of a single molecule that could assume two conformations, one that permits the flow of electrons (ON) and one that prevents such a flow (OFF).

The first single-molecular switch was designed and built in 2001 by Tour (then at Rice University) and Weiss. It consisted of a structure known as a phenylene ethynylene oligomer consisting of alternate phenylene ($-C_6H_4-$) and ethynylene ($-C≡C-$) groups. Tour and Weiss found that the oligomer could assume two different conformations as the result of rotations around single bonds in the molecule. In one conformation, electrical current flows through the molecule; in the second conformation, no current flows. Tour and Weiss were not immediately able to determine the detailed changes that occur in the oligomer to produce these effects, and the problem still had not been definitively solved in the early 2000s.

A third part of an electric circuit is a rectifier, a device that allows the flow of electrons in only one direction. As early as 1974, two researchers, Ari Avram at the IBM Thomas J. Watson Research Center and Mark A. Ratner at Northwestern University, suggested the possibility that single molecules might be constructed that would operate as rectifiers. Some 23 years later, that goal was achieved by a team of researchers at the University of Alabama at Tuscaloosa led by Robert M. Metzger.

Metzger's team synthesized a molecule known as hexadecylquinolinium tricyanoquinodimethanide, whose chemical structure is shown in the figure on page 97. That molecule has three distinct parts: an electron donor region (D), an electron acceptor region (A), and a bridge (σ). In the hexadecylquinolinium tricyanoquinodimethanide molecule, it is the quinolinium segment—the double ring

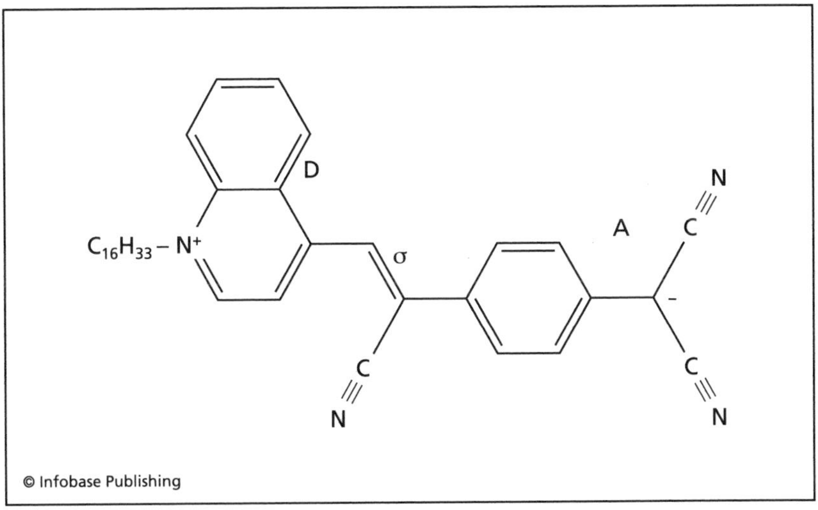

A molecular rectifier

structure at the left of the molecule—that acts as the donor (D). The tricyanoquinodimethanide segment of the molecule, located at the right of the molecule, acts as the electron acceptor (A). And the double bond (=) joining the two segments acts as a bridge (σ) through which electrons can flow.

This compound was tested as a rectifier in two different arrangements. First, a layer only one molecule thick was placed between aluminum electrodes. Next, a multilayer sandwich of molecules was inserted between the electrodes. When a potential of about one volt was applied across each of these systems, a flow of current was observed from "left" to "right," but not from "right" to "left." That observation would, of course, suggest that the molecule had behaved as a rectifier, controlling the flow of electrons in one direction only between the two electrodes.

Computers and circuitry are not the only areas of investigation for nanotechnology, however. Another major area of nanoscale research involves the construction of tiny analogs of macroscale devices, such as pens, motors, balances, tweezers, and even railroad trains. In some cases, the only purpose in making such devices is to demonstrate the ability to do so ("We did it because we could").

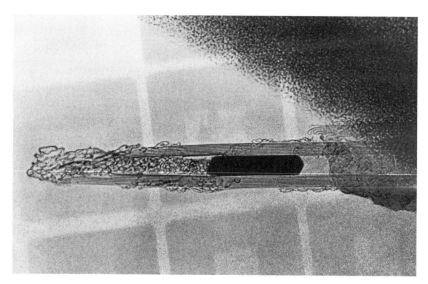

The world's smallest magnet, shown in this photograph, consists of a single crystal of nickel metal inside a carbon nanotube. (Dr. Peter Harris/Photo Researchers, Inc.)

In other cases, such devices are developed based on the premise that they might someday have real-world applications in the manufacture of larger nanoscale devices (such as assemblers and replicators).

One of the first nanoscale "toys" produced was an abacus made by researchers at IBM-ZRL in 1996. The abacus is a very old calculating device consisting of moveable parts (such as wooden rings) that can be slid up and down on fixed rods. The earliest abaci are thought to date to the third millennium B.C.E.

To make their nanoabacus, IBM-ZRL researchers first etched a number of thin grooves on a copper sheet with a laser beam. Next, they used an STM to place 100 buckyballs into these grooves. Finally, they used an STM to slide the buckyballs, one at a time, up and down within the grooves.

One of the basic tools needed for the construction of molecular-size devices is an appliance that would allow an operator to pick up an object, move it, and place it into some predetermined position, much as a crane does during the construction of a building. At least two such devices have now been constructed to operate at the molecular level. The first was made in 1999 by Philip Kim and Charles M. Lieber at Harvard University. To build their device, which they called a nanotube nanotweezer, Kim and Lieber first attached two gold electrodes on opposite sides of a glass micropipette. They then attached a bundle of multiwall carbon nanotubes (MWNTs) to each of the electrodes. Multiwall carbon nanotubes are similar to single-wall carbon nanotubes except that they contain many nanotubes nested inside each other.

To use their nanotube nanotweezer, Kim and Lieber applied opposite electrical charges to the two gold electrodes (and, hence, to the two MWNTs). Since they carried opposite electrical charges, the two MWNTs were attracted to each other with a force that was proportional to the voltage applied to the electrodes. This force of attraction caused the ends of the two MWNTs to approach each other. The stronger the electrical potential applied, the closer the approach of the ends of the nanotweezers. Using this device, Kim and Lieber were able to pick up very small objects, such as polystyrene spheres with diameters of about 500 nm.

A second type of nanotweezer was reported less than a year later by researchers at Lucent Technologies. Lucent researchers used three strands of DNA to make their grasping device. One strand (labeled A in the diagram on page 100) was constructed to have a V-shape, to which two additional strands of DNA (B and C) could be attached. The total length of the device, from the vertex of the A strand to the ends of the B and C strands was about 7 nm.

To produce the closing action needed to make the nanotweezers work, Lucent researchers introduced a fourth strand of DNA (D in the diagram) into the space between the B and C strands. The D strand was constructed so as to be complementary to the B and C strands, causing it to form bonds between both of these strands and drawing them toward each other. In the original experiment, molecules of a fluorescent dye were attached to the ends of the B and C strands, allowing researchers to observe visually the nanotweezer's movement. In a working situation, those dye molecules could be replaced by molecules to be moved into proximity with each other and joined together.

In a final step, the nanotweezers could be opened by introducing a fifth strand of DNA designed to be complementary to the

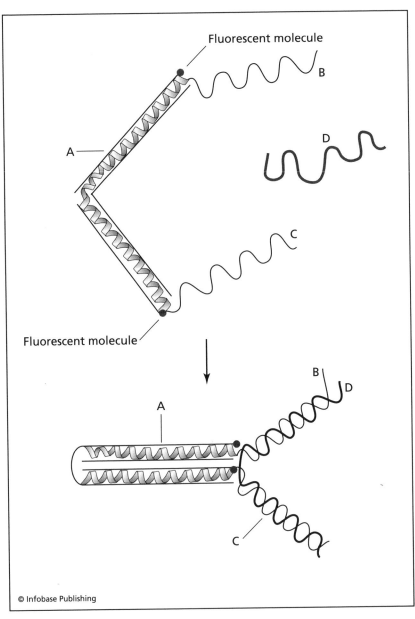

Nanotweezers made of DNA molecules

D strand and to bind more tightly to it than either of the B or C strands. When the strand is introduced into this system, it binds with the D strand, causing the D strand to be released from the

B and C arms of the nanotweezer and returning the device to its original shape.

An example of a nanodevice that might have important practical uses is the molecular motor, a device that will convert electrical, solar, chemical, or some other form of energy into mechanical energy. Many kinds of nanomotors occur in living organisms, but so far relatively little progress has been made in the development of synthetic analogs of such devices.

One exception was the serendipitous discovery in 1998 of a functioning nanomotor by researchers at IBM-ZRL. These researchers were studying the properties of a monolayer (a layer one molecule thick) of the compound hexa-*tert*-butyl decacyclene (HB-DC) laid down on an atomically clean copper surface. The HB-DC molecule consists of a central core made of seven six-membered rings and three five-membered rings, attached to which are six legs made of *t*-butyl [-$C(CH_3)_3$] groups. The legs project from the central core in such a way as to give the molecule a propellerlike structure.

Researchers used an STM to obtain an image of the HB-DC monolayer. The image essentially matched what they had expected: HB-DC molecules were arranged in a crystal-like pattern in which every molecule was held in place by other molecules surrounding it. Because of their shape, the molecules looked like a collection of hexagonal tiles neatly laid out on the copper surface.

The STM image did not precisely match expectations, however. In a few locations, the tile-like pattern was interrupted by a blurred image with a smokey, ring-shaped spot. Researchers hypothesized the following explanation for this phenomenon: In some cases, an individual HB-DC molecule had been slightly displaced by a distance of about 1 nm from the position it would have had in a "perfect" tile pattern. When thus displaced, the molecule was no longer constrained by other HB-DC molecules around it. In such a case, thermal energy in the monolayer was sufficient to cause the displaced HB-DC molecule to begin spinning. The rate of spin was then so rapid that the image obtained with the STM was like that of a spinning propeller. The experiment had accidentally generated a nanoscale motor!

Nanomotors have also been synthesized by more rational, intentional approaches. A research team directed by T. Ross Kelly at Boston College has for some time been studying the synthesis of nanoscale devices, such as molecular brakes, ratchets, and motors. In 1999, these researchers reported on the development of a primitive type of nanomotor. The motor consists of the two parts shown in the figure below, a group of three benzene rings and a four-benzene structure called tetracyclic helicene. The three benzene rings are attached to each other in a paddle wheel–like structure called triptycene. The triptycene "wheel" is designed to rotate around a central axis. The tetracyclic helicene (the four-benzene structure) serves as a housing for the triptycene wheel.

The Kelly device behaves as a motor when a new chemical bond is formed between one of the tripycene "paddles" and the housing. The bond pulls the wheel through an angle of 120° (one-third of a revolution) before it comes to a stop. For the paddle wheel to keep moving, another new bond must form between a triptycene paddle and the housing, and so on. The energy needed for the formation of the new bonds is provided by the compound phosgene (carbonyl dichloride, $COCl_2$). The Kelly nanomotor thus operates by converting chemical energy to mechanical energy, as is the case in an internal combustion engine.

The two most significant features of Kelly's work are the small size of the nanomotor (78 atoms) and the discovery of a mechanism

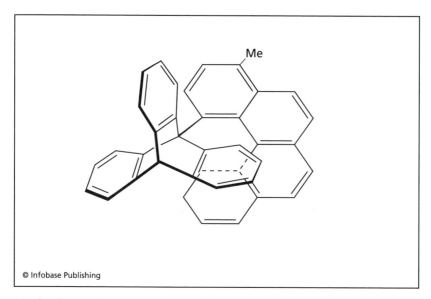

A molecular wheel

by which such a device can operate. The most important limitation of the research is the restricted range over which the nanomotor can operate in any one cycle: one-third of a revolution.

Like most of the research reported in this chapter, the Kelly nano-motor can be viewed from one of two perspectives (or, perhaps, from both). On the one hand, it represents almost the smallest imaginable step forward in the development of nanoscale devices that may one day transform the field of materials science. On the other hand, it *is* a step that has to be taken before larger, more profound discoveries and inventions can be made in that field.

Many scientists predict that nanotechnology will revolutionize the nature of materials research over the next few decades. They believe that a new way of working with materials—from the bottom up, rather than the top down—will result in the development of a host of new materials ranging from paints that change color as a function of temperature to provide automatic heating and cooling to homes; automobile, aircraft, and spacecraft materials that incorporate sensors and repair devices that automatically detect and correct weaknesses; biological nanodevices that can find tumors before they have affected no more than a few cells; and biological nanodevices that can detect DNA structures that may determine a person's susceptibility to certain diseases, infections, or toxins. A 2000 report by the National Nanotechnology Initiative (NNI) listed dozens of near-term breakthroughs like these likely to occur as a result of research in nanotechnology.

In the United States, the federal government has responded to such hopes with a relatively modest level of funding. The National Nanotechnology Initiative received a total of $464 million in 2001, its first year of operation, an amount that increased gradually over the years to $1.303 billion in FY (fiscal year) 2006. President George W. Bush then reduced his request for FY 2007 to $1.278 billion. Much research is also paid for by private funds, of course, but overall the enthusiasm of some researchers for the promise of nanotechnology has not been matched by the levels of funding needed to attain those results.

As a consequence, research in nanotechnology has not produced any remarkable breakthroughs that have transformed materials science. The greatest amount of research and the most important developments so far have been in computer applications of nanotechnology, where the need for smaller, more efficient components is urgent. The development of nanodevices that have widespread impact on the daily lives of people, however, remains a long-term vision.

5
SMART MATERIALS

Your house is dumb. No offense intended, but the structure you call home is able to perform only a limited number of functions. The roof keeps rain and snow from falling on your head. The walls hold up the roof and keep the wind from blowing through your house. The windows let sunlight into the house. And as well as these structures carry out the functions for which they were designed, they do not have much "imagination." They do not "know" how to adjust to changes in conditions.

Suppose an unusually large amount of very wet snow fell on the roof. The roof may not be strong enough to hold the snow, and it may collapse. Or suppose the ground on which the house is built begins to shake and move. The walls may not be able to withstand that movement, and they may crumble and fall. And how well do your windows adjust to very bright days or days when the Sun does not shine? Probably not at all. They transmit the amount of light that is available and no more nor less.

Humans have done very well indeed for thousands of years with the dumb materials they have to work with. Many people live in comfortable homes that offer them protection from the elements,

and they often work in very large complex factories or office buildings that seem to be the most up-to-date products of modern construction techniques. But even today, such buildings continue to be,
for the most part, dumb. They just stand there without the ability to
detect, understand, or respond to significant changes that take place
around them.

But the day of dumb buildings is on its way out, just as is the day
of dumb cars, dumb airplanes, dumb weapons, dumb satellites, and
just about any other kind of dumb structure you can imagine. The
day of smart structures built with smart materials has just about
arrived in the developed world. *Smart materials* have been defined
as materials that respond to environmental stimuli by making some
change in their physical characteristics, such as their size, shape,
electrical or magnetic conductivity, or optical properties. Because
they respond to change in the surrounding environment, smart materials are also sometimes called *responsive materials.*

What Are Smart Materials?

In the broadest sense, *all* materials are smart materials because they
all change in at least some way when exposed to changes in their environment. For example, the volume of any material changes when
the temperature around it changes. In the vast majority of cases, the
volume of the material increases as the temperature increases. This
principle lies at the basis of at least one familiar appliance in your
home that uses responsive materials: a thermostat. A thermostat is
a metal strip consisting of two metals bonded to each other. The two
metals expand at different rates when they are heated. Since they
expand at different rates, the strip bends in one direction or another
as the temperature changes. As it bends, the strip either comes into
contact with a metal electrode and closes a circuit, or it moves away
from that contact and stops the flow of current through the circuit.

So, if all materials change in some way with changes in their environment, what makes smart materials special and different from
not-so-smart or just-plain-dumb materials? One of the major differ-
ences is the rate at which such changes take place. The thermostat in
a house, for example, generally takes at least a few minutes to detect

and respond to changes in the house's temperature. A person may have to wait a half hour or more for a room to warm up, heat up the thermostat, and have the furnace turn off. By contrast, smart materials respond very quickly to changes in the surrounding environment, often in a matter of a few thousandths or millionths of a second. As this chapter will show, however, the kinds of changes observed in smart materials are, in many cases, dramatically different from the more familiar changes (like those that take place in a thermostat).

Smart materials by themselves have a somewhat limited number of practical applications. One of the most familiar of those applications may be the use of photochromic glasses in the manufacture of eyeglasses, windows, and other products. The term *photochromic* refers to any material that changes in color when exposed to changes in light intensity. Photochromic eyeglasses are clear when the wearer is indoors in the presence of reduced amounts of light, and they are dark (like sunglasses) when the wearer is outdoors in the presence of elevated amounts of light. Smart materials that simply respond to environmental changes are generally known as *passive smart materials.* Passive smart materials have the potential for a wide variety of uses as sensors because they are able to detect changes in the environment around them and then undergo some kind of change (such as a change in color) in response.

One example of the sensing capabilities of a smart material is smart concrete, invented by Deborah D. L. Chung at the State University of New York at Buffalo. The product consists of ordinary concrete reinforced by carbon fibers that make up no more than about 0.5 percent of the product by volume. Although concrete itself is electrically nonconductive, the addition of the carbon fibers makes it conductive. This conductivity gives smart concrete properties not present in its dumber version. If tiny, hairline cracks begin to develop in the concrete, its electrical conductivity changes. These changes allow engineers to recognize potentially serious structural problems before they might otherwise be detectable. Smart concrete's electrical conductivity also changes as a function of the pressure placed on it. Increasing pressure on the concrete makes it more electrically conductive. This property is now being used in many states for "weigh-in-motion" systems that allow a monitoring station to determine the

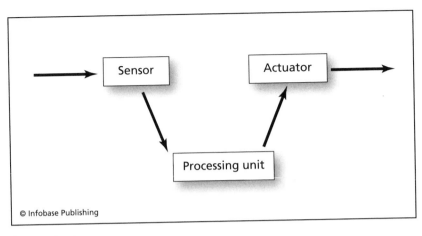

A smart structure

weight of a truck as it drives by on the highway, without the truck's having to stop and be weighed at the station itself.

The most exciting applications of smart materials involve their use in systems, known as *smart structures* or *smart systems*. As shown in the schematic diagram above, a smart structure is one that consists of at least two parts: one or more smart materials and an associated processing unit. When one of the smart materials (the *sensor*) detects a change in the surrounding environment, it sends a signal to the processing unit. The processing unit analyzes the signal received from the sensor and determines the kind of change that has occurred. The unit then determines what changes must be made in response to the external change. It sends a signal to the same or a second smart material (the *actuator*) that initiates changes in the size, shape, or physical properties of that material.

The smart material(s) in this system are usually present in one of two formats: as strips, disks, plates, or other attachments to the surface of a conventional structural material or embedded with the conventional material in the form of a composite. How the system is designed is determined primarily on how and where the smart material will have to act. If it will act on only one portion of a structural unit, it will be attached to that section. If it will act on the whole unit, it will probably be embedded within the whole unit. A smart structure, then, is a kind of feedback system in which a smart material detects a change and then responds in some way to accommodate that change.

The development of structural materials and structural systems represents a dramatic change in the philosophy that guides much of the work in materials science. Before the introduction of smart materials, most structures were built to maintain some given physical shape with certain specific physical characteristics for as long as possible. Change of almost any kind was not considered a good thing in such structures. If the materials of which a bridge, an airplane, a skyscraper, a superhighway, or a nuclear reactor began to break down, develop cracks, or change in some other way, the integrity of the structure was threatened. Specialists had to monitor those structures to find out where and when defects began to appear, and then authorities had to decide how repairs could be made or whether repairs were too expensive to justify.

With smart systems, changes in a material are desirable. They serve as an inherent monitoring system that detects potentially harmful changes in the physical characteristics of a structure before they become serious. And, in many cases, they can actually initiate changes that can be made within the system to counteract those changes and extend the lifetime of the structure and the materials of which it is made.

Types of Smart Materials

The term *smart material* is now used for a rather wide variety of materials, some that have been known and used for many years and some that have been developed only recently. For example, phosphorescent and fluorescent materials are familiar and widely used materials that are sometimes defined as smart materials because they have the capacity to absorb electromagnetic radiation of short wavelengths (X-rays or ultraviolet rays, for example) and re-emit that radiation in the form of visible light. The difference between phosphorescence and fluorescence is that a phosphorescent material continues to emit light after radiation has ceased, while the emission of fluoresced light ends as soon as the source of radiation is removed.

Beyond these two familiar kinds of light-emitting materials are an array of smart materials. The most common ones now being studied are piezoelectric and electrostrictive materials, magnetostrictive materials, shape memory alloys, electro- and magnetorheological materials, photochromatic and thermochromatic materials, and elastomers.

Piezoelectric and Electrostrictive Materials

The piezoelectric effect was discovered in 1880 by two brothers, Jacques (1856–1941) and Pierre (1859–1906) Curie. Piezoelectric materials are materials that change shape when an electric current flows through them and that, in turn, produce an electric current when their shape is altered. Both men were in their early 20s when

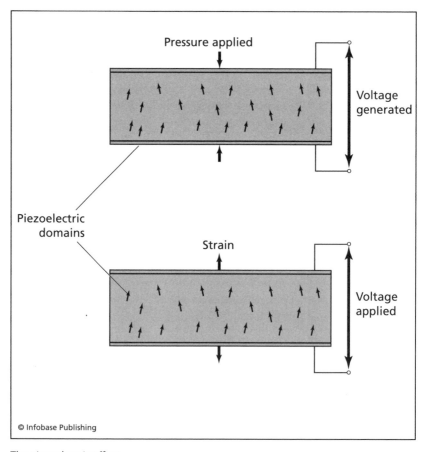

The piezoelectric effect

they made the discovery, which made them famous. Pierre went on to gain even greater fame as a result of his studies on radioactive materials with his wife, Marie.

The Curie brothers were drawn to the subject of *piezoelectricity* because of their familiarity with a phenomenon known for many centuries, that of *pyroelectricity*. Pyroelectricity refers to the tendency of certain materials to generate an electric current when they are heated. The phenomenon was first described in 314 B.C.E. by the Greek philosopher Theophrastus (ca. 370–ca. 285 B.C.E.), who observed the effect with the mineral tourmaline. Little research was done on pyroelectricity until the early 1800s, when the effect was rediscovered and studied in detail by the Scottish physicist Sir David Brewster (1781–1868). Then in 1878, William Thomson, Lord Kelvin (1824–1907), offered an explanation of the atomic changes that take place when pyroelectric effects occur. These developments in the understanding of pyroelectricity led the Curie brothers to study the possibility of producing electricity from crystals by physical means other than heating.

In 1880, they found that the application of pressure in one direction on certain crystals, as shown in the upper diagram on page 110, produces an electric potential (voltage) at opposite ends of that crystal normal (perpendicular) to the direction of pressure. They first discovered the effect in quartz crystals but later found that other materials, including topaz, tourmaline, and Rochelle salts (sodium potassium tartrate tetrahydrate), showed similar effects. Today, about 20 classes of crystals are known to demonstrate piezoelectricity, along with a number of natural materials, including bone, tissue, and collagen. Suspecting that a reverse and complementary behavior might exist in piezoelectric crystals, the Curies set out to discover whether such crystals could change shape if an electric field were applied to them. In 1881, they discovered that effect and named it *converse piezoelectricity*. Converse piezoelectricity is the process in which the application of an electric current to a crystal results in a change in its size and shape that corresponds in magnitude to the magnitude of the potential applied.

Converse piezoelectricity is a specific kind of a more general phenomenon known as *electrostriction*. Electrostriction is the deformation of a material exposed to an electrical field. Nearly all dielectrics (nonconducting materials) exhibit electrostriction. That is, they undergo at least some changes in size and shape when an electrical potential is applied to their surfaces. In most cases, the amount of deformation is relatively small, too small to be of any practical value in the design of useful objects. The major exception involves piezoelectric materials, whose converse effect is sufficiently large to be of practical value. Another important exception involves certain types of polymers in which the deformation produced by an electrical potential is even larger than that of inorganic piezoelectric materials that exhibit converse piezoelectricity. The major difference between the converse piezoelectric effect and electrostriction is that converse piezoelectricity has an inverse effect (the piezoelectric effect itself), but none has been observed for electrostriction.

Today, the atomic mechanism that causes the piezoelectric effect is well understood. Quartz, for example, consists of long chains of silicate (SiO_4^{2-}) groups arranged in a helical pattern, as shown in the diagram below. In any one silicate group, the atoms are arranged

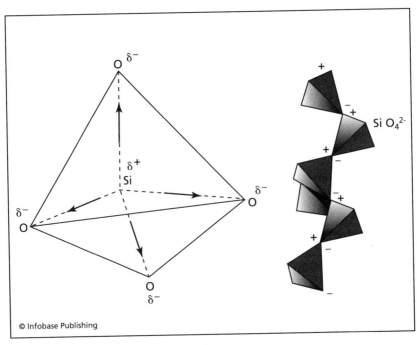

© Infobase Publishing

Atomic mechanism of the piezoelectric effect

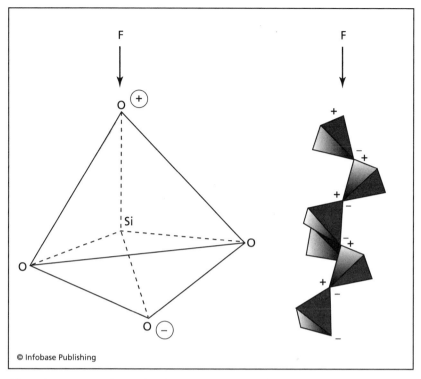

Effect of pressure on charge distribution in a quartz molecule

in a tetrahedron, with the silicon atom at the center and an oxygen atom at each of the four vertices of the tetrahedron. Although each silicon-oxygen bond is polar, the tetrahedron overall is nonpolar, with its outer surface uniformly more negative than its interior.

When pressure is applied to a single tetrahedral unit, as shown in the diagram above, it causes a separation of charges in the tetrahedron, making one side more positive and the other side more negative. If adjacent tetrahedra are not connected with each other (as they are in some silicates) the polarization of tetrahedra occurs so that adjacent units align themselves in a complementary pattern, with positive and negative ends pointing in opposite directions. These silicates show no overall separation of electrical charges, and the application of pressure to such crystals produces no electrical effect. In quartz, however, adjacent tetrahedral units are locked into position on the helix.

All tetrahedra become polarized in the same sense, that is, with the positive and negative ends all pointing in the same direction. In this conformation, the crystal becomes capable of conducting an electric current because of the accessibility of mobile electrical charges.

Of the 32 crystal classes known to scientists, 20 exhibit the piezo-electric effect. What these crystal classes have in common is an asymmetric structure that permits a separation of electrical charges when pressure is applied to them. The extent of the effect varies to a considerable degree among various types of crystals, however, and piezoelectric effects are of practical significance in only a small fraction of all possible cases.

By the mid-20th century, researchers began to discover a number of synthetic materials with piezoelectric properties. In the period 1942–44, for example, chemists in the United States, Japan, and the Soviet Union all found that the ceramic material barium titanate ($BaTiO_3$) demonstrates strong piezoelectric effects. None of these scientists was aware of the work of their colleagues because of the lack of communication during World War II. Piezoelectric sensors made from barium titanate have a piezoelectric constant (a measure of the strength of the piezoelectric effect) almost 100 times as great as that of quartz. The chart on page 115 lists the piezoelectric constants for some common materials. The first applications of such sensors was in the manufacture of phonograph pickups (needles) in 1947. They later found use in a number of other devices, such as vibration detectors; sonar systems; ignition systems; hydrophones; small, sensitive microphones; and relays.

In 1954, the American chemist Bernard Jaffe (1916–86) discovered the piezoelectric effects of the ceramic compound lead zirconate titanate ($PbTiZrO_3$), generally known as PZT. PZT is now commercially available in a variety of forms and is by far the most popular piezoelectric material in use. It has largely replaced barium titanate, which is now used primarily in the manufacture of electrical capacitors. Other ceramics that have been found to produce significant piezoelectric effects and are put to use in some commercial products include lead metaniobate (PN; $PbNb_2O_6$), bismuth titanate (BT; various formulas, including $Bi_4(TiO_4)_3$), sodium potassium niobate (NKN; various formulas, including $Na_{1-x}K_xNbO_3$, where x

◁ PIEZOELECTRIC CONSTANTS FOR SOME MATERIALS ▷

MATERIAL	PIEZOELECTRIC CONSTANT (D_{33}) pC/N*
Quartz	2.3
$BaTiO_3$	57.8
PZT 4	289
PST 5H	593
$(Pm,Sm)TiO_3$	65
PVDF-TrFE	33

*picocoulombs per newton, a charge of 10^{-12} coulomb per newton of force
Abbreviations used:
  PZT 4: One of at least four major types of PZT
  PST 5H: Lead scandium tanatalum oxide
  PVDF-TrFe: Copolymer of vinylidene fluoride and trifluoroethylene

>1), lead titanate (LT; $PbTiO_3$), and lead magnesium niobate (PMN; $Pb(Mg,Nb)O_3$).

Piezoelectric materials have found a number of applications in today's world. These include high-voltage generators, ultrasonic and sonar transducers, intruder alarm systems, remote control systems, record players, deformable mirrors, ultrasonic motors, "smart skis," waste gas generators, and hydrophones. One of the most common applications is as sensors in automotive airbag systems. In case of a front-end collision with another object, an airbag is released from (usually) the dashboard. The airbag inflates when the compound sodium azide (NaN_3) decomposes to produce sodium metal and nitrogen gas:

$$2NaN_3(s) \rightarrow 2Na(s) + 3N_2(g)$$

Inflation of the airbag depends on a somewhat complex process. The process starts with a set of sensors located in a variety of positions in the front portion of the automobile. When these sensors detect a collision of sufficient magnitude, they send an electrical signal to the processing unit, which then signals the airbag to inflate. This whole process generally takes place in less than 50 milliseconds.

The most common airbag sensors are made of piezoelectric materials arranged to form an accelerometer. In its simplest form, an accelerometer consists of a weight suspended in front of a fixed plate. When a force is applied to the weight, it moves toward the fixed plate, changing the electrical properties of the plate and setting up an electric current that can be measured. An automotive accelerometer generally has one of the two designs shown in the diagram below. In one of those designs, the accelerometer consists of a thin disk coated with a piezoelectric material. When a force is applied to the disk (as when the vehicle comes to a sudden stop as the result of striking an object), the piezoelectric material is deformed, creating an electrical current that can be measured. In the second design, a thin bar covered with a piezoelectric material is cantilevered out from a fixed platform. A change in momentum of the device, such as occurs in the case of a collision, causes the cantilevered bar to flex,

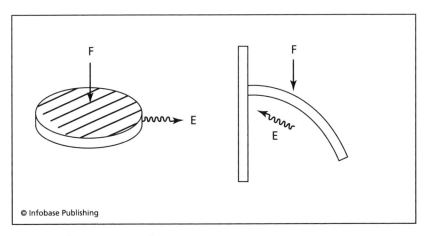

© Infobase Publishing

Two types of automotive accelerometers

creating a measurable electric current. In either of these devices, the electric current that is produced is transmitted to a processing unit, which analyzes the data it receives and transmits instructions to an actuator that releases the airbag. The strength of the electric current produced is a function of the force of the impact, so the processing unit can distinguish between the slow deceleration of the car (such as at a stop light) and the rapid deceleration associated with a collision. Piezoelectric sensors are now used to detect the location of a collision, the size of the object struck, and the speed at which the collision has taken place. All of these factors are important in determining how an airbag should be deployed.

Piezoelectric sensors have a number of other applications in airbag systems. One of the problems in the design of such systems, for example, is determining the weight and position of people riding in the front seat of the car. Although the deployment of an airbag during a collision can save lives, it can actually cause injuries under certain circumstances. For example, young children sitting in the passenger seat may be struck with enough force by an airbag to be seriously injured. Also, studies have shown that adults sitting closer than eight inches to a deployed airbag are likely to sustain serious injury.

Researchers have been exploring a variety of ways in which piezoelectric sensors can be used to help solve such problems. For example, composite fabrics have been developed for use as seat covers in which piezoelectric fibers are embedded in a ground material. The fibers detect the position a person takes on the seat, the person's weight, and any changes the person makes while seated in the car. This information can be used to determine whether an airbag needs to be deployed and, if so, to what pressure it should be inflated.

Piezoelectric sensors have found their way into a number of other applications also. One of the most widely used is a new type of snow ski developed by ski maker K2 of Vashon, Washington. The ski was designed to solve one of the most fundamental problems faced by skiers: that no single ski design is completely satisfactory for all types of skiing. Wide skis work best, for example, on deep, soft powder, but hourglass-shaped skis work best on hard-packed snow. Longer skis work best on straight runs at high speeds, but shorter skis are more efficient when there are lots of turns to make. So which ski design does one choose when one can buy only *one* pair of skis that has to be used in all types of skiing conditions?

K2 found that one of the most difficult problems it had to solve was that of vibration. At high speeds, skis may begin to "stutter" as they strike the ground, change shape (if ever so slightly), and begin to vibrate. As vibrations increase, it becomes more and more difficult to maintain control of the skis.

K2 solved the problem of vibration by installing a system of piezoelectric devices. The piezoelectric devices are attached to the skis just in front of the ski binding, where vibrations usually begin to occur before spreading out through the rest of the ski. As soon as a ski begins to vibrate, it causes the piezoelectric material to change shape. That change initiates a tiny electric current in the material that is transmitted to a small processing unit embedded in the ski. The processing unit analyzes the electric current and determines the change that has occurred in the shape of the piezoelectric device. It then calculates the change in the piezoelectric device necessary to restore the device and the ski itself to its original shape. Finally, it sends an electric current to the piezoelectric device of just the correct magnitude to bring about the desired shape change in the piezoelectric device and the ski to which it is attached.

Some of the most interesting applications of piezoelectric sensors have been in aeronautical engineering. The fundamental problem that aeronautical engineers face, as is the case with designers of skis, is that no single aircraft shape is equally efficient at all speeds and in all flying situations. Aircraft bodies contain a number of special adaptations—ailerons, flaps, elevators, and rudders, for example—that allow the aircraft to adapt to all the different flying conditions it encounters.

Aeronautical engineers have often looked to examples from the natural world, such as birds, for models of the way an aircraft *should* fly. Birds do not have fixed bodies or body parts, of course, but are able to change the shape and size of their wings, the tilt and direction of their wing feathers, the orientation of their legs and feet, and the shape of other body properties to produce the most efficient configurations for takeoff, landing, and a host of different flying conditions.

Piezoelectric devices create the possibility of making aircraft bodies with similar properties. Such aircraft would consist not of dozens of rigid moveable parts but of an airframe each part of which could be altered so as to produce an efficient flying device. In 1995, researchers at Auburn University's Adaptive Aerostructures Laboratory designed, built, and flew a model aircraft with these properties. The Auburn scientists called their invention Mothra after the giant flying insect from Japanese science fiction films that destroyed the character Godzilla in a 1992 film. Mothra was built of a composite material that incorporated piezoelectric devices distributed throughout its body. Electric current applied to these devices caused them to change shape in whatever way the designers wanted. If researchers wanted to make Mothra turn to the left or right, for example, they sent an electric signal to piezoelectric sensors attached to the vertical surfaces of the aircraft's tail, causing them to bend to the left or right. If they wanted to make the aircraft move upward or downward, they sent an electric signal to sensors on the horizontal surfaces of the wings, causing them to bend upward or downward.

About a year later, the Auburn scientists also flew the first helicopter made of smart materials. The helicopter, called Gamera after a fire-breathing turtle from Japanese science fiction movies, used piezoelectric plates on its rotors to change their shape and pitch. Gamera's propulsion system used five primary components rather than the 94 components required in conventional helicopters. The Auburn researchers reported that Gamera experienced a 26 percent reduction in drag, a 40 percent reduction in flight control system weight, and an 8 percent overall reduction in aircraft gross weight.

Piezoelectric devices have found a host of other aerospace applications. For example, one of the most troublesome problems faced by airlines is the detection of tiny hairline fractures in an aircraft body. These fractures often appear long before they can be observed visually during routine maintenance procedures. Yet, once they begin to develop, they can quite suddenly and dramatically lead to much larger cracks and failures that result in disastrous accidents. For this reason, airline companies are constantly searching for methods of identifying hairline cracks before they become serious problems.

Piezoelectric detectors are one of the most promising solutions to this problem. They can be installed at various locations on the aircraft body where they can constantly monitor the integrity of the materials of which the body is made. If cracks begin to develop at any location on the body, they can be detected because they result in the formation of small-scale shock waves as air passes over the aircraft body. These shock waves cause minute distortions of the aircraft's surface. While these distortions are too small to be noticed by most ordinary procedures, they are large enough to create electrical signals in nearby piezoelectric devices that can be picked up and analyzed by processing units attached to them.

When used in this way, the piezoelectric devices operate simply as sensors. In other aeronautical applications, however, they can serve as both sensors and actuators. For example, vibration is a serious problem in aircraft because it tends to weaken the materials from which an airframe is made. In addition, airframe vibration is responsible for much of the noise produced when an airplane is in motion. The solution for this problem using piezoelectric devices is similar to that in K2 skis. When a piezoelectric sensor embedded in the body of an airplane detects vibration, it transmits an electrical signal to a processing unit. That processor then determines the change that is needed to counteract the vibration. Essentially, it sends a signal to another piezoelectric device acting as an actuator to create a force equal to and opposite that causing the vibration. The piezoelectric actuator then makes whatever adjustment is necessary in the airframe to reduce vibration, reducing the risk of damage to the airframe material as well as eliminating the noise created by the vibration. This principle is widely used in a number of industrial, medical, and other applications where vibration is a problem.

Magnetostrictive Materials

Magnetostrictive materials are analogs of electrostrictive materials that change shape when exposed to a magnetic field. The phenomenon was first observed and reported by the English physicist James Prescott Joule (1818–89) in the 1840s. For that reason, *magnetostriction* is now referred to as the *Joule effect*. As with electrostriction, a converse effect can also be observed in which pressures exerted on magnetic materials can change their magnetic properties, a phenomenon called the *Villari effect* or the magnetomechanical effect.

The general mechanism by which magnetostriction occurs is easily explained, although the details of the process are actually quite complex. A magnetic material contains discrete regions known as *magnetic domains* that are oriented randomly, their north and south poles pointed in various directions. When an external magnetic field is applied to the material, however, it forces all those domains to line up in a single direction, with north-seeking poles pointed in one direction and south-seeking poles in the opposite direction. Clearly, the latter arrangement takes up more space and results in an expansion of the material in the direction in which the external magnetic field is applied.

Although most magnetic materials exhibit magnetostriction, the change in volume is quite small, of the order of a few parts per million. This fact suggests that practical applications of magnetostriction may be difficult to develop. That has not been the case, however, since the 1960s, when researchers discovered alloys that demonstrate a significantly greater degree of magnetostriction, called *giant magnetostriction alloys* (GMAs). These alloys show an increase in size of a few thousand parts per million, sufficiently large to permit the development of magnetostrictive-based devices with practical applications.

The first GMAs developed were alloys of iron, terbium, and/or dysprosium. They were discovered by a research group at the Naval Surface Warfare Center (NSWC) in Silver Springs, Maryland, under the direction of A. E. Clark. One of the first and most successful of these alloys had the formula $TbFe_2$ and was given the name of Terfenol (from Te, the symbol for terbium, and Fe, the symbol for iron). Later research showed that an alloy of all three metals had even better magnetostrictive properties. These alloys had the approximate general formula $Tb_x Dy_{1-x} Fe_y$ and were given the name of Terfenol-D (the additional D for the added dysprosium). Terfenol-D is now the most widely used of all magnetostrictive materials. Researchers have developed and tested a number of variations of the basic Terfenol-D formulation, trying to find a product with even better magnetostrictive properties. For example, researchers at the Toshiba Corporation received a patent for a variation of Terfenol-D that contained manganese in addition to terbium, dysprosium, and iron with the formula $Tb_x Dy_{1-x}(Fe_{1-y} Mn_y)$, while researchers at Iowa State University received a patent for a similar GMA that contains silicon rather than manganese. Also, The Etrema Corporation has been given a patent for a Terfenol-D-like alloy that contains various combinations of the rare earth elements lanthanum, cerium, praseodymium, neodymium, samarium, terbium, dysprosium, holmium, erbium, and yttrium. The chart on page 123 shows the relative magnetostrictive strengths of some common magnetic metals and GMAs. The unit of measurement for magnetorestriction is called lambda (λ), with larger values of lambda representing greater amounts of magnetorestriction.

The Clark research team at NSWC has continued its studies of magnetostrictive materials and found that the addition of gallium to alloys also produces strong magnetostrictive properties. The team has called their gallium-iron alloy Galfenol (Ga for gallium, and Fe for iron). Galfenol has demonstrated an increase in volume of 400 parts per million when exposed to low magnetic fields.

Other magnetostrictive materials are being developed by combining familiar GMA technology with another type of smart material, *shape memory alloys* (SMAs). (Shape memory alloys are discussed in greater detail later in this chapter.) The specific SMAs being studied are those made of nickel and titanium or copper and zinc. Some small-scale tests have shown that single crystals of the alloy containing nickel, manganese, and gallium change by as much as 9 percent when exposed to magnetic fields. The search for even better magnetostrictive materials is one of the most exciting in the area of smart materials.

A number of applications of magnetostrictive materials depend on their behavior when exposed to a high-frequency magnetic field: They begin to pulsate synchronously with the changing magnetic field. That is, they change shape in a regular and rapid pattern consonant

◁ MAGNETOSTRICTION IN SOME MATERIALS ▷

MATERIAL	MAGNETOSTRICTION (λ)
Fe	−0.0014
Ni	−0.0050
Permalloy (65 percent Fe, 45 percent Ni)	0.0027
$SmFe_2$	−0.2340
Fe_3O_4	0.0060
$DyFe_2$	0.0650
Terfenol ($TbFe_2$)	0.2630
Terfenol-D ($Tb_xDy_{1-x}Fe_y$)	0.1600–0.2400
TbZn	0.4500–0.5500
TbDyZn	0.5000

Source: Properties of Chosen Magnetostrictive Materials, SmartSITE, http://smartsite.immt.pwr.wroc.pl/index/gmm_02_mag_mat.

with that of the magnetic source. These pulsations may then produce vibrations in the air surrounding the material, creating sound waves of various wavelengths, from ultrasound to audible sound.

The first practical device to make use of magnetostrictive technology, a sonar system developed by researchers at NSWC, used this property. The system consisted of magnetostrictive materials that produced vibrations of sufficient strength to generate a sound wave that could be used for sonar tracking and detection. A similar technology is used to generate ultrasound signals, which are used in applications ranging from diagnostics and medicine to cleaning and testing technologies in various industrial fields.

One of the most recent applications of magnetostriction has been the development of a small device called the Soundbug®, developed by Wave Industries, Limited, of Portland, Oregon. About the size of a computer mouse, Soundbug can be plugged into almost any audio device, such as an MP3, Walkman radio, portable CD, laptop computer, camcorder, or cassette player, and attached via its suction cup to any flat surface, such as a table top or window. The device contains strips of Terfenol-D, which respond to fluctuating magnetic waves from the audio device and produce vibrations that occur as sound waves, turning the flat surface into a loudspeaker. A combination of two Soundbugs attached to two separate surfaces is said to provide a stereophonic effect similar to what a pair of conventional loudspeakers produce.

Electrostrictive and magnetostrictive devices are also finding use in vibration suppression and noise control systems. The principle involved is similar to that employed in the use of piezoelectric devices. When material vibrates in an aircraft, an automobile, or a piece of industrial or medical machinery, an electrostrictive or magnetostrictive sensor detects a change in position (that is, a change in motion) and relays that information to a central processing unit. The processor then determines the correction that needs to be made to compensate for the change and reduce the vibration (and the noise it produces). It relays that information to electrostrictive or magnetostrictive actuators, which generate the shape changes necessary to compensate for the original changes in position detected by sensors.

As this section demonstrates, magnetorestrictive and electrorestrictive devices have potential applications in many different fields, from aeronautics to sports equipment. So far, only modest progress has been made in developing working devices that make use of these materials. A major problem is that the basic science in the operation of such materials is still not well understood. As this fundamental knowledge improves, consumers and industries can expect to see many more uses of magnetorestrictive and electrorestrictive devices in everyday applications.

Electrorheological and Magnetorheological Effects

The term *rheology* refers to the deformation and flow of matter. *Electrorheological* and *magnetorheological* phenomena are, therefore, deformations that occur in matter as the result of the imposition of an electrical or magnetic field, respectively. Electrorheological and magnetorheological effects were discovered at about the same time in the late 1940s, the former by American electrical engineer Willis M. Winslow (then at the University of Colorado at Boulder) and the latter by Jacob Rabinow (then at the U.S. National Bureau of Standards, now the National Institute of Standards and Technology). The electrorheological phenomenon is also called the Winslow effect in its discoverer's honor.

The changes that take place in both materials are very similar. When an electrical current or magnetic force is applied to a liquid, a number of fundamental physical properties change almost immediately. In general, the liquids become much more viscous and change from a watery or oily texture to a thick, syrupy, molasseslike liquid or, in some case, directly to a solid. These changes take place almost instantaneously after the imposition of the external field, generally in a matter of a few microseconds.

Research and development in the understanding and uses of both electrorheological and magnetorheological materials occurred very slowly for a number of reasons. In both cases, research required a broad understanding of a number of disciplines, including chemistry, physics, engineering, and mathematics, that was not especially common at the time. Also, obtaining materials of sufficient purity to obtain the desired results was often difficult. In Winslow's case, the earliest experiments were carried out with finely divided powders, such as starch, silica, gypsum, and lime, suspended in an oily liquid. In the case of magnetorheological liquids, the carrier liquid was also an oil, but the suspended material was finely divided particles of

◁ **JACOB RABINOW (1910–1999)** ▷

Why does a person decide to become a scientist? Ask a dozen scientists and one is likely to get a dozen different answers: to make the world a better place, to find out more about nature, to make a lot of money, and so on. But one answer one is most likely to hear is that scientific works is simply fun. That is the answer Jacob Rabinow gave in March 1999, when asked why he worked so hard as an inventor: "I invent because I get a kick out of it. It's an achievement, where nothing is at stake. If I don't succeed, the world is not going to come to an end. The challenge and the licking of the challenge—all of these inventions are like solving puzzles. I am perfectly happy just to solve a puzzle." At the time Rabinow made this comment, he was 88 years old, officially retired from his job at the National Institute of Standards & Technology (NIST) but still active as an inventor.

Rabinow was born in Kharkov, Russia (now Ukraine), in 1910 as Yakov Aaronovich Rabinovich. When the Russian Revolution moved into his region in 1919, his family fled to China, where his father died. Rabinow and his mother and brother then moved on to the United States, where they settled in Brooklyn in 1921. He enrolled at the City College of New York (CCNY), from which he received his B.S. degree in electrical engineering in 1933. For a few years after graduating from CCNY, he worked at a variety of low-level jobs, including selling hot dogs at Coney Island and working as a wirer in a radio assembly factory. Finally, in 1938, Rabinow passed the U.S. engineering civil service test and got a job as a mechanical engineer at the National Bureau of Standards (NBS, now the National Institute of Standards & Technology, NIST). His beginning salary was $2,000 per year. It was at NBS that he had his first opportunity to try his hand at inventing. He worked in the weaponry laboratory at NBS, where, he later said, "I had problems thrown at me from all sides: guided missiles, parachute releases, safety mechanisms, proximity fuses, generators, speed controls, and recording equipment, so that the opportunity [for invention] was there, the encouragement was there."

In 1954, Rabinow left NBS to found his own company, the Rabinow Engineering Company, so he could develop an idea of special interest, a

iron. Today electrorheological and magnetorheological liquids are usually made of similar suspensions of finely divided particles with diameters of about 0.1–100 μm in which the suspended particles make up 20 to 60 percent by volume of the mixture.

"reading machine." He succeeded, receiving a patent for the reading machine in 1960, and some experts regard it as his greatest invention. The reading machine has the ability to "read" letters and numbers by converting them to patterns of dots, which are then compared to standard letters and numbers. The dot pattern is interpreted when the best match is found between it and the standards. Rabinow's invention is still used widely today to read credit card information, bank checks and deposits, and the vast majority of documents processed by the Internal Revenue Service.

A decade after establishing Rabinow Engineering, Rabinow sold the company to Control Data Corporation. He stayed on as vice president of the company until 1972, when he returned to NBS as chief research engineer at the National Engineering Laboratory. He retired from NIST in 1989, although he continued to maintain an informal relationship with the agency until his death. In 1990, he published his first book, *Inventing for Fun and Profit* (San Francisco Press). When he died, he was still working on inventions. He was trying to improve his pick-proof lock, originally designed in 1938, and was developing a variable-speed hydraulic engine.

Only six months after making the remarks quoted earlier, Rabinow died on September 11, 1999. During his lifetime, Rabinow had received 230 U.S. patents for his inventions, including the automatic letter-sorting machine that is used by the U.S. Postal Service to route mail, a device for regulating the operation of clocks and watches automatically, a magnetic particle clutch used in cars and airplanes, a straight-line phonograph, a new type of Venetian blind, an optical character reader, a pick-proof lock, and a magnetic memory device of the type now used in hard disk drives. Some of his earliest inventions were developed for the military, such as fuses and safety devices for the guidance systems used in missiles. At about the same time, he discovered the magnetorheological effect, whose many possible practical applications are only now being appreciated. Today, the NIST has devoted a whole room at its museum to the display of some of Rabinow's most interesting inventions and discoveries.

Scientists now understand the basic principles that determine the behavior of electrorheological and magnetorheological fluids. They believe that the imposition of an external electrical or magnetic field polarizes the particles suspended in the fluid. In the case of an electrorheological fluid, those particles become dipoles, as shown in the diagram on page 129. Those particles then line up to form long chains, with the positive end of one dipole attached to the negative end of an adjacent dipole. These chains provide a rigid structure that converts the liquid from one with low viscosity to one with much higher viscosity. In the case of a magnetorheological fluid, the effect is similar except that the tiny particles of iron suspended in the liquid are converted into magnetic dipoles, which then self-assemble into long chains with the north-seeking pole of one particle attached to the south-seeking pole of a second particle.

One example of the possible applications of electrorheological or magnetorheological fluids is in automobile shock-absorbing systems. Sensors attached to the car body would detect the presence of an irregularity in the road that would normally jar the car and its occupants. The sensor would then send a signal to a computer that would determine the response needed to counteract the road irregularity. The computer would then send a signal to an electrorheological or magnetorheological fluid contained within the shock absorber, telling the fluid to become more or less viscous and to what extent.

Another possible application that has received considerable attention is the use of a magnetorheological fluid in the design of earthquake-proof buildings. The fluid would be contained in canisters located throughout the building at key structural positions. In the event of an earthquake, sensors would detect the movement of the ground and would send a signal to a central processor communicating the size of the tremor. The processing unit would then transmit to the canisters the changes that would be needed to make the magnetorheological fluid more viscous and rigid, and to what extent that change had to occur.

So far, applications for electrorheological and magnetorheological liquids are rather limited in number, but researchers predict that they will eventually find a number of applications in industry, aerospace, the military, and other fields. As with other fields of materials science, much more basic research is needed to understand the behavior of electrorheological and magnetorheological liquids before everyday applications can be developed.

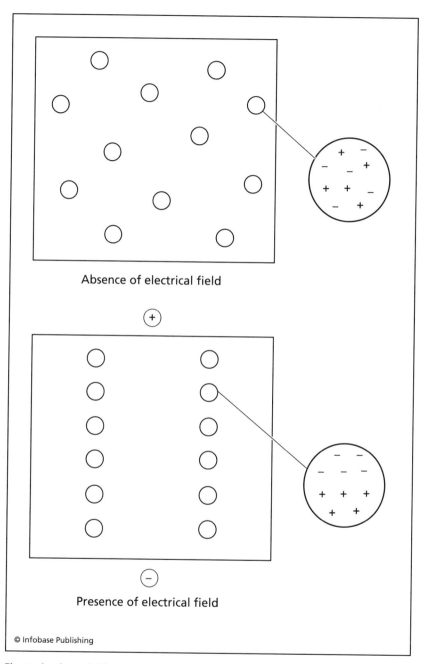

Absence of electrical field

Presence of electrical field

Electrorheological effect

Shape Memory Alloys

Shape memory alloys (SMAs) are metals that, after having been deformed, return to their original shape upon being heated to some characteristic temperature. SMAs were first discovered by the Swedish physicist Arne Olander in the early 1930s. While working with alloys of gold and cadmium, Olander noticed an unusual phenomenon. The alloys could be used to make an object with some given shape, a straight wire or flat plate, for example. These objects could then be bent, twisted, or otherwise reshaped, and the new shape appeared to be permanent. When the alloys were heated to some characteristic temperature, however, the objects spontaneously returned to their original shape. The objects acted as if they "remembered" their original shapes and returned to those shapes once they were provided sufficient energy, represented by the so-called *transformation temperature.*

Relatively little research was conducted on SMAs in the decades following Olander's discovery. In fact, it was not until the early 1960s that the first SMAs with practical applications were developed and studied. The first of these alloys was nitinol, invented by William J. Buehler, a researcher at the Naval Ordnance Laboratory in White Oak, Maryland. The name *nitinol* comes from the two metals of which it is made (nickel, Ni, and titanium, Ti) and the initial letters of the laboratory (NOL) where Buehler was working. It is said that nitinol was discovered quite by accident. During a meeting of researchers, Buehler displayed a strip of the alloy that had been bent a number of times. For some unknown reason, one of the researchers present at the meeting, David S. Muzzey, decided to heat the metallic strip with his pipe lighter. To everyone's surprise, the strip returned spontaneously to its original form. Today, the vast majority of SMA applications make use of one of three alloys: titanium and nickel (TiNi); copper, aluminum, and zinc (CuZnAl); and copper, aluminum, and nickel (CuAlNi).

The behavior of shape memory alloys can be explained on the basis of solid state phase changes that occur within the material. All SMAs exist in one of two phases, known as martensite and austenite, shown in the diagram on page 132. Austenite is the "parent" phase of the two, the one that exists at a higher temperature. It has a body-centered cubic crystalline structure. Austenite is a tough, strong metal with properties similar to that of one of its components, titanium. When the temperature of an SMA is lowered, it begins to undergo a molecular change in which the cubic structure characteristic of austenite is transformed into a stressed form of martensite called twinned martensite. Twinned martensite can exist in any of 24 different crystallographic structures. The change from austenite to twinned martensite is not visually apparent, because both have essentially the same size and shape. Twinned martensite does have significantly different physical properties from austenite, however, since it is very elastic and rubbery, accounting for the term by which it is sometimes known, superelastic SMA.

A further reduction in temperature produces a second phase change in which twinned martensite is converted to deformed martensite. Deformed martensite (or just martensite) can also occur in any of the 24 crystallographic variants as twinned martensite, but as the diagram suggests, it is visually different from both austenite and twinned martensite. It also has significantly different physical properties: It is soft, ductile, and easily deformed, somewhat like the alloy pewter.

The diagram shows the relationship of the three forms of an SMA as a function of the temperature and pressure to which the material is exposed. Notice that it is possible to convert twinned martensite to deformed martensite *without* any change in temperature, but only by increasing the pressure on the material. When deformed martensite is produced by this mechanism, it has only one crystallographic structure, a monoclinic form. Deformed martensite can also be produced directly from austenite by the application of sufficient stress on the latter material.

A host of applications for shape memory alloys have now been developed. Beyond their unusual ability to retain shape, these applications have little in common but human ingenuity. Examples range from aerospace and industrial applications to medical devices to household goods.

As with most other types of smart materials, an important impetus for research on SMAs has been their potential applications in the military and aerospace industry. TiNi Aerospace, for example, has designed and built a number of products used during the launch and deployment phases of space travel. Their Frangibolt® device, for example, consists of a cylinder made of titinol attached to a micro-heating unit. These cylinders are used to hold a variety of devices to a spacecraft, such as antennas, cover doors, solar panels, and experimental payloads. When the time comes to release these objects from the spacecraft itself, the Frangibolt is heated; it returns to its original, reduced size; and the connection between device and spacecraft

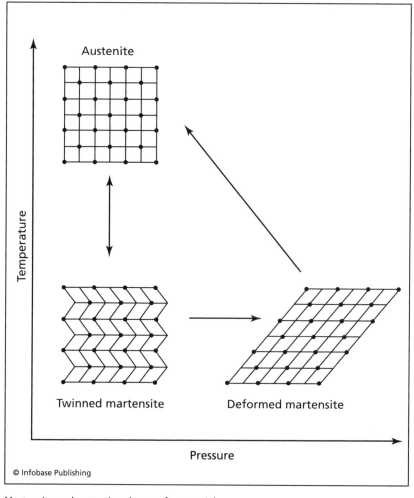

Martensite and austenite phases of a material

is broken. TiNi also makes a Pinpuller device that accomplishes a similar objective with spacecraft devices. The Pinpuller consists of an SMA wire that can be triggered by the input of a small amount of heat; this releases a loaded compression spring that drives the device away from the spacecraft body.

SMAs are also being used to improve the operation of traditional aircraft. For example, the problem of adjusting the shape of an airplane wing so that it will provide maximum lift under a variety of conditions (described earlier in this chapter) can also be solved by using shape memory alloys. SMAs can be attached to the leading and trailing edges of the wing and to its upper and lower surfaces, as shown in the diagram on page 134. Electrical leads to the SMAs are then used to heat the alloys to the temperatures needed to change their shape in some desired manner to achieve maximum flight efficiency.

Splitting apart rocky material is an important step in many activities by which natural resources are extracted from the earth. One example is the quarrying of materials from the ground. The usual process is to drill a series of holes in the side of a mountain (or other source of the material to be quarried) and then expose a block of material using low-yield explosives or rock saws. These methods are relatively efficient, although they tend to be expensive and may result in the production of materials with irregular and undesirable shapes and sizes. An Italian firm, D'Appolonia Engineering Consulting Company, has developed a process for using SMAs in place of drills, explosives, and saws for quarrying. Small pockets are drilled into rock and filled with shells made of shape memory alloys. The alloys are then heated electrically, causing them to change from their martensite to austenite phases. This change results in an expansion of the shells that cracks open the rock and produces the desired product.

The variety of medical applications for shape memory alloys is impressively broad. These alloys are already used as stents inserted into blocked arteries, as vena-cava filters, as orthodontic devices, and in eyeglasses.

Plaque deposits on the inner walls of arteries can lead to the partial or complete blockage of those arteries, restricting the flow of blood to and from the heart and resulting in coronary disease, now the number one cause of death in developed nations around the world. A technically clever and relatively simple solution to this problem involves the insertion of a *stent,* a cylinder-shaped wire mesh, into the blocked artery. The stent is made of an SMA that has been shaped at the alloy's high-temperature austenite phase. It is then cooled to the point that it reverts to its martensite phase. It then has essentially the same shape but a smaller diameter and smaller volume than in the austenite phase. The stent is then surgically inserted into a patient's blocked artery, where it warms up and returns to its austenite phase. As it returns to its original size and

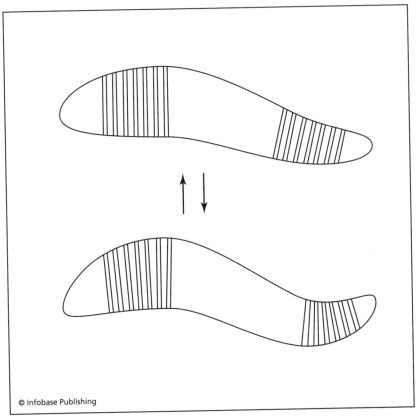

The use of SMAs in adjusting the shape of an airplane wing

shape, it expands to fit snugly against the inner wall of the artery, opening the vessel and allowing blood to flow through freely.

SMAs are also used in another application related to cardiac health problems, as vena-cava filters. In some instances, it is desirable to protect a patient against the possibility that a blood clot formed elsewhere in the body will travel through the circulatory system into the heart, where it may cause a heart attack or stroke. Tiny, umbrella-shaped devices made of SMA materials have proven to be effective in such cases. In these devices, called vena-cava filters, the umbrella portion of the device consists of a mesh of tiny wires made of an SMA material. The device is inserted into the circulatory system in the form of a reduced-size (martensite phase), folded-up umbrella. Once in place, it is opened in such a way that the umbrella fills the vessel leading into the heart. The mesh design allows blood to flow through normally but filters out any blood clots that are carried along with the blood.

Many people are familiar with traditional orthodonture, the process by which steel wires are used to straighten teeth. An orthodontist installs the steel wires, which guide the growth of teeth in some particular, desired directions. The problem with this very popular technique is that stainless steel does not stretch and adjust very well, and a patient may have to visit an orthodontist quite frequently to have adjustments made in the tensions of the wires. The use of SMA materials for orthodontic wires reduces this problem. Such wires exert the force of tension needed to direct the growth of teeth, but they do so with more elasticity and, therefore, less discomfort to patients. Patients must still visit their orthodontist for adjustments, but at much less frequent intervals.

Purchasing a pair of eyeglasses that do the best possible job of improving one's eyesight involves more than simply getting the right prescription for lenses. Those glasses must also fit exactly right on the wearer's face. Before a patient leaves the optometrist's office, then, one of the employees spends some time adjusting the frames of the new eyeglasses. But what happens if the eyeglass wearer accidently puts a book on those glasses or sits on them or does something else that changes the shape of the frames? The eyeglasses will no longer be able to serve as well as they should until the wearer can return to the optometrist's office and have them adjusted. Unless, that is, those frames are made of an SMA alloy. In such a case, deformation of the frames will be only temporary. All the wearer need do is warm the glasses, and the frames will return to their original shape without another trip to the optometrist's!

SMAs clearly have important applications in aerospace technology, industry, and medicine, but as time goes on people will be more likely to encounter these materials in ordinary household devices as well. Japan's Furukawa Techno Material corporation has developed a number of interesting household products that use SMA technology. For example, their SMA rice cooker contains alloys that act as both sensor and actuator, measuring the steam pressure that develops inside the cooker and then opening a valve to release excess steam. Their SMA coffee maker contains an SMA valve that changes shape when water inside the appliance reaches the correct temperature for making good coffee, at which time it releases the water to the coffee filter. Furukawa also uses SMA technology in the louvers they design and build for air conditioners, which sense a room's temperature and then change their position (upward or downward) to produce a flow of air appropriate to that temperature. SMAs are materials that people can expect to see more of in both high-tech applications and consumer goods.

Photochromism

Photochromic materials are materials that change color reversibly with changes in light intensity. The term *reversibly* is of significance here since many chemical systems change color when exposed to light, but in photochromic systems, those changes are never permanent. Self-adjusting sunglasses that are dark when exposed to sunlight and clear in the presence of artificial light are perhaps the most widely known example of photochromism. *Photochromism* is a subset of a larger group of phenomena known as *chromogenism.* Chromogenic reactions are changes in color that take place when a material is exposed to any kind of external stimulus, such as light (photochromism), electricity (electrochromism), or heat (thermochromism). According to some authorities, chromogenic smart materials may represent the "largest marketing opportunity" of all kinds of smart materials. A single photochromic product, self-dimming rearview mirrors, had reached sales by a single company (Gentex) of a million units as early as 1995.

The first observation of the photochromic effect was apparently reported by a German chemist by the name of J. Fritzsche in 1867. He noted that a solution of tetracene was orange in the dark and white when exposed to light. Of special importance was the fact that this change was reversible—the solution changed color from orange to colorless and back again—depending on the amount of light to which it was exposed. Other evidence of photochromic effects were reported by the English chemist T. L. Phipson in 1881, by the Dutch chemist E. ter Meer in 1876, and by the German chemist Markwald in 1899. Phipson reported that a gate painted with a zinc compound appeared to be black during the daytime but then turned white at night. Ter Meer showed that the sodium salt of dintitroethane in the sold state was yellow in the dark and red in bright light. Markwald studied a reversible change in color of the compound 2,3,4,4-tetrachloronaphthalen-1(4H-one). But Markwald's assertion that the change he observed was strictly a physical and not a chemical phenomenon indicates the primitive understanding of photochromism as late as the end of the 19th century.

In fact, relatively little progress in the understanding of photochromic processes occurred until after Wold War II. The process itself was not even named until 1950, when an Israeli chemist by the name of Yehuda Hirshberg suggested the name *photochromism* from two Greek words meaning "light" (*photos-*) and "color" (*chromism*). In the decades that followed, a significant amount of research was conducted in the search for practical applications of photochromism, primarily in the design of "automatic" sunglasses that changed from dark to clear and back depending on the amount of light to which they were exposed. The breakthrough in this research occurred in 1959, when William Armistead, a researcher at Corning Glass Works, discovered a way of making such glasses spontaneously reversible. The first "automatic" sunglasses contained finely divided particles of silver halide, which allowed the glasses to change from clear to dark in sunlight. But the silver halide alone did not permit the glasses to change back once they were removed from the sunlight. Armistead found that the addition of a small amount of copper(I) halide made the reverse transition possible and easy. Since Armistead's work, the design of the vast majority of "automatic" sunglasses has included the use of both silver and copper(I) halides.

Photochromic materials can consist of either inorganic or organic compounds. Some of the best known inorganic photochromic compounds are the silver halides, such as silver bromide and silver chloride, often used in photography. These compounds are now widely used in sunglasses, automobile windshields, and visual display units that change color spontaneously in the presence of greater or lesser amounts of light. The process occurs when visible light provides enough energy to electrons in the halogen atoms to migrate to colorless silver ions, converting those ions to grayish atoms of silver and causing the material to darken:

$$Cl^- - e^- + Ag^+ \rightarrow Ag^0 + Cl^0$$

The copper(I) chloride added to the sunglass material has a dual function. First, it reacts with the atomic chlorine formed in the reaction above, converting it to chloride ion and preventing it from escaping as a gas from the material:

$$Cu^+ + Cl^0 \rightarrow Cu^{2+} + Cl^-$$

Second, the Cu^{2+} ion thus formed reacts with atomic silver formed in light to convert it back to silver ion in the absence of light:

$$Cu^{2+} + Ag^0 \rightarrow Cu^+ + Ag^+$$

The silver halides are by no means the only inorganic compounds to undergo photochromatic reactions, however. An experiment sometimes used in introductory chemistry classes involves the study of the compound mercury dithizonate $[Hg(Dz)_2]$, where the dithizonate ion is equivalent to the diphenyl thiocarbazone group shown in the diagram on page 139. The color change that occurs in this compound, as in all photochromic compounds, involves a shift of electrons that results in the formation of a variant form of the original compound. In this case, the original compound is orange, and the isomer formed is blue.

By far the greatest number of photochromatic compounds, however, are organic. As in the inorganic compound mercury dithizonate, photochromism in organic compounds occurs when one form of a compound is exposed to light, which converts the compound to an isomer of a different color. In most such instances, the two isomers differ in that one is a closed form of the isomer and the other is an open form. In some cases, however, the two isomers differ in that one occurs in a *trans* form and the other in a *cis* form. *Trans* and *cis* isomers are forms of a compound in which two constituent atoms or groups are located on opposite or the same side of a molecule, respectively.

The equations above do not accurately reflect the complexity of the reactions that actually occur when photochromic compounds are exposed to light. In such cases, the low-energy colorless isomer is the more stable form that changes its molecular conformation very

Orange   Blue

Color change in mercury dithizonate

quickly when exposed to light. That change usually occurs in at least two steps that take place very rapidly, generally in much less than a microsecond. Under those circumstances, special techniques must be developed to determine the molecular structure both of the final product and of intermediary species formed during the reaction.

The manufacture of glasses and plastics that change color in the presence of sunlight is almost certainly the most important current application of photochromic materials. A number of research teams are exploring methods for making the use of photochromic materials in such applications even more efficient. For example, scientists at the Lawrence Berkeley National Laboratory at Berkeley, California, are studying the use of nickel hydroxide [$Ni(OH)_2$] and titanium dioxide (TiO_2) in the manufacture of energy-efficient windows that change color automatically when exposed to varying levels of sunlight. Thin layers of the two materials are sandwiched between to panes of glass to make window glass for use in homes, offices, factories, and other facilities. Such windows stay transparent when the sun is low in the sky and on cloudy days but darken automatically as the sun rises and on sunny days.

But photochromic materials are being considered for a number of applications that go beyond sunglasses and "smart" windows. Those who are working with nanoscale devices, for example, are excited about the possibility of constructing molecular switches that operate photochemically. One such device has been investigated by a research group led by B. L. Feringa at the University of Gronigen in the Netherlands. The molecule investigated by the Feringa group exists in two isomeric forms, designated as M-*cis*-nitro and P-*trans*-nitro. When light with a wavelength of about 365 nm is applied to the former structure, it undergoes a rearrangement in which the upper half of the molecule rotates around the double bond joining the two major components of the molecule. That is, the molecule converts from a *cis* orientation to a *trans* configuration. The important point is that any additional components attached to this portion of the molecule would be rotated through a 180° angle during the process, meaning that the molecule could operate as a molecular switch.

Another interesting possible application of photochromic materials is in the construction of new data storage systems for computers. For some time, researchers have been considering the possibility of constructing computing machines that operate with light rather than electricity. Such devices have been called optical computers. Since light travels about 10 times as fast as electricity, optical computers would be able to operate much more rapidly than their electronic counterparts, an appealing feature.

One possible way of constructing the memory devices needed in an optical computer is with photochromic materials. The general approach would be to shine light on this material in such a way as to convert it from one form (e.g., colorless) to a second form (e.g., colored). One form could be designated as an "on" state and the second form an "off" state. A group of Japanese researchers at the Sanyo Electric Company's New Materials Research Center recently constructed a model of an optical computer and found that data could be recorded and read more than a million times faster without causing any damage to the recording material or, hence, to the data itself. The researchers' stated goal was to produce a device in which each bit of information could be stored in a single molecule, resulting in a device that could hold 100 terabits of information per square inch.

This experiment confirmed the fact that photochromic materials are beginning to find a broad range of applications that goes beyond their familiar use in sunglasses, windows, and other everyday devices. As researchers develop a better understanding of the fundamental principles involved in the way photochromic materials operate, advanced applications in molecular switches, nanocomputers, and other nanometer-scale devices are likely to become much more common.

Intelligent Gels

Intelligent, or "smart," gels are materials that expand or contract when triggered by some external stimulus, such as relatively modest changes in light, temperature, pH, pressure, or electrical or magnetic fields. They were first discovered in 1975 by Toyoichi Tanaka, then a professor in the physics department at the Massachusetts Institute of Technology (MIT). A gel is a colloidal material with a consistency somewhere between that of a solid and a liquid. Some common examples of gels include Jell-O, fruit jellies, tofu, yogurt, rubber cement, hair mousse, the material from which soft contact

◁ TOYOICHI TANAKA (1946–2000) ▷

One of the great tragedies of human life is the loss of an unusually great person in the prime of life. In such cases, one looks back at the many achievements of that person's life and can only wonder how much he or she yet had to offer the world. Such was the case with Toyoichi Tanaka, who suffered a heart attack and died while playing tennis on May 24, 2000. Tanaka was the discoverer of intelligent gels in the mid-1970s and had explored both the theoretical basis for the existence of such materials as well as a number of possible applications for these exciting new materials.

Toyoichi Tanaka was born in Nagaoka, in the prefecture of Niigata, Japan, on January 4, 1946. His father was a professor of applied chemistry and founder of the Department of Environmental Technology at Saitama University, located in Urawa, Japan. After completing his secondary education in Nagaoka, Tanaka enrolled at the University of Tokyo, where he earned his bachelor's (1968), master's (1970), and doctoral (1973) degrees in physics. He also spent one semester in fall 1971 as a postdoctoral student at the Massachusetts Institute of Technology (MIT). His work at MIT so impressed his colleagues that he was offered a permanent position and was appointed assistant professor in 1975. He was later promoted to associate professor in 1979 and to full professor in 1982.

Tanaka's discovery of smart gels revolutionized many fields of theoretical and applied science. Their behavior provides an insight on the properties of proteins, and they are expected to have a number of practical applications in

lenses are made, and the cytoplasm present inside a cell. In most cases, a gel is made by preparing a suspension of a finely divided solid (the dispersed phase) in the dispersing phase (the dispersant) at a high temperature that is then allowed to cool. The gel typically forms after a considerable period of time, usually a few hours. *Intelligent gels* differ from ordinary gels in that they change from one phase to another phase almost instantaneously.

Intelligent gels also differ from traditional gels in their extreme sensitivity to changes in external stimuli and their relatively dramatic changes in physical properties. For example, a gel made from the polymer poly(N-isopropylacrylamide) can increase in volume 100 times or more when its temperature changes by a single degree, from the medicinal sciences, the generation of energy, and food production and manufacturing. After his discovery of smart gels in 1975, Tanaka founded or cofounded a number of companies, including GelMed, GelSciences, Smart Gels, and Buyo-Buyo, Inc. to promote research on the nature and applications of intelligent gels. By the 1990s, Tanaka had focused his research on a variety of biomedical applications of intelligent gels. He had also become interested in the clues that intelligent gels might provide to the origin of life on Earth. He was trying to develop proteinlike substances that could synthesize the types of polymers found in living organisms. In 1997, Tanaka was appointed the first Otto and Jane Morningstar Professor of Science at MIT.

Tanaka was widely regarded not only as a brilliant researcher and visionary but a superb teacher. In an article honoring his life, colleagues called him a "brilliant lecturer and teacher of physics, highly appreciated by his students." Thanks to his remarkable artistic gifts, he brought to his lectures vivid and beautiful hand drawings and unforgettable experimental demonstrations. Senior faculty made it a special point to attend research lectures, which one colleague called "masterpieces of elegant exposition, in which he presented his most recent discoveries." Among the awards given to Tanaka were the 38th Toray Science and Technology Prize from Japan's Toray Science Foundation, the 1994 Inoue Prize for Science (Japan), the Vinci d'Excellence Prize (France) in 1993, the Award of the Polymer Society of Japan (1986), and the Nishina Memorial Prize (Japan) in 1985.

32°C to 31°C. Another intelligent gel invented by Sonja Krause and Katherine Bohon at the Rensselaer Polytechnic Institute consists of poly(dimethylsiloxane) and poly(ethylene oxide). This material demonstrates the ability to pulsate back and forth between its expanded and contracted form in less than a millisecond when a small electrical potential is applied to it. Among the most popular materials used to make smart gels are the polymers poly(vinyl alcohol) (PVA), poly(acrylic acid) (PAA), poly(acrylonitrile) (PAN), poly(2-hydroxyethylmethacrylate), and poly(2-hydroxypropylmethacrylate).

The intelligent gels that have been studied most fully at this point are the hydrogels, gels that change shape and volume in aqueous conditions. The polymers that make up the dispersed phase of hydrogels are very long complex molecules with three-dimensional structures consisting of cross-linked chains. Under conditions of low moisture, these chains collapse into themselves, forming a high-density, powdery material similar to what Jell-O is made from. When water is added to this material, however, it fills the interstices between polymer chains, causing the network to swell up, forming a gel.

Changes in the bulk of a smart gel may also occur as a result of the ionization of atoms that make up the polymer chain. Under most circumstances, these chains tend to be electrically neutral, or they may carry modest electrical charges. When water is added, the pH is changed, an electrical potential is added, or some other change is made in the material's environment, however, atoms that make up the polymer chains may gain or lose electrons, becoming positively or negatively charged. When that happens, various portions of the chain may begin to repel each other because they carry similar charges. The diagram on page 145 shows a polymer chain in an uncharged and charged condition.

The first application developed for smart hydrogels was somewhat mundane. They were used as a liner for golf shoes and in-line skates that takes the shape of the wearer's foot as the result of heat released by the foot, but researchers have envisioned a much broader and more significant number and variety of applications for such materials. Proposed applications include optical shutters; actuators and sensors for chemical, heat, and electrical systems; valves; chemical memory systems; fluid switches; absorbents for chemical and petroleum spills; diapers; cosmetics; and desalination systems. Thus far, however, the greatest interest has been in biomedical applications of hydrogels.

The most promising applications of smart hydrogels in the near future are likely to lie in the field of the medical sciences. One suggestion has been for the use of smart hydrogels in the manufacture of artificial muscles. For example, David Brock at MIT has been working for well over a decade on the design of musclelike materials constructed from gels made from N-isopropylacrylamide, polyacrylonitrile-polypyrrole, or a copolymer of polyvinylalcohol and polyacrylic acid. Such materials have already been used successfully on an experimental basis in the production of artificial chemical muscle fibers, an artificial urethral sphincter, and a parallel jaw gripper. Artificial muscles made from these materials have worked

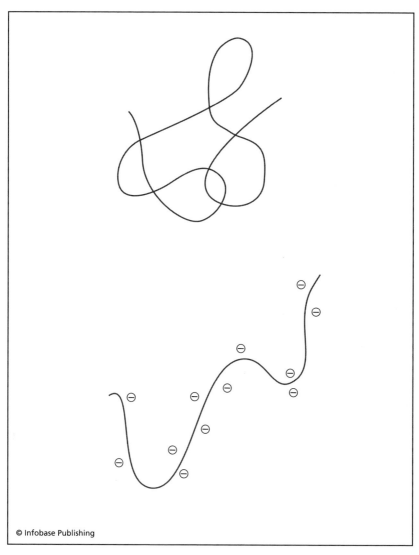

© Infobase Publishing

Changes in configuration of a charged and uncharged polymer chain

satisfactorily in principle, although their action is still far too slow to be used in real situations, with response times ranging from a few seconds up to 20 minutes. These are, of course, far slower than the reaction time of real muscle tissue, about 100 milliseconds. When a way is found to reduce the reaction time of smart hydrogel materials efficiently attached to existing body parts, the day when such materials can be used to replace damaged muscles may be in sight.

Another area in which smart hydrogels are likely to find application is the development of more efficient drug delivery systems. One material that has showed promise in this field is called Pluronic-PAA. Its trade name is Smart Hydrogel™. The material is a mixture of two polymers, one of which is poly(acrylic acid) (PAA), which attaches readily to other biological materials and is responsive to changes in pH. The other polymer is a copolymer of poly(propylene oxide) (PPO) and poly(ethylene oxide) (PEO). This copolymer belongs to a family of polymers known by the trade name of Pluronic polymers.

In dilute aqueous mixture (1 to 3 percent by weight), the Pluronic-PAA copolymer is a clear, colorless, free-flowing liquid. When the mixture is heated to more than 30°C, however, its physical structure changes. The change occurs because one end of the Pluronic-PAA molecule is hydrophobic ("water-hating") and the other is hydrophilic ("water-loving"). As the temperature rises, the hydrophobic ends of adjacent Pluronic-PAA molecules begin to aggregate, forming micelles (small colloidal particles) similar to those formed when oil droplets in water are surrounded by soap or detergent molecules. As shown in the diagram on page 147, the central portion of each micelle consists of the aggregated hydrophobic ends of the Pluronic-PAA molecules, while the hydrophilic ends extend outward from the micelle, like a collection of threads protruding out of a ball of yarn. In this conformation, the hydrophilic ends of adjacent micelles connect with each other to form a network that provides structure and rigidity to the mixture. It changes from a free-flowing liquid into a viscous gel.

The Pluronic-PAA system can be used for long-term drug delivery with a single treatment. The drug to be administered is mixed with free-flowing liquid before injection into a patient's body. Since many drugs are hydrophobic, molecules of the drug tend to collect at the hydrophobic ends of the Pluronic-PAA molecules. When micelles begin to form inside the patient's body (at a normal temperature of about 37°C), the drug molecules are trapped inside the micelles. They are then released from the micelles and into the blood stream at slow, controlled rates to provide long-term treatment that may not be easily produced with other methods of drug delivery.

Like most other smart materials, smart hydrogels are still at a very early stage of development. Scientists often have only minimal understanding of the processes by which these materials work. As a result, widespread commercial applications may still be many years in the future.

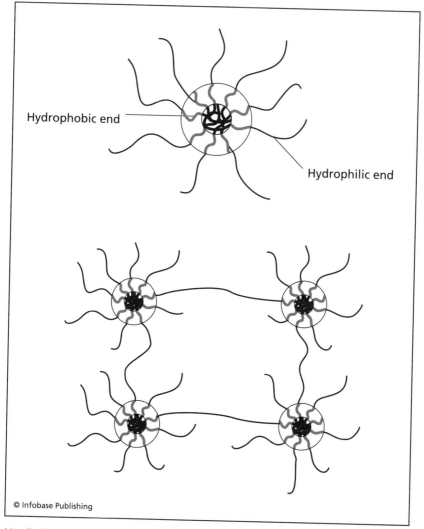

Micelle formation with Pluronic-PAA molecules

Many researchers and engineers see smart materials as the next great breakthrough in materials science. They are expected to have a host of applications in products ranging from military weaponry and aircraft to better performing sports materials. Since research and development costs are, and probably will continue to be, high, the first applications of smart materials are likely to be in areas where cost is less of a factor, such as military and space uses. Within a decade or two, however, many experts expect to see smart materials become part of a host of devices used by consumers in their everyday lives.

NEW POLYMERS

"I just want to say one word to you . . . just one word."
(Spoken by Mr. McGuire, played by Walter Brooke,
to Benjamin Braddock, played by Dustin Hoffman)
"Yes, sir." (Ben)
"Are you listening?" (Mr.McGuire)
"Yes, sir. I am." (Ben)
"Plastics." (Mr. McGuire)
—From The Graduate, *the classic Oscar-winning 1967 film,*
directed by Mike Nichols

Was it really only 40 years ago that a successful businessman (the fictional Mr. McGuire) was recommending to an uncertain college graduate (Benjamin Braddock) to look to plastics as the material of the future? Today virtually unlimited examples of plastics—the colloquial term for chemical materials more accurately known as *polymers*—can be seen in the world around us. They are now used in more applications than one can easily list, ranging from clothing and shoes to hoses and carpeting to sportswear and sporting equipment to structural panels and piping.

And yet, during the decade when Mr. McGuire was offering his advice to Benjamin Braddock, the plastics industry in the United States was truly in its infancy. In 1930, one of the earliest years of the polymer industry's existence, only 15,000 tons of the material were produced in the United States. That quantity grew slowly to 400,000 tons at the end of World War II, in 1945; to more than 2 million tons in 1955; and to 3 million tons in 1960. From the 1970s on,

This high-powered microscopic photograph shows the cross-linking found in some polypropylene fibers. (SPL/Photo Researchers, Inc.)

however, the polymer business has mushroomed steadily such that in 2005 nearly 110 billion pounds of a dozen different classes of plastic were produced in the United States. The growth in the plastics industry is a result of the huge variety of polymeric materials that have been invented with virtually any set of physical and chemical properties one might wish for, resulting in a virtually unlimited list of practical applications.

Polymers are large molecules (macromolecules) that consist of one or two small molecules (*monomers*) joined to each other in long, often highly branched, chains in a process called polymerization. Both natural and synthetic polymers exist. Some examples of natural polymers are starch, cellulose, chitin (the material of which shells are made), nucleic acids, and proteins. Synthetic polymers, the subject of this chapter, include polyethylene, polypropylene, polystyrene, polyesters, polycarbonates, and polyurethanes. In their raw, unprocessed form, synthetic polymers are sometimes referred to as *resins*. Polymers are formed in two general ways: by addition or by *condensation.*

Polymers from Addition Reactions

An addition reaction is a chemical reaction in which two atoms or groups of atoms add to opposite ends of a carbon-carbon double bond (-C = C-). One of the simplest and most common addition reactions is the one that results in the formation polyethylene. This polymer is formed when many ethene (ethylene) molecules combine with each other:

$$CH_2=CH_2 + CH_2=CH_2 \rightarrow CH_2CH_2CH=CH_2$$

followed by:

$$CH_2CH_2CH=CH_2 + CH_2=CH_2 \rightarrow CH_2CH_2CH_2CH_2CH=CH_2$$

followed by:

$$CH_2CH_2CH_2CH_2CH=CH_2 + CH_2=CH_2 \rightarrow CH_2CH_2CH_2CH_2CH_2CH_2CH_2=CH_2$$

This reaction is repeated many times, leading to the formation of a long-chain molecule with the general formula of $-[CH_2CH_2]_n$, where n is typically equal to a few thousand.

◀ SOME COMMON ADDITION POLYMERS ▶

POLYMER	MONOMER(S)
polyethylene $[CH_2CH_2]_n$	ethene* $(CH_2=CH_2)$
polypropylene $[CH_2CH(CH_3)]_n$	propene* $(CH_3CH=CH_2)$
poly(vinyl chloride); PVC $[CH_2CHCl]_n$	vinyl chloride $(CH_2=CHCl)$
polystyrene $[CH_2CH(C_6H_5)]_n$	styrene $(C_6H_5CH=CH_2)$
polyvinyl acetate; PVA $[CH_2CH(OCOCH_3]_n$	vinyl acetate $(CH_2=CH[CH_3COO])$
polytetrafluoroethylene; Teflon $[CF_2CF_2]_n$	tetrafluoroethene $(CF_2=CF_2)$
poly(methyl methacrylate); PMMA $[CH_2C(CH_3)(COOCH_3)]$	methyl methacrylate $(CH_2=C[CH_3][COOCH_3])$

*Ethene and propene are the correct systematic (IUPAC) names for compounds that have traditionally been known as ethylene and propylene, respectively.

A polymer that, like polyethylene, is made of a single monomer is known as a *homopolymer*. A simplified method of describing a homopolymer is as follows:

$$[-A-A-A-A-A-A-A-A-],$$

where A is the monomer from which the homopolymer is formed. Some common homopolymers and the monomers from which they are made are shown in the chart above.

Homopolymers often have considerably more complex structures than the one just suggested. For example, they may contain a number of branches projecting from the main chain, or adjacent chains may bond with each other to form complex networks. Structures such as these may also form with other kinds of polymers than homopolymers.

Branching or networking structures can have significant effects on the physical properties of a polymer. For example, polyethylene that consists entirely of long, linear, unbranched chains can be packed tightly together, forming a high-density product commonly known as high-density polyethylene (HDPE) that is hard, tough, and rigid. If the polyethylene chains are highly branched, they cannot be packed as closely together, resulting in a material that is less dense, softer, and more flexible, a product commonly known as low-density polyethylene (LDPE). Finally, polyethylene in which chains are cross linked with each other has a still more rigid structure that is also tough and hard, a product known as cross-linked polyethylene (CLPE).

Addition polymers can also be produced using two different monomers. In such a case, the polymer formed, called a copolymer, also consists of long chains (that may or may not be branched and/or cross-linked) with two different kinds of monomeric units. An example is the reaction between butadiene ($CH_2 = CH\text{-}CH = CH_2$) and styrene ($C_6H_5CH = CH_2$). The product of this reaction, called SBR or SBS, is one of the most important forms of synthetic rubber now available. There are various forms of SBR rubber with a number of uses, including new and retreaded tires for passenger cars and light trucks, shoe soles and heels, chewing gum, conveyor belts, adhesives and coatings, drain board trays, sealants for food containers, automobile mats, brake and clutch pads, hoses and belts, rubber toys, casings for batteries, cable and wire insulation, and surgical products.

SBR rubber (and other copolymers) can occur in a variety of forms, depending on the arrangement of the monomeric units within the polymeric chains. For example, the monomers sometimes occur in a regular, alternating pattern, of the general structure:

$$- [- A - B - A - B - A - B - A - B - B - A - B - A - B -] -$$

This product is known as an *alternating copolymer.* In other cases, the two monomeric units are arranged randomly in the chain to form a *random copolymer* of the general formula:

$$- [- A - A - A - B - A - B - A - B - B - A - A - B - A - B -] -$$

In still other cases, the monomeric units may be bunched together in groups to form a *block copolymer* that has a structure such as:

$$- [- A - A - A - A - A - B - B - B - B - A - A - A - A - A -] -$$

Finally, *graft copolymers* can be made by attaching a homopolymer made of one monomeric unit to a homopolymer made of a different monomeric unit. For example, a chain made entirely of B units (- B - B - B - B - B -) may be attached at a number of positions along a primary chain made entirely of A units (- A - A - A - A - A - A - A -).

As with the various forms of polyethylene, the molecular arrangement of copolymers affects their physical and chemical properties. For example, block copolymeric SBR tends to be resistant to impact, tough, and flexible, making the material useful for adhesives, roofing and paving materials, and toys. By contrast, random copolymeric SBR is tough and transparent, making it useful in the production of clear bottles and containers, films, and specialized fibers.

Polymers from Condensation Reactions

The second type of polymerization reaction, called a condensation reaction, is one in which two molecules react with each other with the elimination of some small molecule, such as water or hydrogen chloride. Such reactions can be represented, in general, by the following equation:

$$R-H + R'-OH \rightarrow H_2O + R-R'$$

Researchers select the two molecules, RH and R'OH, to obtain a reaction that does not end after a single occurrence, but repeats many times, resulting in the formation of a polymer.

A familiar example of a condensation reaction is one that occurs between phenol (hydroxybenzene, C_6H_5OH) and formaldehyde (methanal, HCHO). In this reaction, shown on page 155, the oxygen atom from a formaldehyde molecule reacts with a hydrogen atom from the benzene rings in each of two phenol molecules to form water (H_2O), allowing the remaining $-CH_{2-}$ group from formaldehyde to bond two phenol remnants to each other. The compound formed in this reaction, commercially known as *Bakelite*, was one of the earliest synthetic polymers made, and the first made from totally synthetic materials.

$$HCHO + C_6H_5OH \rightarrow C_6H_4CH_2OH(OH)$$

$$C_6H_4CH_2OH(OH) + C_6H_5OH \rightarrow C_6H_4OH\text{-}CH_2 - C_6H_4OH$$

$$C_6H_4OH\text{-}CH_2 - C_6H_4OH + HCHO \rightarrow C_6H_4OH\text{-}CH_2 - C_6H_3OH\text{-}CH_2 - \ldots etc.$$

Most condensation polymers fall into one of four major categories: the polyamides, polycarbonates, polyesters, and polyurethanes. One of the first and eventually most popular synthetic polymers to be synthesized was a polyamide called nylon 66, discovered in 1935 by the American chemist Wallace Carothers (1896–1937). Nylon 66 is made in the reaction between adipic acid (hexanedioic acid, $HOOC(CH_2)_4COOH$) and hexamethylenediamine ($NH_2(CH_2)_6NH_2$). The equation for that reaction is as follows:

$$NH_2CH_2CH_2CH_2CH_2CH_2CH_2NH_2 + HOOCCH_2CH_2CH_2CH_2COOH \rightarrow$$
$$- [- NH_2CH_2CH_2CH_2CH_2CH_2CH_2NHOCCH_2CH_2CH_2CH_2COOH -] - + H_2O$$

Notice that as in the reaction between phenol and formaldehyde shown earlier, a molecule of water is split out when the two compounds react with each other, resulting in a new molecule capable of reacting with another adipic acid molecule at one end and another hexamethylenediamine molecule at the opposite end. Over a period of time, a long chain builds up consisting of alternate monomeric units of adipic acid and hexamethylenediamine. (The presence of six carbons in each compound accounts for the *66* in the commercial name of the final product: nylon 66.)

Today, the generic term *nylon* is used for polyamides. The various types of nylon differ in the reagents from which they are made, the method of production used, and, therefore, their physical and chemical properties. The various forms of nylon are designated as different grades, such as nylon 66, nylon 6, nylon 46, nylon 11, and nylon 12. Although the various grades of nylon differ from one another to some extent, they tend to share common physical and chemical properties, such as high tensile strength, good electrical resistance, low flammability, high elasticity, and resistance to alkalies (but not strong acids). Some applications of the nylons include textiles, carpets, food packaging, fishing lines, substitutes for metals in motor vehicles (such as in gears and bearings), electrical insulation, and housing for power tools.

Polyesters are made in the reaction between terephthalic acid ($HOOCC_6H_4COOH$), or one of its derivatives, and ethylene glycol ($HOCH_2CH_2OH$), as shown in the equation below.

$$HOOCC_6H_4COOH + HOCH_2CH_2OH \rightarrow HOCH_2CH_2OOCC_6H_4COOCH_2CH_2OH$$
$$(\text{polymerized}) \rightarrow - [- OOCC_6H_4COOCH_2CH_2 -]_n - + H_2O$$

In this reaction, a molecule of water is eliminated, resulting in the formation of a compound belonging to the family of esters. An ester is an organic compound formed from an alcohol (such as ethylene glycol) and an acid (such as terephthalic acid). Notice that terephthalic acid is a dicarboxylic acid (that is, it contains two carboxyl groups, -COOH), and that ethylene glycol is a dihydroxy alcohol (it contains two hydroxyl groups, -OH). In the reaction between these two reagents, then, the ester formed still has one carboxyl group and one alcohol group. It is able to react at one end with a second molecule of terephthalic acid and, at the other end, with a second molecule of ethylene glycol. As the reaction continues, then, the molecule continues to grow by adding new units at both ends. The final product of the reaction is a very long, linear molecule consisting of many ester linkages, a molecule known as a polyester. The name for the product of this specific reaction is poly(ethylene terephthalate), or, as its more commonly known, PET or PETE.

Although the reaction shown above works satisfactorily in the laboratory, it is not the process by which PET is made commercially. Instead, the methyl ester of terephthalic acid, dimethyl terephthalate ($H_3COOCC_6H_4COOCH_3$), is used in place of terephthalic acid. In this reaction, methyl alcohol, rather than water, is eliminated during the reaction between the two reagents. The two reactions are in principle, however, nearly identical.

PET is one of the most versatile of all polymer materials now in use. MetWeb, an internet source of materials properties and products, lists more than 1,600 different forms of the material. In addition to the most common PET form, polyesters produced from other reagents are also available. Some of the most common include poly(butylene terephthalate, PBT), poly(cyclohexylenedimethylene terephthalate, PCT, PCTG, and PCTA), poly(trimethylene terephthalate, PTT and PTI), poly(trimethylene naphthalate, PTN), and poly(ethylene naphthalate, PEN). The various forms in which polyesters occur are available as fibers, films, or in bulk form that can be molded or extruded. They are sold under a number of trade names, including Arnite®, Dacron®, Hostaphan®, Impet®, Melinar®, Melinex®, Mylar®, Rynite®, Teijin®, Teonex®, Terylene®, and Trevira®. Although the properties of polyesters vary depending on the form in which they are prepared, they tend to be hard, stiff, and strong, with little or no tendency to absorb water. They are resistant to most chemicals (but not alkalis) and tend to be opaque to gases. In most cases, they are transparent and colorless, although they may develop an off-white cast in thicker sections. Polyester products are used in a host of applications, including medical products, such as artificial skin and blood vessels; many types of fabrics and fibers; tires; seat belts; magnetic tape; photographic film; food packaging; beverage bottles; coatings for appliances and furniture; automotive parts and accessories; ducts, flues, and other structural components; hoses; boat hulls; and foams.

The next group of condensation polymers, the polycarbonates, are a special family within the polyesters. They are usually formed in the reaction between phosgene (carbonyl chloride, $COCl_2$) and bisphenol A (4,4'-isopropylidenediphenol, $HOC_6H_4C(CH_3)_2C_6H_4OH$), a compound containing two benzene rings. An equation for that reaction is given below. This reaction results in the elimination of a hydrogen chloride molecule from the two reagents, a process repeated a number of times until a polymer is formed. The polymer gets its name from the characteristic carbonate unit ($-CO_3-$) that repeats within the molecule.

$$HOC_6H_4C(CH_3)_2C_6H_4OH + COCl_2 \rightarrow -[-OCOOC_6H_4C(CH_3)_2C_6H_4-]-_n$$

Polycarbonates are strong, stiff, hard, tough, and transparent, with the ability to maintain these properties at temperatures as high as 140°C and as low as −20°C. One of the earliest polycarbonates ever made was produced in Germany in 1953. It was given the trade name Lexan® or Merlon®. Some uses of the polycarbonates include bullet-proof windows and shields, compact discs for computers and audio devices, covers and housings for power tools and household appliances, mobile telephones, casings for batteries, automotive lighting systems (including both headlamps and dashboard lighting), interior paneling, exterior parts (such as bumpers and body panels), bottles and containers (especially baby bottles and water dispensers), garden equipment, office furniture, and medical equipment.

Polyurethanes, the last group of condensation polymers, are formed by a reaction quite unlike that of any other type of polymer, a reaction known as rearrangement. Consider the general reaction between the two compounds shown below. One of these compounds is a diisocyanate, an organic compound with two isocyanate (-N = C = O) groups. The other compound is a diol, an organic compound with two hydroxyl groups. In this reaction, a hydrogen atom from the hydroxyl group in the diol moves to the nitrogen atom of the diisocyanate, while the oxygen from the same hydroxyl groups shifts to the adjacent carbon atom. As a result of this arrangement, a new compound is formed in which the two reagents are joined to each other to form a product known as a urethane.

$$O=C=N\text{-}R\text{-}N=C=O + HO\text{-}R'\text{-}OH \rightarrow -\ [\ -\ CO\text{-}NH\text{-}R\text{-}NH\text{-}CO\text{-}O\text{-}R'\text{-}O\ -\ ]_n$$

Urethanes are named after a parent compound with the formula $CO(NH_2)OC_2H_5$. Since the functional groups involved in the rearrangement are still present in the urethane product, the reaction can be repeated again with additional molecules of either diisocyanate and/or diol, eventually resulting in the formation of a long chain molecule of polyurethane. A portion of a relatively complex polyurethane molecule, made from 4,4-diisocyanatodiphenylmethane ($O = C = N\text{-}C_6H_4CH_2\text{-}C_6H_4\text{-}N = C = O$) and ethylene glycol (HO-CH_2CH_2-OH) is shown below.

$$O=C=N-C_6H_4CH_2-C_6H_4-N=C=O + HO-CH_2CH_2-OH \rightarrow$$
$$- [- CO-NH-C_6H_4-CH_2-C_6H_4-NH-CO-O-CH_2CH_2-O -]_n$$

Polyurethanes are probably the most versatile of all polymers. They can be made as fibers, coatings, flexible and rigid foams, adhesives, sealants, and rubberlike materials called elastomers. Each type of polyurethane has characteristic properties that determine the uses to which it is put. Polyurethane fibers, for example, tend to be very elastic with high resistance to moisture and electrical conductivity. As coatings, polyurethanes tend to be very hard, flexible, and glossy and resistant to abrasion, wear, weathering, and most chemicals. Foams can be made in a variety of forms, ranging in density from two to 50 pounds per cubic foot, with very low thermal conductivity. And in their elastomeric form, polyurethanes are usually resistant to wear and abrasion, although they tend to become hard and brittle at low temperatures.

The list of uses to which polyurethanes have been put is impressive. It includes furniture and bedding; carpeting and carpet pads; automotive interiors; seat cushions; insulation for homes, commercial buildings, railroad cars, trucks, and trailers; roofing systems; automobile coatings; adhesives and sealants; apparel (one of the most popular of which is spandex, or Lycra®); synthetic wood; coatings for wires and masonry; paints; boat hulls and components; structural panels; packaging materials; hospital bedding, dressings for wounds, catheter tubes, and other medical applications; absorbents for crude oil spills; cigarette filters; and soundproofing.

Thermoplastic and Thermosetting Polymers

Apart from the type of reaction (addition or condensation) that is used to produce them, polymers can be classified into two general categories based on their behavior when heated. Polymers in the first category, called the *thermoplastics,* soften and begin to flow when they are heated. When cooled, they once again solidify. The temperature at which softening begins in a thermoplastic material is called its *glass transition temperature* (T_g). Some common thermoplastics and their glass transition temperatures are shown in the

◄ SOME COMMON THERMOPLASTICS AND THEIR GLASS TRANSITION (T_g) AND MELTING (T_m) TEMPERATURES ▷

POLYMER	T_g (°C)*	T_m (°C)
Polyethylene (LDPE)	−125	130
Polyethylene (HDPE)	−125	135
Polypropylene (PP)	−10	175
Polystyrene (PS)	100	240
Poly(vinyl chloride) (PVC)	65–80	227
Polycarbonate (PC)	150	–
Poly(ethyelene terephthalate) (PET)	70	265
Nylon 6	50	215
Poly(methylmethacrylate)	105–120	200
Polytetrafluoroethylene (Teflon)	117	327

*Values are approximate because composition of materials differs considerably depending on method of production
Sources: "Polymer Properties," *Polymer Products from Aldrich,* online at http://www.sigmaaldrich.com/img/assets/3900/Thermal_Transitions_of_Homopolymers.pdf and "Thermoplastics—An Introduction," abstracted from the Materials Information Service, edited by Justin Furness, online at http://216.239.41.104/search?q=cache:BI7epgbl1pgJ:www.azom.com/details.asp?ArticleID=83+tg+table+"glass+transition +temperature"&hl=en&ie=UTF-8

chart on page 160. The glass transition temperature is not the same as the melting point. The term *melting point* applies to a crystalline material that, when sufficient heat is added, changes from a solid to a liquid. Softening occurs in amorphous (noncrystalline) materials in which molecules gradually become more disordered. Polymers differ considerably in the degree to which they contain crystalline and amorphous domains (regions). The glass transition temperature refers only to the softening effect that occurs in the amorphous portions of those materials.

By contrast with thermoplastics, *thermosetting polymers* are materials that are soft and plastic when first prepared but then become permanently hard and rigid once they cool. All thermosetting polymers are condensation polymers. Some well-known members of this group are Bakelite and other formaldehyde-based polymers and epoxy resins, including the epoxy group, a three-membered ring that contains one oxygen atom and two methylene (CH_2) groups. Thermosetting polymers differ from their thermoplastic counterparts primarily because they readily form many cross-links between adjacent polymer chains. A typical example is the reaction between phenol and formaldehyde to form Bakelite, described earlier in this chapter. Once a long-chain polymer is formed with these two reagents, there is a strong probability that hydrogen atoms from one chain will react with hydroxyl groups from an adjacent chain to form water, which is then eliminated, resulting in the formation of a cross-link between the two chains. The cross-linking that develops among many chains in the polymer results in the formation of a rigid structure that is unaffected by further heating, the identifying characteristic of a thermosetting resin.

So many kinds of polymers exist that scientists have developed ways of categorizing them to make it easier to study and describe them. Polymers formed by addition or condensation reactions, for example, are placed in the same category because they are formed by a common chemical reaction and, in many cases, have common physical and chemical properties. Similarly, thermoplastic and thermosetting polymers are grouped together primarily because of their behaviors when exposed to heat, and, hence, applications for which they are likely to be most suitable.

Recent Developments in Polymer Science

Any search for polymer products on the internet will reveal the staggering number and variety of materials now available. It would seem that every type of polymer imaginable for just about any possible application already exists. Yet research in polymer science is among the most active in any field of chemistry. Today researchers are still inventing many new kinds of polymers with a host of specialized properties and uses. Some of the most exciting research involves the development of conductive and semiconductive polymers, dendrimers, and synthetic proteins.

Conductive Polymers

Many of the applications in which polymers are used are based on the fact that they tend not to conduct an electrical current very well. For example, one reason for the enormous popular success of the first entirely synthetic polymer, Bakelite, in the early 1900s was its outstanding electrical insulation properties, just the characteristic needed for a host of applications in the new and growing field of electrical appliances. Within a decade after its discovery, Bakelite was being used for housing and casings for industrial and household electrical equipment and for insulation on electrical wires and structures. For the past century, the applications of many different kinds of polymers in electrical insulation have become legendary.

It was thus a considerable surprise in the late 1970s when two research groups, one at the University of Pennsylvania and one at the Tokyo Institute of Technology, announced the discovery of a polymer that conducted electricity as well as most metals. The events leading to that discovery were rather remarkable. In Tokyo, Hideki Shirakawa and his colleagues were studying the preparation and properties of a polymer known as polyacetylene. As shown in the diagram on page 163, polyacetylene made by the polymerization of ethyne (acetylene) can exist in either of two forms, *trans* or *cis*. It usually occurs as a rather ordinary looking brownish-black powder. On one occasion, however, one of Shirakawa's assistants, a graduate student from Korea, misunderstood the directions for preparing polyacetylene. The polymer that formed precipitated not as a brownish-black powder, but as a beautiful silvery film. Because of his limited knowledge of Japanese, the Korean student had added 1,000 times the amount of catalyst normally used to make polyacetylene!

Instead of bemoaning the error, Shirakawa decided to learn more about this fascinating new version of an old familiar polymer, poly-acetylene. He soon discovered that the silvery film consisted of the *trans* form of polyacetylene and that a comparable copper-colored film could be produced with large quantities of catalyst at different temperatures. The copper-colored film was found to consist of the *cis* form of the polymer.

Cis and *trans* forms of polyacetylene

◄ HIDEKI SHIRAKAWA (1936–) ►

Are there ways to look for new information, unexpected discoveries, or happy results out of research that has suddenly gone wrong? Such was the dilemma that faced Hideki Shirakawa in 1967 when one of his students added far too much catalyst to an experiment being conducted in his laboratory. Even to this day, no one is quite sure who actually made the mistake: Shirakawa in giving directions or the graduate student for misunderstanding them. In the end, it did not make any difference. The result of the error was the synthesis of an entirely new kind of polymer that had never been seen before, a polymer that was as highly conductive as some metals. And with that unexpected discovery, a whole new field of protein research opened up. Fortunately, Shirakawa had the intelligence and imagination to see that the mistake that had occurred was not a disaster, it was an opportunity!

Hideki Shirakawa was born in Tokyo on August 20, 1936. He was the third of five children born to Hatsutarou Shirakawa, a physician, and his wife, Fuyuno Shirakawa. In the first dozen years of his life, Hideki Shirakawa moved frequently with his family, first to the rural city of Takayama, then to the province of Manchu on the Chinese mainland (then recently conquered by the Japanese army), and finally back to Tokyo and Takayama after the end of World War II. As early as junior high school, Shirakawa was thinking about a career in the field of polymers. He wrote an essay in which he expressed a desire to "conduct research on plastics useful for ordinary people."

Where this information might have led had Shirakawa continued to work on his own in Tokyo is not clear, because in another twist of fate, he happened to meet two Pennsylvania researchers, Alan G. MacDiarmid and Alan J. Heeger, during a coffee break at a seminar being held in Tokyo in 1976. MacDiarmid and Heeger told Shirakawa about a fascinating new silvery polymer of sulfur and nitrogen they had been working with in their laboratories. The three researchers saw some promising commonalities in the work they were doing, and MacDiarmid and Heeger invited Shirakawa to join them in Pennsylvania later that year. Within a year, the three had synthesized, studied, and explained the first of an exciting new group of

After completing secondary school, Shirakawa enrolled at the Tokyo Institute of Technology (TIT), from which he graduated with a bachelor's degree in chemical engineering in 1961. He then continued his studies at TIT and was awarded his Ph.D. in engineering in 1966. He stayed on at TIT as a research assistant in the Chemical Resources Laboratory, where his first assignments involved very routine work in the synthesis of polymers. It was not until the "unfortunate accident" of 1967 that Shirakawa began his foray into a new and entirely different field of polymer research, *conductive polymers*.

After a chance meeting in Tokyo in 1976 with Alan MacDiarmid, then working in the Department of Chemistry at the University of Pennsylvania, Shirakawa left TIT for a three-year residency with MacDiarmid at Pennsylvania. In 1979, he returned to Japan, where he assumed the post of associate professor in the Institute of Materials Science at the University of Tsukuba. Three years later he was promoted to full professor, a post he held until his retirement in March 2000. Only seven months later, he was chosen one of the three winners (along with MacDiarmid and Alan Heeger of the University of California at Santa Barbara) of the 2000 Nobel Prize in chemistry for their discovery of conductive polymers. In addition to the Nobel Prize, Shirakawa has been honored with the 1983 award of the Society of Polymer Science of Japan and the Japanese government's Order of Culture in 2000.

polymers: polymers that conduct electricity with an efficiency equal to that of most metals. For their work, the three were awarded the 2000 Nobel Prize in chemistry.

The discovery of conductive polymers was an important breakthrough in materials science because it provided researchers with a whole new category of materials with properties very different from those of traditional conductors, which are all metals or alloys. For example, polymeric materials can be made into a greater variety of shapes more easily than can metals. Thus, it should be possible to make thin films, hollow spheres, flat strips, and particles of irregular shape of conductive polymers, when similar objects made of metal would produce more challenging production problems.

So what is it that makes it possible for a polymer like polyacetylene to become conductive, when it is normally nonconductive? The answer to that question lies in the electronic structure of polyacetylene molecules. Such molecules consist of alternating single and double bonds (conjugated systems) consisting of sigma bonds and sigma and pi bonds, respectively. The electrons that make up a sigma bond are tightly held within the bond. Since they are very difficult to move, they are unable to transport an electric current through the molecule. The electrons in a pi bond, while somewhat more mobile, are still held too tightly to move through the molecule under normal circumstances. In its normal state, polyacetylene contains enough mobile electrons to carry an electrical current weakly. That is, it is a semiconductor.

The change that converts the polyacetylene molecule from a nonconductive to a conductive state involves the addition of some foreign material, a dopant, to the polymer. Two kinds of dopants are used: those that attract electrons and remove them from the bonds that make up a polymer molecule, and those that donate electrons to the molecule. In either case, the normal electronic structure of the molecule is disrupted, and individual electrons within the molecule become more mobile. As their mobility increases, they tend to flow through a molecule and from one molecule to the next when an external electrical potential is applied to the polymer.

For example, iodine atoms have a strong attraction for electrons, and when added to polyacetylene, they pull on the electrons in pi bonds strongly enough to remove some of them from those bonds:

$$I_2^0 + [CH]^0 \rightarrow I^- + [CH]^+$$

The space left behind by the loss of an electron is known as a positive hole. The negative iodide ion and the positive hole in the polyacetylene chain associated with it is known as a polaron. A disturbance of this kind may then lead to a disruption of electron patterns in nearby portions of the molecule, resulting in a reversal of single and double bonds, producing a pattern known as a *soliton*. The now unbonded electron from the pi bond left behind from this reaction has a much greater tendency to move out of position and travel down the polymer chain. When an electrical potential is applied at one of the chain, then, those "abandoned" single electrons set up an electrical current that flows through the polymer.

The addition of an electron-accepting material, such as iodine, to a polymer is known as oxidative doping because electrons are lost from the polymer. Reductive doping is the process by which an electron-donating material, such as sodium, is added to a polymer. In this case, the polymer gains an electron and becomes negatively charged.

$$Na^0 + [CH]^0 \rightarrow Na^+ + [CH]^-$$

The end result is the same with both oxidative and reductive doping, however, because it is not the sodium or iodide ion formed that is mobile, but the deformation of the polymer chain itself that results in a flow of current through the molecule.

Although the original research on conductive polymers was done with polyacetylene, a number of other conjugated polymers have been developed for such uses. Among these products are the polythiophenes, polyanilines, polyphenylenevinylenes, polyethylenedioxythiophenes, polypyrroles, and polydialkylfluorenes. These products are now beginning to find applications in a number of industrial, research, medical, and consumer devices.

For example, there has been a great deal of interest in the production of organic light-emitting diodes (OLED) similar to the inorganic LEDs now found in many types of electronic devices. OLEDs have a number of advantages over traditional LEDs, such as ease of fabrication, flexibility, light weight, thinness, low power demands, and broadness of viewing angle. An OLED is much simpler to make than a traditional LED. It generally consists of a conductive polymer sandwiched between two electrodes. As an electrical potential is applied to the electrodes, current flows through the polymer, and light is emitted.

OLEDs can be made in either of two forms: passive or active. In the passive form, electrical currents are passed through rows and columns that define each pixel in a display, much as in traditional LEDs. Variations in the current supplied affect the intensity of the light produced in each pixel and, hence, the intensity of the display itself. In the active form, a thin transistor film is laid down on top of the OLED itself. The film controls the amount of current flowing through each pixel of the OLED at every instant the device is turned on.

One of the first possible applications considered for conductive polymers was in the manufacture of so-called plastic batteries. Batteries, of course, have a multitude of important applications in everyday life, ranging from the powering of spacecraft and satellites to the operation of portable radios and compact disc players. Although battery technology has evolved dramatically over the past 200 years, the general principle on which they operate has not. Electrons released from one electrode in the battery pass through a conductive material, the electrolyte, and into a second electrode. They then travel out of the battery, through an external circuit, and back into the battery again.

As important as batteries are to modern civilization, a number of inherent problems are associated with them. For example, the lead-storage battery present in all modern motor vehicles is very heavy (it contains one of the densest of common metals, lead): and it must be continually recharged, eventually wears out, and presents serious environmental problems during its manufacture and disposal. After the discovery of conductive polymers, many scientists hoped and dreamed that these materials could be used to make efficient, lightweight plastic batteries.

For a variety of reasons, this hope has not come to fruition. Although researchers have designed a number of batteries made of conductive polymers that work satisfactorily in the laboratory, significant commercial production has not yet occurred. For example, researchers at Johns Hopkins University reported in 1996 on the development of the first all-plastic battery, a project funded by the U.S. Air Force's Rome Laboratory in Rome, New York. The Johns Hopkins battery, shown in the diagram on page 169, consisted of five primary elements, two outer support sheets made of teflon about 50 μm thick, an anode made of poly(3,4,5-trifluorophenylthiophene), a cathode made of poly(3,5-difluorophenylthiophene), and a permeable gel electrolyte containing an organic compound of boron. The battery looked like a small credit card and was able to generate about 2.5 volts. (By comparison, the common AA battery used in many electronic devices generates about 1.5 volts.) It had many attractive characteristics, including the ability to be made into virtually any size or shape: It could be produced as a large sheet that could be hung on a wall or in the form of a small tube that could be rolled up and carried around in one's pocket. The possibilities seemed endless. Unfortunately, more than a decade after the Johns Hopkins invention, plastic batteries still had found virtually no commercial market. They tend to be at least as expensive as more traditional batteries, and their other desirable qualities have not yet made up for this basic economic drawback.

Conductive polymers have found other applications, however, often in areas where their relatively high cost is justified by highly specialized uses for which other products are not nearly as effective. For example, a variety of such polymers have been used as antistatic agents on photographic film, in carpeting, and in surgical rooms;

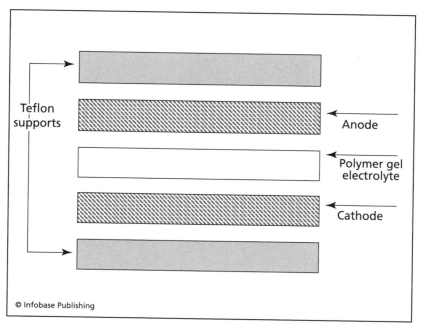

All-plastic battery developed at Johns Hopkins University

in the plating of circuit boards for electronic devices; in flat-panel displays for televisions, computer screens, and mobile telephone displays; as biosensors and chemical sensors; in "smart membranes" that can be used in gas separation, environmental cleanups, pharmaceutical separations, and other applications; as antiradiation coatings; as de-icer paneling; as radar dishes; and in scanning systems for items sold in supermarkets. Some of these conductive polymers have already found substantial commercial application, while others are still in the research and development stages and may not reach the marketplace for many years.

The outlook for conductive polymers is similar to that for other new materials discussed in this chapter. Researchers must still solve a number of technical problems before the products are likely to find significant commercial applications. Conductive polymers, for example, tend to develop large amounts of static electricity, which can interfere with the products in which they are used. This problem must be solved if wide applications of the material are to occur. Still, the market for conductive polymers is promising, with experts predicting growth rates of about 5 percent per year over the next decade. As more types of conductive polymers become available and as researchers solve the technical problems associated with them, consumers are more likely to encounter these exciting substances in the products they use in their daily lives.

Dendrimers and Hyperbranched Polymers

Dendrimers were discovered in 1979 by the American chemist Donald Tomalia and his colleagues at the Dow Chemical Company. The name for these polymers, from the Greek word *dendron,* for "tree," comes from their highly branched, treelike shape. In their simplest form, dendrimers consist of a single, basic unit with two or more branches, from which additional branches project. Dendrimer researchers foresee a number of possible applications for the new material. These include a variety of medical applications, such as drug delivery systems, for diagnostic and therapeutic uses, and as carriers of genetic material. Industrial applications include electronic and photonic devices; surface coatings; and a variety of chemical, petroleum, drug, cosmetic, and pharmaceutical products.

A variety of methods is available for the production of dendrimers. For example, one type of dendrimer is made by reacting 1,4-diamino-butane with four molecules of acrylonitrile ($CH_2 = CHCN$), as shown

© Infobase Publishing

Divergent synthesis of a dendrimer

in the diagram on page 171. The product of this reaction consists of the four-carbon core provided by 1,4-diaminobutane, to which are attached the four molecules of acrylonitrile. In the next step of the synthesis, the four cyano (-CN) groups are reduced to form amino (-C-NH$_2$) groups. As a result of this reaction, each of the groups protruding from the central core consists of an amino group that readily reacts with an additional molecule of acrylonitrile. The molecule now consists of eight projecting groups, rather than the four projecting groups of the molecule from which it was formed. The reduction of the projecting cyano groups again produces amino groups, each of which can react with yet another group of acrylonitrile molecules. After this step, the molecule contains 16 projecting groups. Clearly, each time the process is repeated, the number of projecting groups doubles. Since each iteration of dendrimer synthesis can be thought of as a generation, each new shell that is formed is called a generation of that dendrimer.

In the first few generations of dendrimer synthesis, the molecules produced are not so different from other types of organic molecules. They tend to be flexible and have relatively little clearly defined structure. After about generation five, however, they begin to develop the more rigid, clearly defined shape of a sphere with concentric shells corresponding to each of the generations through which the dendrimer has grown. The outer surface of each shell consists of amines, while the partial shell within each shell consists of the cyano groups from which the amines are formed. The surfaces of both the outer shells and the inner half-shells have, therefore, functional groups (amino groups or cyano groups) with which other groups can be reacted. Because of the "explosive" manner in which dendrimers are formed by this process, they are sometimes known as starburst dendrimers.

This brief description provides only the simplest overview of the way in which dendrimers can be synthesized. Many variations on this scheme have been explored. For example, one might begin with a core molecule that consists of three functional groups (such as ammonia, NH$_3$) rather than the two functional groups found in 1,4-diaminobutane. One could also provide a direction for the growth of the dendrimer by blocking one or more of the functional groups at one or more generations of its growth. In such a case, the molecule would continue to grow in unblocked directions, where functional groups remained available, but could no longer grow where those functional groups had been "sealed off." By using a great variety of such techniques, researchers have now produced dendrimers with more than 50 different shapes, including spheres, cubes, rectangular boxes, long tubes, and hollow, basketlike objects.

One of the earliest questions researchers had about dendrimers was whether there was some limit to the size they could grow. They wondered whether a dendrimer molecule could get so large that further generations of growth were no longer possible. At this point in time, the answer to that question appears to be "no." Dendrimers with diameters of more than 10nm and molecular weights of more than 1 million daltons are now routinely produced.

A great appeal of dendrimers is that they have a set of unique and valuable physical, chemical, and biological properties. For example, their molecular structure is so precise that one can be virtually certain exactly where every atom of every kind in the molecule is located. Materials made from such molecules are, therefore, likely to be both uniform and pure. The ability to manipulate functional groups in a dendrimer molecule makes it possible to augment its chemical properties in a variety of ways, increasing or deceasing its solubility in hydrophilic or hydrophobic solvents, for example, or providing mechanisms by which it can bind to other molecules. Also, one can synthesize a multifunctional dendrimer molecule by modifying some functional groups in some parts of the molecule in one way, modifying other functional groups in other parts in a different way, and blocking other functional groups in other parts of the molecule to form a product that can perform various functions in various segments of the molecule. One of the dendrimer molecule's most intriguing assets is the hollow cavity typically found at its center. This cavity provides a place where atoms, molecules, ions, and other chemical species can be stored and transported, much the way coins are deposited and carried about in a coin purse.

Some scientists have suggested, for example, that dendrimers could constitute the basis of a very highly specific drug delivery system. The drug needed by a patient would first be inserted into the central cavity of a dendrimer and the outer surface of the molecule modified to "recognize" and locate a specific type of cell (such as a cancer cell) where the drug is needed. Once inside the body, then, the dendrimer-drug package would find its way exclusively to cells where treatment was needed and not to other cells where the drug might cause damage. Once it had located its target cell, the dendrimer molecule would then open up and release its drug to that cell. A similar process could be used for the transfection of DNA into a cell. Transfection is the process by which foreign genetic material is inserted into some host cell, as, for example, in an attempt to treat a genetic disorder. Dendrimer molecules with the ability to transport drugs, genes, and other materials have been designed and built. At this point, however, the technical and economic problems involved in making them widely available have not been solved.

The method for synthesizing dendrimers developed by Tomalia, described at the beginning of this section, is known as *divergent synthesis* because one begins with the core of the dendrimer and works outward until a full molecule has been produced. In the early 1990s, J. M. M. Fréchet, at the University of California at Berkeley, suggested an alternative method of making dendrimers now known as *convergent synthesis*. In the convergent approach, the process begins with the outer shell of the dendrimer and builds inward until, in the final step, the core of the dendrimer is inserted in the molecule.

In principle, there are many similarities between the divergent and convergent methods of making dendrimers. In convergent synthesis, one begins with a multifunctional (in this example, bifunctional) molecule, such as the molecule RX_2 shown in the diagram on page 175. It is combined with a second molecule capable of reacting at both of the reactive sites of the first molecule. The core portion of the bifunctional molecule is then converted to an active form, producing the first generation product of the reaction. This molecule is then reacted with a second molecule of the original bifunctional species, producing a second generation molecule. As these two reactions are repeated over and over again, an umbrella-shaped structure with the appearance of the outer shells of a dendrimer begins to form. At some point, when the shells are large enough, they are joined to each other and to a central core molecule (or group of molecules) to produce a complete dendrimer.

Convergent synthesis of a dendrimer

Both methods of synthesizing dendrimers have their advantages and disadvantages. For example, there appears to be virtually no limit to the size of a divergent dendrimer, but the size of a convergent dendrimer is determined by the maximum size of the wedges that can be made before they are joined to each other. The likelihood of errors in the synthesis of a divergent dendrimer is much greater, however, than it is with convergent dendrimers, where the addition of new units can be more carefully controlled. Also, it tends to be easier to add various functional groups to the exterior shell of a convergent dendrimer than it is to its divergent counterpart.

Some researchers see a bright future for dendrimers in many different industrial, medical, research, and consumer applications. One company that produces dendrimers lists applications in drug delivery systems, gene transfection, biotechnology, sensors for diagnostics and detection systems, carbon fiber coatings, microcontact printing, adhesion, molecular batteries, catalysis, separation systems, lasers, composites, and ultrathin films used in optics.

Thus far, few of these applications have been commercially successful, but current trends appear to support the enthusiasm for more widespread uses of dendrimers in the near future. Dendritic Nanotechnologies reports that the number of publications on dendrimers has grown from essentially zero in 1980 to well over 2,000 annually in 2003. And a recent study by the legal firm of Foley-Lardner shows that the number of dendrimer patents has increased from zero during the period 1976–80 and two during the period 1981–85 to 433 in 1996–2000 and more than 1,000 in 2001–05.

Probably the most important factor holding back a more rapid development of dendrimer applications is the time and expense required to produce these molecules. One possible solution to that problem is the production of dendrimerlike molecules that can be made more easily and at less cost. A group of molecules that meet those criteria is the *hyperbranched polymers*. In this context, the term *hyperbranched* refers to a molecule in which a number of linear chains are attached to a single core structure. By that definition, dendrimers are one kind of hyperbranched polymer in that they contain large numbers of chains extending outward from a central core. The difference between dendrimers and other types of hyperbranched molecules, besides ease of production, is that dendrimers tend to be nearly perfect structures. One might compare a dendrimer to a perfectly sculpted piece of topiary and a hyperbranched polymer to a free-growing tree. In the former, every leaf, branch, and twig is in some precise location, while in the latter, branches and twigs have different sizes and shapes, resulting in a somewhat disordered structure.

For example, Anja Mueller and Karen L. Wooley at Washington University in St. Louis have made a hyperbranched polymer starting with 3,5-di(pentafluorobenzyloxy)benzyl alcohol. As shown in the diagram below, the single hydroxyl group in this monomer reacts readily with a fluorine or other substituent on a benzene ring of

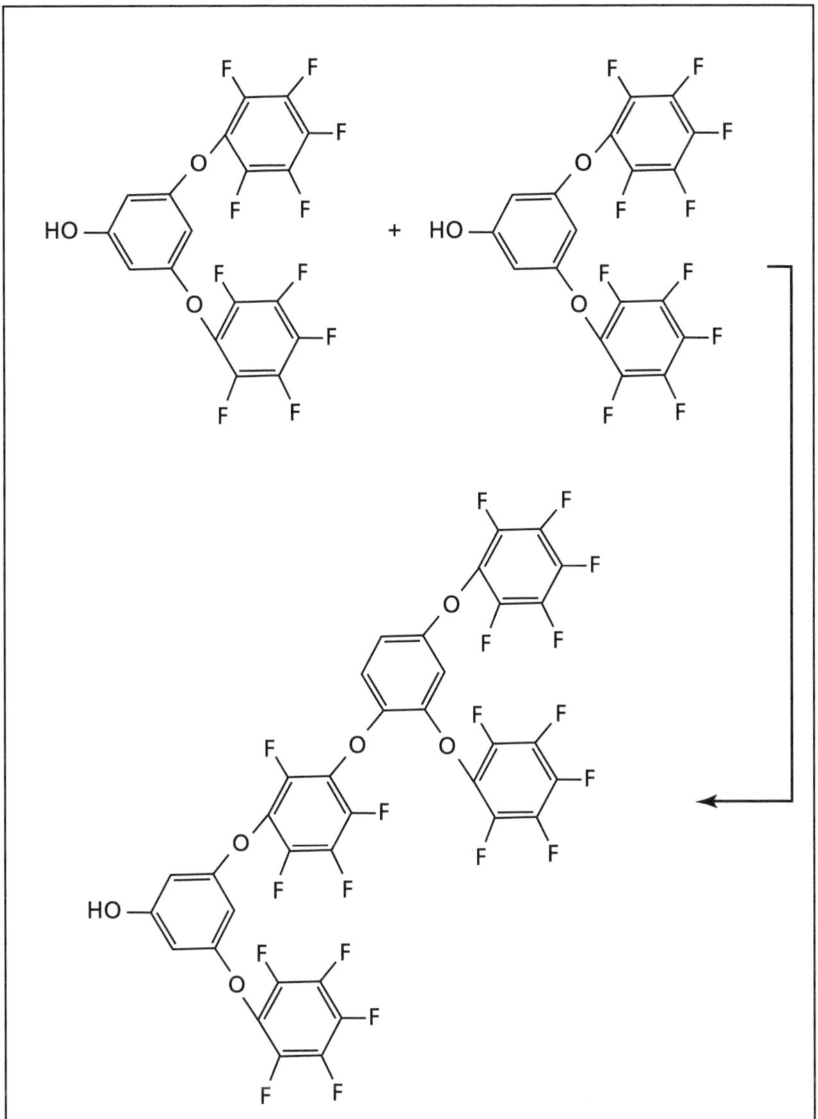

Example of a hyperbranched polymer

an adjacent molecule to form a dimer; this dimer then reacts in a similar fashion with another adjacent molecule. In actual practice, a series of such reactions occurs very quickly, and the hyperbranched polymer is formed essentially in a single step. This type of reaction contrasts dramatically with the formation of dendrimers, which occurs over an extended period of time in many discrete steps.

Hyperbranched polymers are now commercially available from a German company, Hyperpolymers GmbH, in Freiburg. Among the applications the company suggests for its products are retention of moisture in cosmetics, templates for nanoporous materials, supports for organic syntheses, specialized coatings, controlled drug release, encapsulation of compounds for slow release, use as crosslinking agents, and use as hydrogels in tissue-growth systems.

Dendrimers and hyperbranched polymers are among the newest and most unusual substances being explored. Both products are currently in their earliest stages of development, and widespread applications are not likely to appear for some time.

Synthetic Proteins

Chemists have synthesized an amazing array of new materials in the last few decades, materials that include conductive plastics, dendrimers, and hyperbranched polymers, but those accomplishments are actually quite modest compared to the staggering range of molecules synthesized every moment of every day by bacteria, viruses, cabbage leaves, fireflies, and every other type of living organism. Even the simplest organism easily manufactures nucleic acids, carbohydrates, lipids, proteins, and other biochemical molecules with structures and functions so complex that chemists may be unable to replicate them or even to understand them. It is hardly surprising then that for many chemists the greatest challenge imaginable is to find ways of mimicking the synthesis of complex natural molecules. For many years, some of the most exciting research in that field has been on the design and production of synthetic proteins.

Proteins are of special interest to synthetic chemists because of the great variety of functions they have in living organisms. First, they are the primary structural component of most plant and animal material, making up, on average, at least half the dry weight of cells. Second, proteins carry out a number of functions essential to living organisms, including the transmission of nerve messages (neurotransmitters), regulation of metabolism (hormones), defense against attack by outside invaders (antibodies), catalysis of biochemical reactions (enzymes), and transport of oxygen (hemoglobin and related compounds). Understanding and replicating by synthetic means the ways in which proteins are made and the ways in which they carry out this diverse set of functions is, therefore, an important challenge for many chemists in today's world.

Proteins are naturally occurring polymers made of various combinations of amino acids. The amino acids that are most familiar to the average person are the alpha-amino acids, carboxylic acids that contain an amino ($-NH_2$) group attached to the first ("alpha") carbon attached to the carboxyl ($-COOH$) group, as shown in the diagram. (Other kinds of amino acids exist, but they do not occur in the proteins made by living organisms).

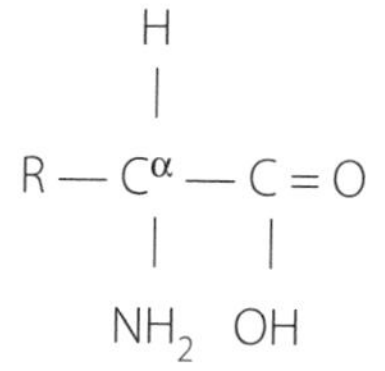

$$\begin{array}{c} H \\ | \\ R - C^\alpha - C = O \qquad R\text{-}CH(NH_2)\text{-}COOH \\ | \quad | \\ NH_2 \ \ OH \end{array}$$

Living organisms form polymers (proteins) out of at least 20 different amino acids by combining them in an endless variety of ways. The general reaction by which proteins are formed is shown below. Notice that the hydroxyl groups in one molecule (bold in the formula below) and a hydrogen atom in the second molecule (also bold) combine to form a molecule of water, leaving behind a dipeptide, a molecule consisting of two amino acid fragments. The sequence of amino acids present in a protein is known as the protein's *primary structure*.

$$R - CH - NH_2 - CO\textbf{OH} + R' - CH - N\textbf{H}_2 - COOH \rightarrow$$
$$H_2O + R - CH - NH_2 - CO - NH - CH - R' - COOH$$

A long-chain polymer made of hundreds or thousands of amino acids is not a particularly interesting molecule because it is unable

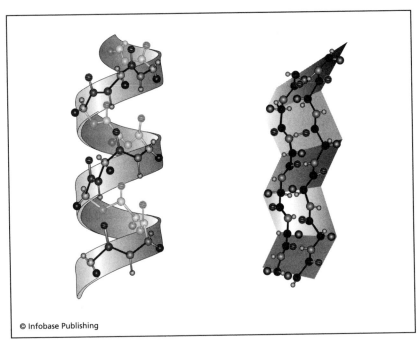

Helical and pleated-sheet conformations in proteins

to perform any of the functions carried out by proteins. Those functions are made possible because the protein, once its primary structure has formed, spontaneously assumes one of a number of possible three-dimensional shapes. The shapes a protein can assume are known, in order of increasing complexity, as its *secondary structure, tertiary structure,* and, in some cases, *quaternary structure.*

Two of the most common secondary structures found in proteins are helical and pleated-sheet conformations, shown in the diagram above. One might compare the helical structure of a protein, for example, with the spiral-shaped cord found on many home telephones. These structures form when atoms, ions, or other chemical species in one part of the protein's primary structure are attracted to other atoms, ions, or chemical species with opposite electrical charges in another part of the structure.

Most proteins also assume a higher level of organization, a tertiary structure. Again, the development of a tertiary structure results from the strong attraction of opposite-charged portions of the protein molecule, which, in some cases, form chemical bonds within the molecule. The secondary, tertiary, and quaternary structures that proteins assume tend to give these molecules very complex shapes, often with specialized regions adapted to carrying out particular functions for which the protein is designed.

Consider enzymes. Enzymes are proteins that act as catalysts in biochemical reactions. They are able to do this because enzyme molecules contain one or more *active sites,* regions with a characteristic shape designed to fit some particular molecule (the *substrate*) on which the enzyme operates. Suppose the function of the enzyme is to break apart a large molecule. That reaction is made possible when the large molecule "docks" in the active site, prompting some chemical mechanism in or around the active site that cleaves it. If the function of the enzyme is to join two small molecules, the reaction takes place when both small molecules take their places in the active site, which generates chemical bonds between the two molecules.

As impressive as living cells are in manufacturing the proteins they need, they have certain inherent limitations. Specifically, they make only the proteins they need for their own survival and reproduction. They do not make other kinds of proteins that people might find helpful and desirable for other purposes. For example, humans might really like to have a protein molecule with an active site that could recognize and bind to a molecule of RDX explosive. Such a protein might be a powerful tool in efforts to detect the presence of RDX in locations where it ought not to be, such as commercial airports.

The problem many chemists have chosen to attack, then, is to find out how proteins are made naturally in cells and then develop methods for replicating those methods in the laboratory. This field of study has now been given the name *proteomics.* According to a definition suggested by Stanley Fields at the University of Washington, proteomics is the science that seeks to identify and quantify proteins and to determine localization, modifications, interactions, activities, and, ultimately, their functions. Knowledge of this kind is essential, of course, not only in understanding how natural proteins function, but also how their synthetic analogs might be built and how they might operate in a variety of conditions.

The science of designing, building, and studying synthetic proteins—sometimes called *protein engineering*—generally takes one of three primary directions. First, some researchers are interested in working with natural proteins, modifying various regions of the protein to see how such changes affect the protein's function. Second, other researchers focus on only certain portions of a protein molecule, a chain of amino acids known as an *oligopeptide,* for study and analysis. Since protein molecules are so large, focusing on some specific oligopeptide with an important function can make a researcher's work simpler. Finally, still other researchers prefer to design, build, and study proteins that are not found in nature, totally synthetic proteins that may have functions similar to natural proteins but may also have totally new structures and properties. This field of research is referred to as the de novo approach to protein synthesis, a Latin phrase meaning "from the beginning." De novo protein engineering is, in some ways, the most challenging of all three fields of protein research because it involves working with proteins with no natural analogs, proteins about which a researcher starts out knowing little or nothing.

The design and construction of synthetic proteins tend to follow one of two general approaches. In the first approach, bacteria and other simple organisms are genetically engineered to produce proteins that are normally not part of their repertoire. For example, a bacterium might naturally produce an enzyme for the hydrolysis of glucose as one of its normal biochemical functions. Researchers can alter that bacterium's genome, however, to make it produce an enzyme that performs some other kind of chemical change with glucose. They can then study the artificial enzyme (protein) produced by means of this genetic transformation.

Second, researchers can synthesize proteins without the use of living systems at all, employing only chemical techniques familiar to any chemist. A number of techniques have been developed for the chemical synthesis of proteins. Perhaps the simplest and most obvious (but definitely not the fastest) has been called *stepwise synthesis.* In this procedure, amino acids are added to each other, one at a time, until a chain of the desired length has been attained. The technique was first developed by Bruce Merrifield, then at Rockefeller University in New York City, who was awarded the 1984 Nobel Prize in chemistry for this achievement.

In the Merrifield method, also called *solid-phase peptide synthesis* (SPPS), a researcher selects some amino acid as the beginning point for the new protein and attaches that amino acid to a solid polymer by reacting the carboxyl group of the amino acid with a basic group in the polymer. A second amino acid is then reacted with the first amino acid, resulting in the formation of a two-residue structure known as a dipeptide. The dipeptide (still attached to the polymer base) is then washed to remove by-products and extraneous reactants, and the process is repeated. The product of the second step is a tripeptide (three-residue compound); the product of the third step a tetrapeptide (four-residue compound); the product of the fourth step a pentapeptide (five-residue compound); and so on. When the product has reached some desired length, it is chemically treated to break the bond between the first amino acid from the solid support, releasing the oligopeptide or polypeptide for further study. (The term *oligopeptide* refers to amino acid polymers with some small number of amino acid residues, usually fewer than about 12. A *polypeptide* is an amino acid polymer with many, often hundreds or even thousands, of amino acid residues; in other words, a protein.)

The Merrifield technique is probably the most popular single method for synthesizing synthetic proteins now available to chemists. It does have some drawbacks, however. For example, since so many steps are required to produce a complete protein, the efficiency of the process overall is very sensitive to the efficiency of each individual step. Chemists have calculated that a system that is 99.9 percent efficient at each individual step can result in an overall yield of 90 percent of the desired product, but an otherwise identical system that is only 97 percent efficient in each step will result in a final yield of only 5 percent.

Obtaining a protein that develops just the right secondary, tertiary, and quaternary structures (that "folds" correctly) with stepwise synthesis is also a problem. Indeed, getting proteins to fold correctly—or in many instances, to fold at all—is one of the most challenging problems in all of protein engineering. A possible solution to this problem in protein synthesis has been suggested by Manfred Mutter at the Ecole Polytechnique Fédérale de Lausanne. Mutter's method is called the template-assembled synthetic protein (TASP) approach. TASP is based on the assumption that proteins grown by synthetic methods are more likely to fold properly if they are provided with some structural guidelines to follow as they are synthesized. A number of compounds have been studied as possible guidelines for use with TASP syntheses. TASP techniques used in conjunction with SPPS methods have been quite successful in producing proteins that are very similar to naturally occurring materials as well as those for which there are no natural counterparts.

Protein folding is one of the most frustrating and difficult of all issues facing those working in the field of protein engineering. Ironically, the problem does not exist for cells. As soon as a new protein is synthesized within a living system, it twists and turns until it achieves some three-dimensional shape required to carry out its normal functions. Chemists know that that process is made possible by a host of possible chemical interactions among various parts of the protein molecule (hydrogen bonding, disulfide bonding, van der Waals forces, and so on), but they do not really understand the kinetics by which folding actually occurs in most proteins. And there is little point to designing and building novel proteins by the SPPS and/or TASP methods if, ultimately, those proteins do not fold properly. It is hardly surprising, then, that large numbers of chemists are now spending their time and energy on learning more about protein folding.

Certainly, there are some clues to the folding puzzle that chemists can use to encourage novel proteins to assume some three-dimensional shape. Researchers have known for some time, for example, that amino acids tend to fall into at least two general groups: hydrophilic ("water loving") and hydrophobic ("water hating"). When a natural protein assumes some three-dimensional shape, it often does so by twisting and turning so that hydrophobic amino acids point inward, toward the center of the molecule, and hydrophilic amino acids point outward, toward the aqueous solution they tend to occupy. If a researcher could arrange the primary structure of a synthetic protein in such a way as to achieve a similar result, perhaps the folding problem could be at least partially solved.

The problem is that the size and complexity of polypeptides is so great as to make such predictions extraordinarily difficult. Recall that any one of 20 different amino acids can occupy each location in the polypeptide, and each amino acid can assume a number of different positions (called *rotamers*) at that site. As many as about a dozen possible rotamers at each location is not unusual. In a polypeptide of about 15 amino acids, then, the number of different arrangements that can exist is on the order of $1,000^{15}$. How is one to know which of those possibilities are likely to result in a protein that will fold in such a way as to make it functional, that is, able to carry out some predetermined task?

Prior to the existence of high-speed computations, there was no answer to that question. It was simply impossible to calculate the potential energy of all possible arrangements to find out which were low enough for a structure to exist and which were so high that the protein would not assume a stable conformation. Since the mid-1990s, however, scientists have been working on a variety of computer programs designed to sort through the very large number of possible conformations a protein can take and decide which of those conformations are at least theoretically possible from the standpoint of energy considerations. The scientists can then use the result of these computations to design and build a synthetic protein that meets those requirements.

One of the first breakthroughs in this field was the design of a computer program by B. I. Dahiyat, then a graduate student in the Division of Chemistry and Chemical Engineering at the California Institute of Technology (CalTech) and S. L. Mayo, professor of biology at the Howard Hughes Medical Institute at CalTech. Dahiyat and Mayo decided to write a program that would predict a possible structure for a naturally occurring protein known as a *zinc finger*. They chose the protein because it is relatively simple (it contains only 28 amino acid residues), yet it is capable of folding in such a way as to produce the three basic structures found in proteins: an alpha helix, a beta sheet, and segments that connect the two.

◄ DAVID A. BAKER (1962–) ►

At one time, researchers thought that Mother Nature provided all or most of the clues they needed to know how to make new proteins, but that simplistic view has changed. Today, scientists know that they can produce a virtually unlimited number of proteins, many of which do not exist in nature. One of the leading researchers in this field is David A. Baker at the Howard Hughes Medical Institute at the University of Washington. Baker's work suggests that the proteins found in nature represent only a hint of the possibilities that exist.

David A. Baker was born in Seattle on October 6, 1962. After attending local schools, he enrolled at Harvard University, from which he received his B.A. degree in 1984. He then began his doctoral studies in biochemistry at the University of California at Berkeley and received his Ph.D. there in 1989. After spending three years in a postdoctoral program at the University of California at San Francisco, Baker was appointed assistant professor in the Department of Biochemistry at the University of Washington, Seattle. In 2000, he was promoted to associate professor and was appointed assistant investigator at the Howard Hughes Medical Institute in Seattle. He is now professor of biochemistry, adjunct professor of bioengineering, and adjunct professor of genome sciences at Washington.

Baker's primary research interests have been in the use of computer programs to predict protein folding. He has authored and coauthored more than 100 papers in the field in just over a decade, and in 2003 he was lead scientist in a research team that synthesized the first completely synthetic protein, a molecule that does not exist in nature with a three-dimensional structure that is also unknown in the natural world. This accomplishment was widely regarded as one of the most significant breakthroughs in the field of protein engineering in the brief history of the science. In recognition of his work in protein engineering, Baker was awarded the 2002 Overton Prize for Computational Biology and the 2004 Feynman Prize from the Foresight Institute.

The problem with which the program had to deal was staggering. There are roughly 2×10^{27} different ways in which 28 amino acid residues can be combined and about 1×10^{62} arrangements of all possible rotamers. The Dahiyat-Mayo program was successful, however, at least partly because it made use of a special program known as the dead-end elimination (DEE) theorem, which eliminated at the outset a very large fraction of the 1×10^{62} possibilities because they did not meet some basic energy requirements. Still, the program ran for more than 90 hours before it selected a structure (later given the name of full sequence design 1, or FSD-1) that appeared to meet the requirements established by the zinc finger.

Somewhat surprisingly, the structure recommended by the computer program for FSD-1 was quite different from that of the zinc finger itself. It contained only six of the 28 amino acids found in the zinc finger and five more that are chemically similar, but not identical. Still, even with the nonnatural set of amino acids, FSD-1 folded in precisely the same way as the zinc finger, resulting in an artificial protein that met a set of predetermined conditions.

The Dahiyat-Mayo program is by no means the only computer program to have been designed for the manufacture of synthetic proteins. David A. Baker, at the Howard Hughes Medical Institute at the University of Washington, has been working on such programs for more than a decade. He has used one of those programs, called Rosetta, to predict the structure of proteins that will fold in some predetermined way. In December 2000, Baker and his colleagues competed with about 100 other research groups from around the world in the fourth Critical Assessment of Techniques for Protein Structure Prediction (CASP4) held at Asilomar, California. Contestants were awarded two points for each structure that was "among the best" generated by their program for matching the structures of natural proteins, one point for structures that were "pretty good," and no points for structures that were too different from natural proteins. Baker's team earned a total of 31 points overall, compared to the next most successful group, with eight points.

Nearly three years later, Baker and his colleagues demonstrated the practical significance of their computer modeling. In November 2003, they announced the synthesis of the first completely artificial protein, which they called Top7. They used Rosetta to design a protein of 93 amino acid residues with a geometric structure consisting of two α-helices and five β-strands never before seen in any other protein. They then proceeded to synthesize the protein in the laboratory and found that its structure was "strikingly similar" to that predicted by Rosetta. According to Baker, the synthesis of Top7 "open[s] the door to the exploration of the large regions of the protein universe not yet observed in nature."

The possible applications of synthetic proteins appear to be extensive. In some cases, it may be possible to redesign natural proteins to allow them to function more efficiently than they do in nature. For example, most proteins carry out their normal functions only in rather narrow environmental conditions, often near body temperature of 37°C and a pH close to 7.0. But there may be circumstances under which it would be helpful if those proteins functioned over a broader range of temperature, acidity, and other conditions. The ability to rearrange the primary sequence of the protein may make changes of this kind possible.

An example of this kind of work involves the enzyme subtilisin, frequently used as an additive in laundry detergents because it attacks the proteins that soil clothing. The problem, however, is that subtilisin is easily destroyed by bleaches with which a detergent is often used. Research showed that subtilisin is sensitive to bleach because a single amino acid in its primary structure—a methionine at position 22—is destroyed by bleach. By replacing this methionine with an amino acid that is not sensitive to attack by bleach, then, researchers were able to synthesize a new form of subtilisin that did not degrade in the presence of bleach for use in laundry detergents.

Synthetic proteins may also have applications in the field of medicine, mimicking the behavior of natural proteins in a host of ways or providing entirely new mechanisms for carrying out essential biological functions. For example, researchers hope to design synthetic proteins that can deliver drugs to specific sites in the body to treat specific problems. For example, one might design a synthetic protein that could be opened to allow the insertion of some form of medication and then resealed for delivery in the patient's body. Once the protein had reached its target organ in the body—a group of cancer cells, for example—the protein would once more open up, releasing the drug it carried to the target cells.

A number of applications of synthetic proteins may be completely different from those of natural proteins. One of the most active areas of research is in the design of artificial proteins as sensors. The concept is a simple one. A protein could be designed to contain an active site, like any enzyme, that would be built to recognize and bond to some very specific molecule. When the sensor protein found and bonded to that molecule, it might initiate an electrical current or other signal that would alert a human observer. In one example of this line of work, David A. Tirrell, a researcher active in the field of protein engineering, has developed an engineered form of the enzyme phosphotriesterase, found in the *Pseudomonas dimuta* bacterium, that is able to detect pesticides in the organphosphate family as well as a variety of agents used in chemical warfare. The protein is attached to an electrode or an optical fiber, through which it releases a message that a suspect molecule has been detected.

Chemists have long admired the ability of cells to manufacture a huge variety of complex proteins that perform a host of complex biochemical functions. For a long time, the primary goal of chemists was to learn how cells accomplish this task and to replicate the processes involved in a laboratory. In recent years, researchers have gone far beyond that challenge, discovering ways to make not just natural proteins but also proteins that are partially or entirely synthetic. This research is resulting in the production of very specialized molecules that can be designed to carry out precise functions with medical applications. As with other fields of materials science, such as nanotechnology and smart materials, many of the first applications of synthetic proteins will, therefore, be in the field of medicine. Thus far, no product using synthetic proteins has yet been approved for use with humans. However, tests with experimental animals on a number of new products is under way. And like other new materials described in this chapter, synthetic proteins hold great potential for changing and improving human health and life.

CONCLUSION

It is easy to take rock, stone, clay, and hunks of iron for granted. These materials exist abundantly in the Earth's surface, and they have been used by humans for millennia to construct homes, tools, kitchen implements, and other objects needed in everyday life. The task of recovering these materials from the ground and learning how to shape them into useable forms may seem a drab and uninteresting activity. Who, with any initiative, imagination, and ambition, would want to become a materials scientist?

The answer to that question today is "Lots of people." The study of both natural and synthetic materials has changed so dramatically in the past few decades that some of the most exciting research in the chemical sciences is now taking place in the field of materials science. In some ways, one of the most surprising accomplishments in materials science has been reported in research on composites, possibly the oldest type of material used by humans for construction purposes. Scientists are beginning to learn that "boring" materials like stone and clay can be reformulated and reshaped in a variety of ways, often with the use of synthetic materials, to produce products with superior chemical and physical properties to those found in nature or those that people had historically developed.

Biomaterials are another field in which researchers are finding ways of improving on the natural products in the world around us, this time in the area of living organisms. Nature has done a remarkable job in designing materials needed to carry out the endless array of tasks that living organisms perform in order to stay alive, remain healthy, and reproduce successfully, but the compounds and structures that nature has produced through evolution are not perfect, nor do they meet every requirement that living organisms have. Cells grow old and become "sick," that is, they lose the ability to function as they must if an organism is to survive. So human researchers are faced with the challenge of learning how living organisms produce the chemicals they need to operate correctly and efficiently and then of improving on the materials and techniques that nature has developed. Scientists have met this challenge very successfully, producing synthetic cells, skin, bone, blood vessels, and other body parts that can be used to replace damaged or diseased tissue and organs and extend human life.

For some researchers, the most exciting field of materials science today involves research at the nano level. In many respects, the most fundamental secrets of the way matter is put together and the way it functions can be unraveled only by looking at the atoms and molecules of which matter is made. As recently as the 1980s, the idea that humans would be able to carry out such research—to "look at" and manipulate individual atoms and molecules—would have seemed to be fantastical. But scientists have shown that such is not the case. They have developed the tools and techniques needed to work at the atomic level with increasing efficiency, providing an opportunity for future researchers to build new materials in ways that have never been possible and making it likely that types of materials that were once only the subject of science fiction novels will be created.

As exciting as nanomaterials may be for many researchers, smart materials may present an even more promising future. With the ability to sense changes in the environment around them, analyze those changes, and then develop appropriate responses, smart materials have some of the fundamental qualities that people associate with "life." Will smart materials someday act so much like living materials that the difference between "life" and "nonlife" becomes unclear? As smart materials become smarter, people wonder.

Finally, scientists have shown that imaginative research can restore and revitalize "old" and "boring" topics in the field of synthetic materials like plastics, just as it can with natural materials like stone and clay. Despite the enormous impact polymers have made on human life in the past half century, they, like stones and clay, have become such an ordinary, routine part of everyday life that few people think seriously about them anymore. But new developments in the field of polymer science have begun to change that situation. Today, scientists are beginning to learn about many new kinds of polymers, such as conductive polymers, dendrimers and hyper-branched polymers, and synthetic proteins, whose applications in everyday life are difficult to appreciate.

In some ways, then, the evolution of materials over the millennia is one of the clearest mirrors of the evolution of human society itself. Since the day when the first human learned how to chip a rock to produce a useful tool, people have continuously learned more about the materials that nature has given, the ways in which those materials can be manipulated and used, and the ways people can go one step more in producing new and better materials.

GLOSSARY

active site   The region within an enzyme molecule at which a substrate has a tendency to bond.

active smart materials   Smart materials that analyze environmental stimuli and then respond to those stimuli in some way.

actuator   Any device in a smart system that initiates a change in the size, shape, color, or other property of a material.

addition polymer   A polymer formed as the result of an addition reaction between two molecules, each of which contains at least one multiple bond.

addition reaction   A chemical reaction in which two atoms or groups of atoms add to opposite ends of a carbon-carbon double bond.

advanced composite   *See* HIGH-PERFORMANCE COMPOSITE.

allograft   A graft in which tissue or bone is transplanted from one human to another human. *See also* AUTOGRAFT; XENOGRAFT.

alternating copolymer   A copolymer in which the monomeric units alternate with each other in a regular pattern.

assembler   A hypothetical nanoscale device, first suggested by K. Eric Drexler, that would have the ability to construct other nanoscale devices by following some predetermined instructions.

autograft   Tissue or bone transplanted from one site on an individual's body to another site.

biomaterial   A nonliving material that can be used in a medical device intended to interact with a biological system.

block copolymer   A copolymer in which monomeric units are grouped together in blocks within the polymeric chain.

buckminsterfullerene   An allotropic form of carbon in which carbon atoms are arranged in large, closed structures with shapes like that of a soccer ball.

buckyball   The nickname given to a buckminsterfullerene molecule.

carbon nanotube   A cylindrical form of carbon only a few nanometers in diameter, consisting of a single wall or a series of concentric walls of carbon atoms.

cast iron   A form of iron that contains up to about 5 percent carbon.

ceramic   A claylike material often made of nonmetallic oxides.

chromogenism   The tendency of a material to change color when exposed to some external stimulus, such as light (photochromism), electricity (electrochromism), or heat (thermochromism).

composite   A mixture of two or more substances that are mutually insoluble and that differ from each other in their physical and chemical properties.

condensation polymer   A polymer formed by the reaction between two molecules during which some small molecule, such as a molecule of water or ammonia, is split out.

conductive polymer   A polymer capable of conducting an electrical current to at least some minimal extent.

convergent synthesis   A process for making dendrimers in which one begins by constructing the outermost shells first and then attaches these shells to a central core.

converse piezoelectricity   The process in which the application of an electric current to a crystal results in a change in its size and shape.

copolymer   A polymer that consists of more than one (usually only two) kinds of monomers.

dendrimer   A complex molecule generally with a spherical shape consisting of many concentric shells and an overall branching shape.

de novo synthesis   Literally, the synthesis of a compound "from the beginning," that is, from its basic components.

divergent synthesis A process for making dendrimers by beginning with a central core and adding outer shells, one at a time, to this core.

doping The process of adding some impurity to a material to change its electrical properties.

electrorheological effects Deformations that occur in a material as a result of its being exposed to an electrical field. Also known as the Winslow effect.

electrostriction The deformation of a material when exposed to an electrical field.

extracellular matrix The scaffolding to which cells are attached in an organism, produced by materials secreted by the cells into the surrounding medium.

filler The material embedded in the matrix of a composite; also called reinforcement.

giant magnetostriction alloys (GMAs) Alloys that demonstrate unusually large degrees of magnetostriction when exposed to pressure. *See also* MAGNETOSTRICTION.

glass transition temperature The temperature at which softening begins in a thermoplastic material.

graft copolymer A copolymer in which monomeric chains of one type are grafted on to a main chain containing a different monomer.

gray goo A term used to describe a hypothetical material made of nanoscale particles that has the general appearance of a cloud.

heme The nonprotein portion of a hemoglobin or myoglobin molecule.

hemoglobin analog A synthetic molecule that mimics the chemical and physical properties and structure of natural hemoglobin.

heterograft *See* XENOGRAFT.

high-performance composite Structural materials designed for applications for which more traditional materials, such as aluminum alloys and steels, are not satisfactory.

homograft *See* ALLOGRAFT.

homopolymer A polymer that contains only one kind of monomer.

hyperbranched polymer   A molecule in which a number of linear chains are attached to a single core structure.

intelligent gel   Any liquid material that expands or contracts when exposed to some external stimulus, such as changes in light, temperature, pH, pressure, or electrical or magnetic fields.

interphase   An intermediary phase that sometimes exists between the filler and matrix in a composite.

Joule effect   *See* MAGNETOSTRICTION.

living blood vessel equivalent (LBVE)   A synthetic material that mimics the structure and function of blood vessels.

macroscale   With dimensions of a macroscopic object.

macroscopic   Visible to the naked eye.

magnetic domain   A region within a magnetic material in which atoms tend to align themselves in a uniform direction.

magnetomechanical effect   *See* VILLARI EFFECT.

magnetorheological effects   Deformations that occur in a material as a result of its being exposed to a magnetic field.

magnetostriction   The deformation of a material when exposed to a magnetic field. Also called the Joule effect.

matrix   That portion of a composite that gives it body, shape, and bulk and that holds the material together.

microtechnology   Research that is conducted on materials with dimensions in the range between about 10 and 1,000 nm.

modulus of rupture   The ability of a material to withstand breaking such as, for example, when it is bent.

molecular electronics   A term used to describe the design and construction of electronic components consisting of individual molecules or small groups of molecules.

molecular manufacturing   The process of constructing a material from the "bottom up," beginning with individual atoms and molecules.

molecular nanotechnology   A term that is sometimes used to describe "bottom-up" construction of materials that begins with the manipulation of individual atoms and molecules.

monomer   A small molecule that is capable of reacting with itself in such a way as to produce a very large molecule (polymer) in which the molecule is repeated many times over.

nanobot   A term used to describe nanometer-size robots.

nanometer   One billionth of a meter.

nanotechnology   Research conducted with materials having dimensions at the nanometer scale.

neointima   The interior lining of nerve cells.

oligopeptide   A chain of amino acid residues consisting of fewer than about a dozen amino acids.

osseointegration   A process by which a nonliving material is integrated into normal bone.

passive smart materials   Smart materials that simply respond to environmental stimuli to which they have been exposed.

perfluorocarbons   A family of hydrocarbons in which all hydrogen atoms have been replaced by fluorine atoms.

photochromism   The tendency of a material to change color when exposed to changes in light intensity.

piezoelectricity   The tendency of a material to generate an electric current when pressure is applied to it.

polyhemoglobin   A molecule consisting of two or more hemoglobin molecules attached to each other.

polymer   A very large molecule consisting of one or two basic units (monomers) repeated many times over.

polypeptide   A chain of amino acid residues consisting of many—generally at least a few dozen and typically a few hundred or few thousand—amino acids.

potential (electric)   The difference in electrical charge between two points in a circuit, expressed in volts.

primary structure (of a protein)   The sequence of amino acid residues that make up the structure of a protein molecule.

protein engineering   The science of designing, building, and studying synthetic proteins.

proteomics   The science that involves the identification and quantification of proteins and the determination of their localization, modifications, interactions, activities, and, ultimately, their function.

pyroelectricity   The tendency of certain materials to generate an electric current when they are heated.

quaternary structure (of a protein)   The overall three-dimensional structure of a protein molecule produced when two or more macromolecules combine to form a higher-order molecule.

random copolymer   A copolymer in which monomeric units are arranged randomly in sequence with the polymeric chain.

regenerative medicine   *See* TISSUE ENGINEERING.

reinforced concrete   A form of concrete whose strength is increased by the addition of steel bars embedded within it.

reinforcement   *See* FILLER.

reparative biology   *See* TISSUE ENGINEERING.

replicator   A theoretical nanoscale device imagined by K. Eric Drexler as having the capability of making exact copies of itself.

resin   Any solid or semisolid material made of organic material produced naturally or synthetically. The term has a somewhat ambiguous meaning and is often applied to the raw form of a synthetic polymer.

responsive material   *See* SMART MATERIAL.

rheology   A term that refers to the deformation and flow of matter.

rotamer   One of the many three-dimensional configurations an amino acid residue can take on a polypeptide chain.

scanning probe microscope (SPM)   Any one of a number of devices, such as the scanning tunneling microscope and atomic force microscope, that can be used for observing and manipulating individual atoms and molecules.

scanning tunneling microscope (STM)   A device for observing and manipulating materials at the atomic level.

secondary structure (of a protein)   The linkages produced by hydrogen bonding between peptides in a protein molecule that stabilize the structure.

sensor   A device that is capable of detecting some external stimulus; commonly used in smart materials systems.

shape memory alloy (SMA)   A metal that after having been deformed returns to its original shape upon being heated to some characteristic temperature.

smart gel   *See* INTELLIGENT GEL.

smart material   A material that responds to environmental stimuli by making some change in its physical characteristics, such as size, shape, electrical or magnetic conductivity, or optical properties.

smart structure   A structure that contains two parts, one of which is a smart material and the second a processing unit that can analyze data and act on it.

smart system   *See* SMART STRUCTURE.

solid-phase peptide synthesis (SPPS)   A method for synthesizing proteins by attaching an amino acid to a solid polymer support, reacting a second amino acid to that amino acid, washing the dipeptide formed to remove extraneous reactants and by-products, and then repeating that process a number of times.

soliton   An electrical disturbance (wave) in a molecule that accompanies a shifting back and forth between single and double bonds in the molecule.

stainless steel   A form of steel that contains chromium, making the alloy more resistant to corrosion.

steel   An alloy of iron that contains small amounts of carbon and usually other metals.

stent   A cylinder-shaped device inserted into a blood vessel in order to help keep it open.

stepwise synthesis (of a protein)   The synthesis of a new protein by the addition of one new amino acid at a time to a growing chain.

substrate   A molecule on which an enzyme tends to act.

tertiary structure (of a protein)   The three-dimensional shape of a protein molecule produced as the result of various types of bonding between portions of the polypeptide chain.

tetramer   A molecular structure that consists of four units bonded to each other.

thermoplastic polymers   Polymers that, once formed from the liquid state, become solid and are then capable of being melted at a later time.

thermosetting polymers   Polymers that, once formed from the liquid state, remain solid when heated at a later time.

tissue engineering   The application of principles and methods of engineering and life sciences toward fundamental understanding of structure-function relationships in normal and pathological mammalian tissues and the development of biological substitutes to restore, maintain, or improve tissue functions.

toughness The ability of a material to absorb energy by bending or otherwise changing its shape without breaking.

tow A bundle of carbon fibers used as filler in a composite material.

transformation temperature The temperature to which a shape memory alloy must be heated to return to its original shape.

transistor An electronic device used to control the flow of electricity.

Villari effect Changes in the magnetic properties of a material when pressure is applied to the material. Also known as the magnetomechanical effect.

Winslow effect *See* ELECTRORHEOLOGICAL EFFECT.

wrought iron A form of iron that contains no more than about 1 percent carbon.

xenograft Transplantation of bone or tissue from one species to a different species. *See also* ALLOGRAFT; AUTOGRAFT.

zinc finger A particular kind of naturally occurring protein containing 28 amino acid residues and an atom of zinc.

◆ BIBLIOGRAPHY

PRINT RESOURCES

Aldissi, M. *Intrinsically Conducting Polymers: An Emerging Technology.* Hingham, Mass.: Kluwer Academic Publishers, 1993.

Ball, Philip. *Made to Measure: New Materials for the 21st Century.* Princeton, N.J.: Princeton University Press, 1997.

Baum, Rudy. "Nanotechnology: Drexler and Smalley Make the Case for and against 'Molecular Assemblers.'" *Chemical and Engineering News* 81, 8, December 1, 2003, 37–42. Also available online at http://pubs.acs.org/cen/coverstory/8148/8148counterpoint.html.

Bhat, Sujata V. *Biomaterials.* Boston: Kluwer Academic Publishers, 2002.

Bonassar, Lawrence J., and Charles A. Vacanti. "Tissue Engineering: The First Decade and Beyond." *Journal of Cellular Biochemistry Supplements* 30–31, 1998, 297–303.

Callister, William D. *Materials Science and Engineering: An Introduction.* New York: Wiley, 2003.

Chandrasekhar, P., ed. *Conducting Polymers, Fundamentals and Applications: A Practical Approach.* Hingham, Mass.: Kluwer Academic Publishers, 1999.

Drexler, K. Eric. *Engines of Creation.* Garden City, N.Y.: Anchor Press/Doubleday, 1986.

Editors of *Scientific American. Understanding Nanotechnology.* New York: Warner Books, 2002.

Friend, R. H. *Conductive Polymers: From Science to Applications.* Toronto: ChemTech Publishing, 1993.

Gandhi, Mukesh V., and B. S. Thompson. *Smart Materials and Structures.* New York: Chapman & Hall, 1992 .

Gay, Daniel, Suong V. Hoa, and Stephen W. Tsai. *Composite Materials: Design and Applications.* Boca Raton, Fla.: CRC Press, 2002.

Grant, Gregory A., ed. *Synthetic Peptides: A User's Guide.* New York: Oxford University Press, 2002.

Hull, Derek. *An Introduction to Composite Materials.* Cambridge: Cambridge University Press, 1981.

Janocha, Hartmut, ed. *Adaptronics and Smart Structures: Basics, Materials, Design, and Applications.* New York: Springer, 1999.
Kroschwitz, Jacqueline I., ed. *Encyclopedia of Polymer Science and Technology.* 3d ed. New York: Wiley Interscience, 2004.
Mazumdar, Sanjay K. *Composites Manufacturing: Materials, Product, and Process Engineering.* Boca Raton, Fla.: CRC Press, 2002.
McIntire, Larry V., et al. *WTEC Panel Report on Tissue Engineering Research.* Baltimore: International Technology Research Institute, 2002. Also available online at http://wtec.org/loyola/te/final/te_final.pdf.
Newton, David E. *Recent Advances and Issues in Molecular Nanotechnology.* Westport, Conn.: Greenwood Press, 2002.
Park, Joon B., and Joseph D. Bronzino, eds. *Biomaterials: Principles and Applications.* Boca Raton, Fla.: CRC Press, 2003.
Poole, Charles P., Jr., and Frank J. Owens. *Introduction to Nanotechnology.* Hoboken, N.J.: John Wiley, 2003.
Ratner, Buddy, et al., eds. *Biomaterials Science.* San Diego: Academic Press, 1996.
Ratner, Mark, and Daniel Ratner. *Nanotechnology: A Gentle Introduction to the Next Big Idea.* Upper Saddle River, N.J.: Prentice Hall, 2003.
Roylance, David, and Margaret Roylance. *Understanding Composites.* Cincinnati, Ohio: Hanser Gardner Publications, 2003.
Schwartz, Mel, ed. *Encyclopedia of Materials, Parts, and Finishes.* 2d ed. Boca Raton, Fla.: CRC Press, 2002.
———. *Encyclopedia of Smart Materials.* New York: J. Wiley, 2002.
Skotheim, Terje A., Ronald L. Elsenbaumer, and John R. Reynolds. *Handbook of Conducting Polymers.* New York: Marcel Dekker, 1998.
Teegarden, David M. *Polymer Chemistry: Introduction to an Indispensable Science.* Washington, D.C.: NSTA Press, 2004.
Wilson, Michael, et al., eds. *Nanotechnology: Basic Science and Emerging Technologies.* Boca Raton, Fla.: Chapman & Halland CRC Press, 2002.

INTERNET RESOURCES

About.com. "Composites/Plastics." Available online. URL: http://composite.about.com/cs/aboutcomposites/. Accessed on October 10, 2006.
Advanced Polymer Courses. "Inherently Conductive Polymers." Available online. URL: http://www.conductivepolymers.com/. Last updated on September 29, 2006.
"Biomaterials Network." Available online. URL: http://www.biomat.net/. Accessed on October 10, 2006.
Bone Tissue Engineering Center. "Tutorials" (on bone tissue engineering). Available online. URL: http://www.btec.cmu.edu/reFramed/tutorial/mainLayoutTutorial.html. Accessed on October 10, 2006.
Bonsor, Kevin. "How Smart Structures Will Work." Available online. URL: http://science.howstuffworks.com/smart-structure.htm. Accessed on October 10, 2006.

Design inSite. "Composites." Available online. URL: http://www.
designinsite.dk/htmsider/inspinfo.htm. (Go to Materials section.)
Accessed on October 10, 2006.

——. "Responsive (Smart) Materials" Available online. URL: http://www.
designinsite.dk/htmsider/inspinfo.htm. (Got to Materials section.)
Accessed on October 10, 2006.

Eads Composites Atlantic. "What Are Composites?" Available online. URL:
http://www.compositesatlantic.com/index_whatcomp.html. Accessed
on October 10, 2006.

European Commission. "Biomaterials for Health, Wealth and
Employment." Available online. URL: http://ec.europa.eu/research/
growth/gcc/projects/in-action-biomat01.html. Accessed on October 10,
2006.

Foresight Nanotech Institute. "Advancing Beneficial Nanotechnology."
Available online. URL: http://www.foresight.org/. Accessed on October
10, 2006.

Goodrich. "Why Composites?" Available online. URL: http://www.epp.
goodrich.com/why.shtml. Accessed on October 10, 2006.

Merkle, Ralph. "Nanotechnology." Available online. URL: http://www.
zyvex.com/nano/. Accessed on October 10, 2006.

"Nanotechnology Now." Available online. URL: http://nanotech-now.com/.
Accessed on October 10, 2006.

National Aeronautics and Space Administration. "Aviation Research; You
Decide; Smart Materials." Available online. URL: http://virtualskies.
arc.nasa.gov/research/youDecide/smartMaterials.html. Accessed on
October 10, 2006.

National Nanotechnology Initiative. "Leading to a Revolution in
Technology and Industry." Available online. URL: http://www.nano.
gov/. Accessed on October 10, 2006.

Sensors Research Consulting, Inc. "Resources for Sensors, Measurements,
Instrumentation and Related Sciences," Available online. URL: http://
www.sensors-research.com/senres/materials.htm Accessed on October
10, 2006.

ScientificAmerican.com. "Browse by Subject: Nanotechnology." Available
online. URL: http://www.sciam.com/nanotech/. Accessed on October
10, 2006.

SMA/MEMS Research Group. "Smart Materials." Available online. URL:
http://www.cs.ualberta.ca/~database/MEMS/sma_mems/smrt.html.
Last modified on August 17, 2001.

INDEX

Italic page numbers indicate illustrations.

A

accelerometer *116,* 116–117
acrylonitrile 171, 172
active site 181
actuator 107, 108
addition polymers 151–154
adipic acid 155
advanced composites 25–39
Advanced Tissue Sciences 52
aeronautical engineering 118–120, 133
aerospace industry 33–35, 118–120
AFM. *See* atomic force microscope
airbags, automotive 115–117
aircraft, SMAs for 133, *134*
alcohol 10
Allard, David 95
Alliance Pharmaceutical Corporation 67
allograft 47
alloys 2–3, 12–18, 21, 43, 58–59. *See also* shape memory alloys
allyl toluidine 8
alternating copolymers 154
aluminum 17
aluminum oxide 5, 28
amino acids 179–180, 182–188
amino group 172
ammonium cyanate 6
amorphous materials 161
aniline 8
apatite 23
Apligraf® 52
aramid 26. *See also* Kevlar®
Aristophanes 42
Armistead, William 137–138
aromatic polyamide 27
artificial materials. *See specific material, e.g.:* bone, artificial
Aspdin, Joseph 5
assemblers 69, 73–75, 80
atherosclerosis 53, 133–135
atomic force microscope (AFM) 88, 92
austenite 130–131
autograft 47
automotive airbags 115–117
automotive rear-view mirrors 137
automotive shock absorbers 128
Avram, Ari 96

B

Baekeland, Leo Hendrik 10–12
Bakelite 11–12, 154–155, 161, 162
Baker, David A. 186–188
barium titanate 114
basal cells 51
batteries, plastic 168–169
benzene 27, 95, 102
Berzelius, Jöns Jakob 6–7
Bessemer, Henry 14–16
Bessemer process 15, 16
β-tricalcium phosphate (β-TCP) 61
billiard balls 9–10
bimetal strip 106
Binnig, Gerd 86, 88
bioceramics 57

biomaterials x, 40–67, 190–191
Biopure 66
biotin 85
Biryukovich, K. L. and D. L. 33
bisphenol A 157
blast furnace 15
block copolymers 154
blood, artificial 42–43, 62–67
blood vessel, synthetic 43, 53–56, *55*
boats, composite materials for 35
body parts, bioengineered 52–61, *55, 57, 58, 60*
Bohon, Katherine 143
bone *22*, 22–23, 43
bone, artificial 56–61
bone plates 43–44
bonsilate 11
boron 28
boron filaments 33–34
bottom-up nanotechnology 72. *See also* Drexlerian nanotechnology
Branemark, Per Ingvar 58
Braun, Erez 83
Brearley, Harry 17
Brewster, David 111
brick ix, 24–25
bridges 37–38
Brock, David 144
bronze 2–3
Bronze Age 3
buckminsterfullerene (buckyball) *91, 92,* 98
Buehler, William J. 130
Burke, John F. 47–49, 51
burns, to skin 46–47
Bush, George W. 103
butadiene 153

C

cadmium 130
calcium phosphate 61
camphor 10
carbon 3, 13, 15, 16
carbon-carbon composite 32
carbon fibers 27, 107
carbon filaments 33–34
carbon nanotube 83, 85, 89–93, 95
carbon steel 16
Carothers, Wallace 155
Carrel, Alexis 43, 53
cast iron 13, 15
celluloid 9–11
cellulose 9, 24
ceramic-matrix composites 31–32, 35
ceramics 31, 114–115
Chang, Thomas 63, 64
chondroitin sulfate 50
chromium 17
chromium alloy steel 16–17
chromogenism 136–137
Chung, Deborah D. L. 107
cis isomer 140, 163
Clark, A. E. 121, 122
clay 1–2, 24–25
coal tar 8
cobalt 58
collagen *22*, 23, 49–52
collodion 63
composite fabric 117
composites ix, 20–39, 119
computers 76, 93–94, 140–141, 185–188
concrete 4–5, 25, 33, 107–108
condensation polymers 154–161
conductive polymers 162–170, *163, 169*

conductivity. *See* electrical conductivity
convergent synthesis 174–176
converse piezoelectricity 111, 112
copolymers 28, 30, 153–154
copper 2, 3, 17
copper chloride 138
Crick, Francis 83
cross-linked polyethylene 153
cross-linking 161
crystals, and piezoelectric effect 112–114
Curie, Jacques and Pierre 110–111
Curie, Marie 111
cyano group 172

D

Dacron® 53–55
Dahiyat, B. I. 185–187
Dai, Hongie 95
D'Appolonia Engineering Consulting Company 133
dead-end elimination theorem 187
Dekker, Cees 90
dendrimers 170–176, *171, 175*
Dendritic Nanotechnologies, Inc. 176
de novo synthesis 182
dentistry 135
Dermagraft-TC® 52
detergent 188
1,4-diaminobutane 171, 172
dielectric 111–112
diisocyanate 158
dinititroethane 137
diol 158

dipeptide 183
dipole 128
disassemblers 74
divergent synthesis 174–176
DNA (deoxyribonucleic acid) 75–76, *82*, 82–86, *87*, 99–101, 174
doping 166–167
double helix 83
Dow Chemical Company 170
Drexler, K. Eric 69, 72–74, 77–79
Drexlerian nanotechnology 73–82, *75*
drug delivery systems 146–147, 173–174, 188
DuPont 26
duralumin 17
dye, synthetic 7–9

E
early humans x
early synthetic materials x, 1–5
earthquake-proof buildings 128
Edison, Thomas 18
Egypt, ancient 2, 32–33, 41, 42
Eigler, Donald M. 73, 88
electrical conductivity
    conductive polymers 162–170
    in metal-matrix composites 31
    and polyphenylene wire 95–96
    of smart concrete 107
    through carbon nanotubes 90–92
electrical insulation 162

electric motor, nanoscale 72
electrorheological effects 125–130, *129*
electrostriction 111–112
electrostrictive materials. *See* piezoelectric materials
enzymes 181
epidermis, artificial 51
epoxies 161
ethanol 8
ether 10
ethylene glycol 156
Etrema Corporation 122
evolution, of materials 1–19
extracellular matrix 50–51
eyeglasses, photochromic 107
eyeglass frames 135–136

F
F-14 fighter plane 34
Faraday, Michael 16–17
feedback system 108–109
Feringa, B. L. 140
Feynman, Richard 68–72, 79
fiber 21
Fiberglas® 36–37
fiberglass 35–37
fiber-reinforced polymers (FRPs) 34
fibrils 24
fibrin 54
Fields, Stanley 181
fillers 20, 21, 23, 28–29
flax fiber 28–29
Fluosol-DA 66–67
formaldehyde 11, 30, 154–155

Frangibolt® 132–133
Fréchet, J. M. M. 174
Fritzsche, J. 137
fuchsin 9
Furukawa Techno Material 136

G
GAGs (glyco-saminoglycans) 50
Galfenol 122
Gamera (helicopter) 119
Garfinkel, Simon 77
gels. *See* intelligent gels
General Bakelite Company 12
genetic engineering 182
Gerber, Christoph 88
giant magneto-striction alloys (GMAs) 121, 122
glass 2, 27, 33
glass-aramid composite 38
glasses. *See* eyeglasses, photochromic
glass fiber 27
glass fiber-reinforced concrete 33
glass transition temperature 159–161
glycosaminoglycans (GAGs) 50
GMAs. *See* giant magnetostriction alloys
gold 41, 130
golf shoes 144
graft copolymers 154
graphene 90
gray goo 80–81
Green Cross Corporation 66–67
Greene, Ray 35
gum acacia 42

H

Hadar, Africa 1
Harvey, William 42
Haversian system 23
HDPE (high-density
  polyethylene) 153
heart disease 53,
  133–135
Heeger, Alan J.
  164–165
helicopter 119
hemicellulose 24
hemoglobin 62–66
HemoPure® 66
hexamethyl-
  enediamine 155
hexa-*tert*-butyl
  decacyclene 101
high-density
  polyethylene
  (HDPE) 153
Hirshberg, Yehuda 137
Hittites 4
Ho, Wilson 89
Hoffmann, August
  Wilhelm von 7–8
homopolymer 30,
  152–153
household appliances,
  SMAs for 136
Hyatt, John Wesley
  9–11
hydraulic concrete
  4–5
hydrogels 143–147
hydroxyapatite 56,
  60, 61
hyperbranched
  polymers 176–178,
  177
Hyperpolymers
  GmbH 178

I

IBM 73, 86, 96, 98, 101
Iijima, Sumio 89, 90
immune system,
  implants and 44, 45
implanted medical
  devices 44

Industrial Revolution
  4, 11–12, 14
inflammation 45
infrastructure, public
  37–38
inorganic materials
  28, 138
insulation, electrical
  162
Integra® 51
intelligent gels
  141–148, *145, 147*
interphase 21
Interpore
  International 60
intraocular lens
  implants 44
iodine 166, 167
iron 3–4, 13–17
iron dicarbonyl 89
Isis Innovation
  Limited 61
isomers 140–141

J

Jaffe, Bernard 114
jet engines 34
Johnson, Alan 92
joint replacement
  57–58, *58*
Joule, James Prescott
  121
Joule effect 121

K

K2 Corporation
  117–118
Kelly, T. Ross 101–103
Kevlar® 26–28
Kim, Philip 99
Krause, Sonja 143
Kwolek, Stephanie
  26

L

LBVE (living blood
  vessel equivalent)
  54–55
LDPE (low-density
  polyethylene) 153

lead zirconate titanate
  (PZT) 114
Lee, Hyojune 89
leg, prosthetic 41, 42
lens implants 44
Lexan® 158
Lieber, Charles M. 99
lignin 24
lime mortar 4–5
limestone 4, 5
liposome 64–65
liquid, effect of
  electromagnetic
  forces on 125
living blood vessel
  equivalent (LBVE)
  54–55
long-chain polymer
  161
low-density
  polyethylene
  (LDPE) 153
Lucent Technologies
  99

M

MacDiarmid, Alan G.
  164–165
macromolecules 151
macroscale 72
magenta 9
magnesium 17
magnet, nanoscale *98*
magnetic domain 121
magnetorheological
  effects. *See*
  electrorheological
  effects
magnetostrictive
  materials 120–125
manganese 17
Marsh, Albert 17, 18
martensite 130, 131
materials research,
  future of 18–19,
  190–192
matrix 20–21, 23, 31,
  56
mauve dye 7–8
Mayo, S. L. 185–187

medicine 133–136,
144–147, 188. *See also*
tissue engineering
Meekeren, Job van 57
Megagraft 1000 61
melamine 33
melting point 160, 161
mercury dithizonate
138, *139*
Merlon® 158
Merrifield, Bruce 183
metallurgy, early 2
metal-matrix
composites 31, 34
methane 95
Metzger, Robert M. 96
micelles 146, *147*
microfibrils 24
micron 69
microprocessors
93–94. *See also*
processors
Middle Ages 5
military aircraft 34
mining 133
missiles 34
modulus of rupture 25
molecular electronics
94–97
molecular motor
101–103
molecular
nanotechnology
72–73, 77, 80–81
molecular switch 96,
140
molecular wheel *102*
molecular wires 95–96
molybdenum 43
Monier, Joseph 25
monitoring system
109
monomers 9, 151, 153
Moore, Gordon 93
Moore's law 93
Mothra (aircraft) 119
mucopolysaccharides
23–24, 50. *See also*
glycosaminoglycans
Mueller, Anja 176–177

multiwalled
nanotubes
(MWNTs) 90, 99
muscles, artificial
144–146
Mushet, Robert
Forester 16
Mutter, Manfred 184
Muzzey, David S. 130
MWNTs. *See*
multiwalled
nanotubes

N
nanoabacus 98
nanobot 80–81
nanocomputers 76
nanomagnet *98*
nanomaterials/
nanotechnology x,
68–104, *75*, 191
nanomotor 101–103
nanorope 92
nanoscale devices
97–103
nanotile 85, *87*
nanotransistor 83–85,
84, 86
nanotube, carbon *91*
nanotube
nanotweezers
99–101, *100*
nanowires *94*
native metals 2
natural polymers
151
nature, composites in
22–24
neointima 54
nichrome 17–18
nickel 17, 122
nickel hydroxide 140
nitinol 130
nitric acid 9
noise control systems
124
Nomex® 26
nonferrous alloys 17
North America 2
Northfield Labs 66

nose repair 46–47
nylon 155–156

O
oil drilling platforms
38
Olander, Arne 130
OLEDs (organic light-
emitting diodes)
167–168
oligomer 96
oligopeptide 182, 183
Olympus Optical 61
o-phosphoserine 61
optical computer 141
optometry 135–136
organic chemistry
6–12
organic light-emitting
diodes (OLEDs)
167–168
Organogenesis 52, 54
orthodonture 135
OSferion 61
osseointegration 58
osteoblasts 56, 60
osteoclasts 56
osteocytes 56
Osteo Medica 61
osteon 23, 24
Owens-Corning
Fiberglas® 36–37
oxidants 65
oxidative doping 167
oxygen 15, 16, 62
Oxygent™ 67
Oxyglobin® 66
oxyhemoglobin 64

P
Parkes, Alexander 9
parkesine (Xylonite)
9, 11
particulate fibers 29
passive smart
materials 107
peptides 27
perflubron 67
perfluorocarbons
(PFCs) 66, 67

Perkin, William
Henry 7, 8
PET. *See* poly(ethylene
terephthalate)
Phelan and Collender
Company 9–10
phenol formaldehyde
11, 30, 154–155
phenylene ethynylene
oligomer 96
phenylpropane 24
Phipson, T. L. 137
phosgene 102, 157
o-phosphoserine 61
phosphotriesterase
189
photochromic
materials 107,
136–141, *139*
photochromism
(origin of term) 137
pi bonds 166, 167
piezoelectric constant
114, 115
piezoelectric effect 87,
110, 112, 113
piezoelectric materials
110–120, *116*
Pinpuller (SMA
device) 133
plasma, blood 62
plastic batteries
168–169
plastics 9–12. *See also*
polymer(s)
platelets 62
Pluronic-PAA 146–147
PMMA (polymethyl-
methacrylate) 44
polyacetylene 162–163,
166–167
poly(acrylic acid) 146
polyamides 155–156
polycarbonates
157–158
poly(dimethyl-
siloxane) 143
polyesters 156–158
polyethylene 29–30,
151, 153

poly(ethylene oxide)
143
poly(ethylene
terephthalate)
(PET) 53, 156–157
polyglycolides 59
PolyHeme® 66
polyhemoglobin 65–66
polylactides 59
polymer(s) xi, 149–
189, *150*
for biomaterials 44
for bone
implantation
59–60
lignin as 24
for matrices 29–30
for smart hydrogels
143–144
in World War II 25
polymer chain
144–145
polymer chemistry
9–12, 26
polymer fiber 27–28
polymer matrix
composite 38
polymethyl-
methacrylate
(PMMA) 44
poly(N-
isopropylacryla-
mide) 142–143
polypeptide 23, 50, 62,
183, 185
polyphenylene chains
95
polyphenylene wire
95–96
polytetrafluoro-
ethylene 54
polyurethanes
158–159
Portland cement 5
primary structure
(of a protein)
179–180
processors 93–94, 108,
117, 128
Pro Osteon 60

prosthetic devices
41–42
protein(s), synthetic
178–189, *180*
protein engineering
178–189
protein folding
183–187
proteomics 181–182
public infrastructure
37–38
Pullars of Perth 8
pyroelectricity 111
pyrolysis 27
pyroxylin 9, 64
PZT (lead zirconate
titanate) 114

Q
quarrying 133
quartz 112–114
Quate, Calvin 88
quaternary structure
(of a protein) 180,
181
quicklime 4
quinine 8

R
Rabinow, Jacob
125–127
random copolymers
154
Ratner, Mark A. 96
rear-view mirrors,
self-dimming 137
RecA protein 83, 85
rectifier, molecular
96–97, *97*
red blood cells,
artificial 62–64
reductive doping
167
regenerative
medicine. *See* tissue
engineering
reinforced concrete
25, 33
reinforced plastic 20,
21

reinforcements. *See* fillers
rejection, of implants 44, 45
reparative biology. *See* tissue engineering
replicators 69, 73, 75–76, 80–81
research, future of 18–19
resins 30–31, 151
responsive materials. *See* smart materials
reversibility 136
rheology 125
Ridley, Harold 44
RNA (ribonucleic acid) 76
Rohrer, Heinrich 86
Rome, ancient 5
Rosetta program 187–188
rotamers 185
rubber, synthetic 153
rustless steel 17

S

Sanyo Electric Company 141
SBR rubber 153, 154
scaffolding 60, 61
scanning probe microscope (SPM) 88, 93
scanning tunneling microscope (STM) 73, 86–89, 98
Schweizer, Erhard K. 73, 88
secondary structure (of a protein) 180
Seeman, Nadrian 83
semiconductors 92–93, 166
sensors 108, 117–120, 189
shape memory alloys (SMAs) 122, 130–136, *132, 134*

Shirakawa, Hideki 162–165
shock absorbers 128
sigma bonds 166
Silby, Robert J. 77
silicate groups 112–113
silicon boride 35
silicon carbide 32, 35
silicon dioxide 95
silicone 49, *50*, 51
silicon oxide 5
siloxane 49, *50*
silver halide 137–138
single-molecular switch 96
single-walled nanotubes (SWNTs) 90, 92
skates, in-line 144
ski(s) 117–118
skin, synthetic 48–52
skin grafts 46–52
slaked lime 4–5
Smalley, Richard 77, 92
smart concrete 107–108
smart gels. *See* intelligent gels
Smart Hydrogel® 146
smart hydrogels 143–147
smart materials x–xi, 105–148
smart structures (smart systems) *108*, 108–109
SMAs. *See* shape memory alloys
Smith-Peterson, Marius 57–58
snow skis 117–118
sodium azide 115–116
solid-phase peptide synthesis (SPPS) 183
soliton 166
Soundbug® 124
sound waves 123–124
South America 2
spacecraft 132–133

space program, U.S. 33
space travel 132–133
SPM. *See* scanning probe microscope
sporting equipment 36
SPPS. *See* solid-phase peptide synthesis
stainless steel 17, 43, 58
stainless steel 316L 59
static electricity 170
steel 4, 13–17, 25, 43, 58, 59
stents 133–135
stepwise synthesis (of a protein) 182–183
STM. *See* scanning tunneling microscope
Stodart, John 17
straw 24, 25
streptavidin *84, 85*
styrene 153
styrene-maleic anhydride 28
substrate 94, 181
subtilisin 188
sunglasses, "automatic" 137–138
superelastic SMA 131
Sushruta 46, 47
suspensions 125–128, 142
switch, molecular 96
SWNTs. *See* single-walled nanotubes
synthetic material. *See specific type of synthetic material, e.g.:* skin, synthetic

T

Tagliacozzi, Gaspare 47
Tanaka, Toyoichi 141–143
Teflon® 54
template-assembled synthetic protein (TASP) synthesis 184

tensile strength 25, 90
terephthalic acid 156
Terfenol-D 121–122, 124
ter Meer, E. 137
tertiary structure (of a protein) 180–181
tetracene 137
2,3,4,4-tetrachloro-naphthalen 137
tetracyclic helicene 102
tetramer 62, 64
Theophrastus 111
thermoplastic polymers 30, 159–161
thermosetting polymers 30, 161
thermostat 106–107
Thomson, William (Lord Kelvin) 111
tin 2, 3
TiNi Aerospace 131–133
Tirrell, David A. 189
tissue engineering 45–61, 50
titanium 58, 59, 130
titanium dioxide 140
titinol 132
toasters 17–18
Tomalia, Donald 170, 174
tools, earliest recorded 1

tooth implants, gold 41
Top7 187–188
top-down manufacturing 72
Toshiba Corporation 122
toughness, of composites 22
Tour, James 95–96
tourmaline 111
transformation temperature 130
trans isomer 140, 163
transistor 83–85, 84, 86
β-tricalcium phosphate (β-TCP) 61
triphenylmethane 9
triptycene 102
tungsten steel 16
tunneling current 88
twinned martensite 131

U
ultrasound 124
urea 6
urethanes 158

V
vanadium steel 43
vena-cava filters 135
Verguin, Emanuel 9
vibration 107, 118, 122–124

Villari effect 121
viscosity 125, 128

W
Watson, James 83
Weiss, Paul 95–96
whiskers 21
white blood cell 62
Wilm, Alfred 17
windows, energy-efficient 140
Winslow, Willis M. 125
Winslow effect 125
Wöhler, Friedrich 6, 7
wood 22, 24
wood fiber 28
Wooley, Karen L. 176–177
World War I 12, 42–43
World War II 25, 37
wrought iron 13, 15

X
xenograft 47
xenon 88
Xylonite (parkesine) 9

Y
Yannas, Ioannis V. 48–53

Z
zinc 137
zinc finger 185–187